The Year-Round, All-Occasion
Make Your Own
Greeting Card Book

Created by
Charles Bennett, Gerald Taylor and Peggy Yatabe

JEREMY P. TARCHER, INC.
Los Angeles
Distributed by Houghton Mifflin Company
Boston

ACKNOWLEDGMENTS

We wish to thank these friends for the hours of testing, rewriting, revising, drawing and redrawing to make this "how-to" book really work.

Patty Taylor
Janet Rulec
Helen Holden
Denise Minobe
David Dexter
Lucy Barajikian

And last, but not least, an understanding publisher,

Jeremy Tarcher.

Library of Congress Cataloging in Publication Data

Copyright © 1977 by Charles Bennett, Gerald Taylor, & Peggy Yatabe

Bennett, Charles.
    The year-round, all-occasion make your own greeting card book.

    1. Greeting cards.   I. Taylor, Gerald,
1949–   .   II. Yatabe, Peggy. III. Title.
TT872.B46   1984   745.594   84-8459
ISBN 0-87477-321-0

Copyright © 1984 by Charles Bennett, Gerald Taylor, & Peggy Yatabe

Jeremy P. Tarcher, Inc.
9110 Sunset Blvd.
Los Angeles, CA 90069

Designed and illustrated by
The Committee

Manufactured in the United States of America
S 10 9 8 7 6 5 4 3 2

Contents

Introduction

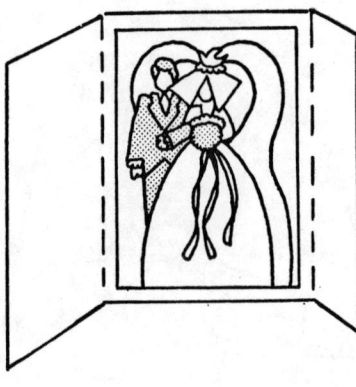

For years, we three have been designing and producing greeting cards for ourselves and our families, to send to friends and clients, and we never tire of being told that our handmade greetings are remembered above all others. We know that you will enjoy creating and giving this kind of personal card, too, and so we are happy to welcome you to the *MAKE YOUR OWN GREETING CARD BOOK.*

We have designed this book for the non-artist as well as for the arts and crafts person, because we know that you don't need drawing ability in order to be creative.

Our techniques have been tested and our card designs refined over the years, and in this book we have compiled the results of all of our experience together with helpful hints to give *you* the professional edge.

We have often found that the mistakes that occur when making a card are just as interesting as what you would have gotten if the card had come out letter perfect. The variations give you a one-of-a-kind effect. When you're producing a greeting card, perfection is not the goal. Making an individual statement is! The real challenge is to start with a blank sheet of paper and transform it into something that communicates an emotion or idea that only you, the creator, have in mind.

You will surely find (as we have) that no matter how much your cards are enjoyed by others, no one can possibly get as much pleasure from receiving them as you have had in creating them.

Charles Bennett, Gerald Taylor, Peggy Yatabe

How to Use This Book

The most important instruction we can give you for using this book is: HAVE FUN. Making your own greeting cards is a relaxed and pleasant pastime, full of the joy that you find when you make something with your own two hands. It is a personal, creative activity; not a competition. Your reputation as a human being is not on the line when you create your own cards. So relax and enjoy it. If something doesn't please you, it can simply be thrown away. Then try again. Most of the materials you will be using are inexpensive, and you can practice without any concern about cost. Practice leads to success. And success is exciting and fun.

Once you get involved, you will find that being creative is a form of play. Even just laying out the materials can give you pleasure. Assembling your pencils, paints, scissors, foils, fabrics, and paper is all part of the pleasure of making your own greeting cards.

Put the play into the card itself. Each time you begin a new technique, do it first as it is described. Then vary the elements as your spirit dictates. Try different materials. See what effects you get. Use more. Use less. Make it bigger or smaller. Change colors. Play. Have fun.

Don't hesitate to experiment. What others might call "mistakes" are all part of the game. Be bold. If you are timid about applying the techniques or using the materials, your caution will show up in the card. Each experiment will teach you something you didn't know before. The use of color, for instance. Don't be afraid to use color. Bright colors. Contrasting shades. In fact, don't just *use* color— *create* color. Experiment with unusual combinations. Mix different paints or layers of tissue paper. Mix and match fabrics, foils, and doilies. Use your imagination and let it do wonderful things for you.

Ideas will come from the materials themselves: the texture and feel of various kinds of papers, the shape of a tool, the combination of certain paint colors—all will indicate how they might be used.

Don't feel that you must match the quality of machine-made cards. *Your* quality is the handcrafted, personal look that no store-bought card can give you. Those of you who really want a professional look will soon discover that, as you learn and master the techniques shown in this book, the quality of your cards will improve remarkably. You may even need to sign each design to prove to the recipient that *you* were the card artist who made it.

All you need for this entertaining process of making your own greeting cards are easily obtainable materials and, for the most part, inexpensive tools. You will find many of these items already in your home. Those you do not have can be purchased for little cost. You will also discover new uses for commonplace things—a potato, a toothbrush, a paring knife.

If cardmaking is new to you, be ready to have fun and to get dirty. The dirt is not permanent. Paints wash off with water. (Just keep your materials clean.) It helps to have a supply of paper towels or rags on hand. Then roll up your sleeves and begin.

We believe that you will enjoy creating greeting cards so much that you will make cards not only for traditional holiday occasions but find excuses to make up your own occasions. You'll want to get your friends and family together to join in the fun. Then you'll want to branch out and begin making your own stationery, gift-wrapping paper, and party invitations.

You will see as you glance through the book that instructions for making each card follow the same format. All of them require that you pay attention to some basic techniques and a general card-making procedure. So before you begin, please read the following material, which follows the outline of this book and shows you where to find everything you'll need to know to make your own greeting cards.

BASIC TECHNIQUES

Some steps in card making are basic to almost every technique. These include cutting, scoring, and folding the card, as well as transferring and gluing the design. Rather than repeating these instructions in each card section, we have explained and illustrated them for your convenience in the Techniques section which follows this section.

USING OTHER DESIGNS

The designs in this book were created with two ideas in mind: to give you appropriate cards to send on any occasion and to introduce you to the card-making techniques. Once you master a process, however, you need not limit yourself only to the designs in that section. Most of the designs in this book are applicable to any number of techniques. And if you are on the lookout for them, you will find designs everywhere. One of the best places, of course, is in a commercial card shop. Choose a card you like. Take it home. Study it. Then reproduce it your way or use it as a model to create an entirely new card by adding your own touches to it.

Some good sources for card designs are book, magazine, and catalog illustrations; wallpaper samples; old photographs; gift-wrapping paper; fabric—anything that has been printed. Or if you have a particular gift for drawing, get your idea from nature—a bird, a flower, a tree—and draw your own design.

There is one thing to remember: not every design is suitable for every type of card-making process. If you look at a specific design in this book, you will see it has a certain character that makes it ideal for that particular card process. So when you see a design you would like to use, compare it to a similar one in these pages. This will lead you to just the right process to which it can be adapted. For instance, if you find an interesting silhouette in a magazine, leaf through this book and you will see there are similar designs in the Embossed Cards section. You have found a design that will make a wonderful Embossed Card—but not a very good Collage Card. An intricate drawing might make an exciting Collage Card—but not a very workable Paraffin Print Card.

When you have found your design, use one of the transfer methods described in the Techniques section (see How to Transfer), then follow the instructions in the appropriate card section to complete your card.

To help you find a card design for a specific occasion, we have prepared an Index of Cards by Occasion which appears at the back of the book. You will find, for instance, that all the Christmas cards are listed together, according to the technique used. Each of the 23 occasions listed is handled the same way. Then just refer to the card sections listed to find the card you want to make.

FINDING THE CARD
FOR THE OCCASION

Paper is the basic material for every card and envelope, so it is easy to understand that the kind of paper you use—its weight, texture, and color—in part determines the kind of card you will get. Changing any one or all of these elements can dramatically change the quality of your card.

To help you as you begin, paper recommendations have been made in each section. In addition, we have prepared an All About Paper listing at the back of the book outlining many other paper choices. The most common types are described and suggestions made on how they are best used.

PAPER

Throughout the book we refer to easily obtainable tools and materials that are necessary for a particular card or technique. Some of these are used for other techniques as well, so they make practical items to purchase and keep on hand. We have illustrated, described, and explained how to use these items in the Glossary at the back of the book.

TOOLS AND MATERIALS

Many people take the approach that if all else fails, they read the instructions. Don't do it that way. We have made our instructions as clear and easy to follow as we can, and our best suggestion to you is to read through this section and the Techniques section that follow before making your first card. We have tried to anticipate many of the questions that may arise and answered them here.

Then when you decide on the card you would like to make, read through the general and individual card instructions. Look at all the pictures. Follow the instructions in your mind so you have a sense of the overall process and can plan your work accordingly. Take special note of the hints. They are the result of the experiences (mistakes) of first-time card makers. Following those hints with care will help you become accomplished very fast.

When you have mentally followed the process, collect your materials and tools. This is a trick professionals use to achieve their best results. Having everything you need at hand makes for a smooth operation.

When you try a technique that is new to you, make a practice card first. You will quickly see the areas in which you need to take care and can avoid problems when you sit down to make your "send out" card. After you make your first card, try the variations we suggest in the card instructions—or make up your own.

These new techniques may contain unfamiliar terms. When you run into one, turn to the Glossary at the back of the book where tools and materials are defined, explained, and illustrated.

HOW TO MAKE THE CARD

THE MESSAGE

Every card needs a message. Sometimes the *card* is the message, as you will see in Letter Cutouts, where words themselves ("THANKS" "NOEL") make the card. More often, you will need to look for a way to express the thought that prompted you to send the card in the first place. Of course, you can write your message with calligraphy, transfer type, or by putting together letters traced from the alphabets we have provided in the Lettering and Typefaces section at the back of the book. Each of these methods is described, including an easy transfer technique for the typefaces.

ENVELOPES

Some of our cards can be folded so that they turn into their own mailer. Others need envelopes. Each card instruction specifies the envelope size (or name, if any) needed for that particular card. If you consult the Easy Envelopes section at the back of the book, you will find charts illustrating most commercially available sizes, and will see what the envelope looks like. If the envelope you want is not available, or you prefer a more personal touch, you can make one of your own by following the instructions for the two easy-to-make ones we have designed to fit any size card.

MAKING QUANTITIES OF CARDS

If you are planning to make cards for a group, a section called Making Cards in Quantities at the back of the book provides hints and suggestions to make your venture successful.

ENGLISH OR METRIC

The dimensions of each card are given in the English system so if you live in a country where the metric system prevails, use the conversion chart shown here.

If you want to make a particular card, it might be best to check the standard metric commercial envelope sizes first to see if there is one that will fit the card you have chosen. If not, make an envelope from the make-your-own section, since the two envelopes shown may be adapted to fit any size card.

You might also wish to check with the post office in your country to see if there are any postal restrictions with regard to envelope sizes. Sometimes very small-sized cards are prohibited (see Easy Envelopes.)

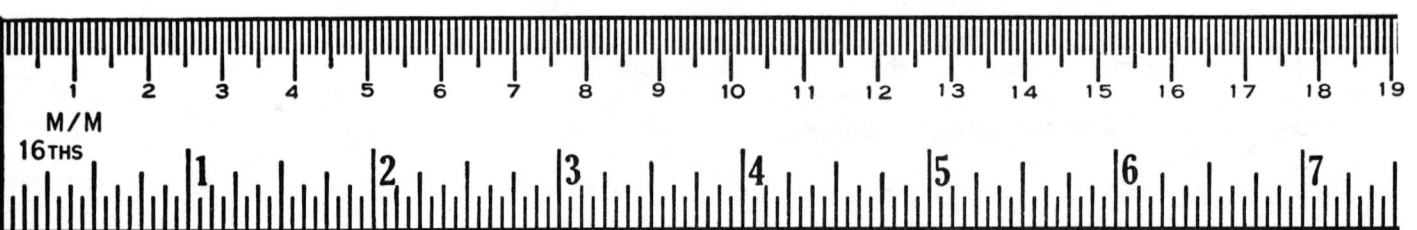

Basic Techniques

Materials (depending on transfer technique): sharp pencil, tracing paper, carbon paper, light cardboard, card paper.

**CARBON PAPER
TRANSFER**

1. Cover the design you want to transfer with tracing paper to protect your book from pencil marks.
2. Place the carbon paper underneath the design, with the dull (un-inked) side up.
3. Beneath the carbon paper, place the light cardboard (or card paper or other surface) onto which you want to transfer the design. Center the cardboard on your design.
4. Now trace firmly along the lines of the design with a sharp pencil. Your design now appears on the cardboard.

**TRANSFER TO
REVERSE A DESIGN**

1. Place the tracing paper on top of the design you want to reverse.
2. Trace the design onto the tracing paper with a soft, sharp pencil.
3. Now turn the tracing paper over and place the traced side against your printing surface in the position you want the design to appear.
4. Retrace along the lines of the design (which you can see through the tracing paper) with a soft, sharp pencil. The pressure of the second tracing transfers the pencil lead from your original tracing to your printing surface, and the design is reversed.

**TRACING PAPER
TRANSFER**

1. Place the tracing paper on top of the design you want to transfer.
2. Trace the design onto the tracing paper with a soft, sharp pencil.
3. Now turn the tracing paper over. Using the side of your pencil (rather than pressing on the point), shade the lines of the design (which you can see through the tracing paper) to make a penciled area about ¼" wide along each line.
4. Turn the tracing paper back over and position it on your card paper. Retrace the design. The pressure of the second tracing transfers the pencil lead from the shaded area on the back of the tracing paper to your card paper, in the shape of your design.

**HOW TO CUT,
SCORE, AND FOLD**

Cutting. The paper for your cards (your "card paper") must first be cut to the proper size as indicated in the individual card instructions (the "unfolded card size"). The cards in this book are designed to take advantage of standard paper sizes to eliminate waste, but a certain amount of cutting is usually necessary.

The easiest way to cut your card paper is to use the large paper cutter available at an art supply store. The people there will probably be happy to cut the paper for you or let you use the cutter. Before you cut, however, double-check the individual card instructions—some card designs require that the card paper be larger than the finished, unfolded card size. Also, check your paper needs for envelopes so you can cut everything you need at the same time. In any case, to save repeated work try to cut the paper for as many cards as possible at one time.

If you are cutting only a few cards or do not have access to a paper cutter and are cutting your paper at home, use an X-acto knife and a ruler (see How to Use an X-acto Knife in this section). This is especially necessary if your paper has been cut larger than the final unfolded size and you must trim it further at home. If you are cutting a large number of cards (over a hundred), it might be worthwhile to take your paper to a printer. A printer's power cutter can cut up to 500 cards at a time for about $2 per cut.

Another way to cut your card paper and produce an interesting effect is to tear it against a ruler. To tear your paper, lightly pencil the outline of the unfolded card size onto your card paper, lay a ruler or straightedge along one of the lines, and then quickly tear the paper against the ruler. Repeat on all sides until the whole card is outlined with rough, but straight, edges. If the pencil lines do not disappear with the tearing, erase them. Or to give your card an elegant "deckle edge," fold your paper along the penciled outline of the unfolded card size, dip the folded edge you want to deckle into ¼" of water, and let it saturate. Then with the paper lying flat, carefully pull the paper apart along the wet fold. You may then cut or deckle the other edges of your card to its unfolded size.

If you dip the wet, torn edge into watercolor or ink, the color will travel up the edge until it fades into the card paper. Let the paper dry before making your card. Note: Before giving an edge to your paper, be sure that the card instructions do not call for smooth edges. Some cards need smooth edges (cut with a paper cutter or X-acto knife) to be constructed properly.

Once your card paper is cut to size, the design of the card (the "card design") usually calls for cutting of design shapes. These may be cut with an X-acto knife or scissors. See How to Use an X-acto Knife in this section to learn to use this tool. If you use scissors, they should be strong and sharp. When purchasing scissors, avoid loose or dull blades, which give a ragged, undesirable cut.
Note to teachers: Most of the card designs in this book can be cut with scissors, but some of them require an X-acto knife (as in the Silk Screen section) which is very sharp. Before you assign a card to your students be sure that it can be made using scissors or that your students are able to handle the knife.

1. **Scoring and Folding.** Most paper is made with a grain, like the grain in wood, and when you fold paper it is best to fold in the direction of the grain. Folding against the grain creates uneven or broken folds. To find the grain in lightweight paper, hold it up to the light to see which way the fibers run. To find the grain in heavy paper, fold it. If the fold is against the grain it will be ragged and perhaps tear the paper; if the fold is with the grain it will be smooth and straight. But wherever possible, try to plan your card and its folding to take advantage of the paper grain.

2. The technique of scoring helps get the best fold possible. Before folding, a scoring tool—dry ball-point pen, dull screwdriver or butter knife, smooth nail point—is used to make an indentation in the paper along the fold line. This prevents the paper from breaking when it is folded. To score, lightly pencil your fold line and then lay a ruler

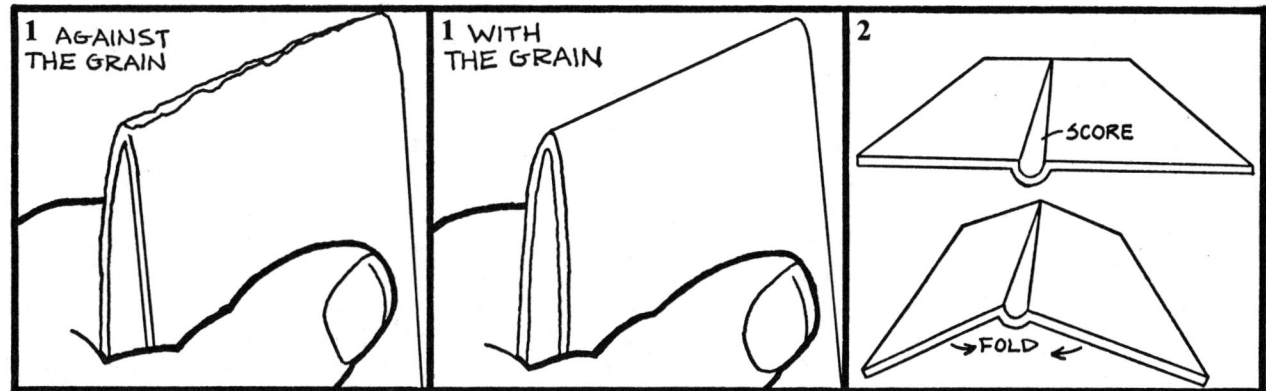

beside it. Keep your scoring tool pressed against the ruler and pull it across the paper with a firm, even pressure to make an indentation. Don't press so hard that you cut the paper fibers; this is what you are trying to prevent. Once scored, your paper is easily folded. Heavy-weight paper and coated paper always need scoring; lightweight paper does not.

**HOW TO USE
AN X-ACTO KNIFE**

1. The X-acto knife is an excellent cutting tool. It cuts best when the blades are sharp, so change blades often as you work. Before you begin cutting, protect your work surface by laying a piece of heavy cardboard (not corrugated) underneath your paper. To cut out a design shape, hold the knife like a pencil, press down firmly, and carefully follow the lines to be cut. Always cut in the direction of the sharp edge of the blade, cutting toward you as much as possible. If necessary, turn your hand, body, or paper so you can follow the lines most accurately.

2. Since the X-acto knife is very sharp, it may often try to follow a path you do not intend. To guard against this, use an object to help guide the blade around the design. A hard, curved shape like a dinner plate for curves and a metal ruler for straight lines are good examples of "cutting guides." Align the edge of the cutting guide with the line you want to cut, keep the side of the X-acto blade against the guide and the point on the line, and then cut. Always be aware of the direction of the blade—this will help you avoid cutting anything other than the paper.

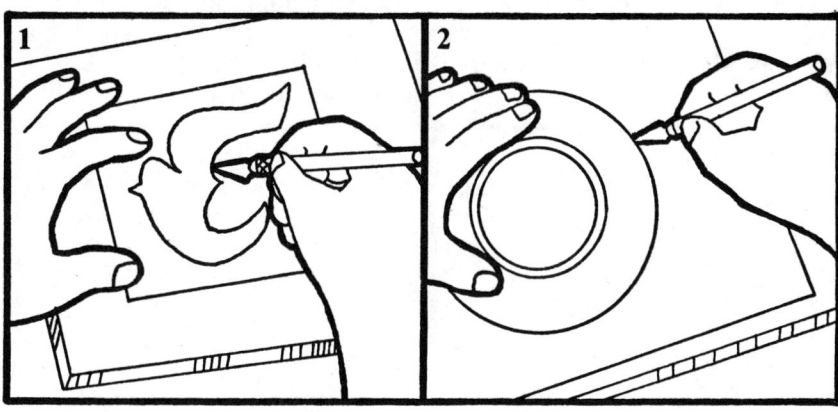

8

HOW TO MAKE DRAWING AND CUTTING GUIDES

In card making, a "drawing guide" is a design shape cut out of cardboard that is used to guide a pencil to draw the same shape onto card paper. A "cutting guide" is a shape cut out of cardboard that is used to guide an X-acto knife to cut out the same shape from card paper (see How to Use an X-acto Knife in this section for another kind of cutting guide). A cardboard shape can be a guide for either drawing or cutting and is used to save repeated work. Once the guide is made, you can draw or cut great quantities of one shape.

Specific instructions are given in each card-making section on how to make these guides. In general, the design shape is transferred to cardboard and then cut out. Then a pencil is traced around the guide to outline the shape on card paper, and the shape is then cut out of the paper (usually with scissors). Or the guide is placed on top of the card paper and an X-acto knife follows the outline to cut out the shape from the paper.

HOW TO GLUE

1. **White Glue.** This is the standard permanent glue for paper. The trick to using white glue is to use as little as possible in as thin a coat as you can apply. Squirt a small amount of glue onto your paper and spread it around with a short strip of heavy paper or cardboard. This gives you a very thin layer, which lessens the likelihood of bumps or the papers buckling. You must work fast, because the thin layer of glue dries quickly, so have everything you need at hand before you begin.

For troublesome corners and edges that just won't stay down, put some glue on one side of your cardboard spreader. Then with the glue-side up, slide the spreader underneath the corner or edge. Press the paper down until it rests on the spreader and then pull it out, leaving some glue on the paper. Now push the paper down and hold for a moment until it sticks.

2. **Spray Adhesive.** This new product is probably the easiest and cleanest way to adhere paper to paper. Pieces can be peeled up and repositioned without damage, and the drying time is very short. The spray tends to drift, however, so always cover your work area with scrap paper (not newspaper—the adhesive will dissolve the ink onto your hands). There are several brands on the market, but we have found Photo Mount to be the best.

To use, follow the instructions on the can. The most important point is to spray lightly in a back and forth motion. After spraying, just press the paper down where it is to be glued. Be sure to keep the spray nozzle clean, or the adhesive will drip.

3. Glue Stick. There are advantages to this solid-stick adhesive. It goes on dry (and so will not pucker lightweight paper), is not messy, and takes less time to dry than white glue. To use, twist the bottom of the stick to expose the glue, and rub on.

4. Rubber Cement. The advantages of rubber cement are that the paper can be repositioned easily and that any excess cement can be picked up cleanly with an eraser or even your finger. Its disadvantage is that it is not permanent and in time it will dry out and lose its adhesive quality. Therefore, it is not recommended for techniques such as Collage, where you want the pieces to stay put for a long time, but it is highly recommended for Machine-Printing, where it allows you to prepare a pasteup with great accuracy.

5. To use, brush the cement (most containers come with brushes) onto one of the pieces of paper to be adhered. Then quickly, before the cement dries, press the papers together, sliding them back and forth slightly to position before letting them dry. To remove a rubber-cemented piece of paper, use rubber-cement thinner (a good brand is Bestine). Pour a small amount underneath one edge of the piece to be removed. As the cement dissolves pull the piece away, adding more thinner as needed. The thinner will dry without a trace, and the cement itself can be picked up with an eraser to leave a clean surface for recementing.

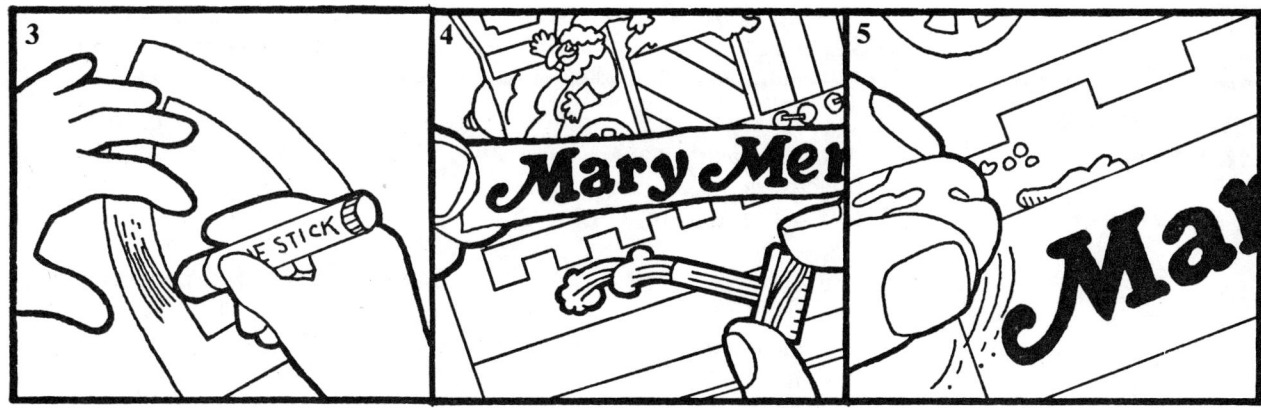

Collage Cards

Appearance: Very handmade look. Layered, multicolored, multi-textured effect.
Skill required: Lots of careful cutting, gluing, and positioning.
Quantity/Time: One at a time, fairly slow.

MATERIALS	• Recommended paper: medium-weight cover paper (see All About Paper) • Easy Envelopes • Assorted colored papers • Old gift wrapping, paper doilies, foil, fabrics, gummed stickers, sequins, glitter, dried flowers	• Tracing paper • Carbon paper • Light cardboard • Back side of a breadboard, or heavy cardboard (to protect your table when cutting) • White glue or glue stick
TOOLS	• Scissors or an X-acto knife • Sharp pencil	• See individual cards for additional materials and tools

HOW TO MAKE THE CARD

1. Trace one of the card designs and its rectangular border onto a piece of tracing paper. Use coins, jars, and plates as drawing guides for circles and curves.
2. Cut, score, and fold your card paper. Unfold your card for the next steps.
3. Lightly tape one edge of the traced design to the card paper, using two small pieces of masking tape to make a hinge. The tracing should be positioned properly on the card according to the card design.
4. Now trace each design element onto its own piece of tracing paper. These tracings are your cutting guides. The design elements will be shown either within the card design or in illustrations accompanying the design (see individual cards).

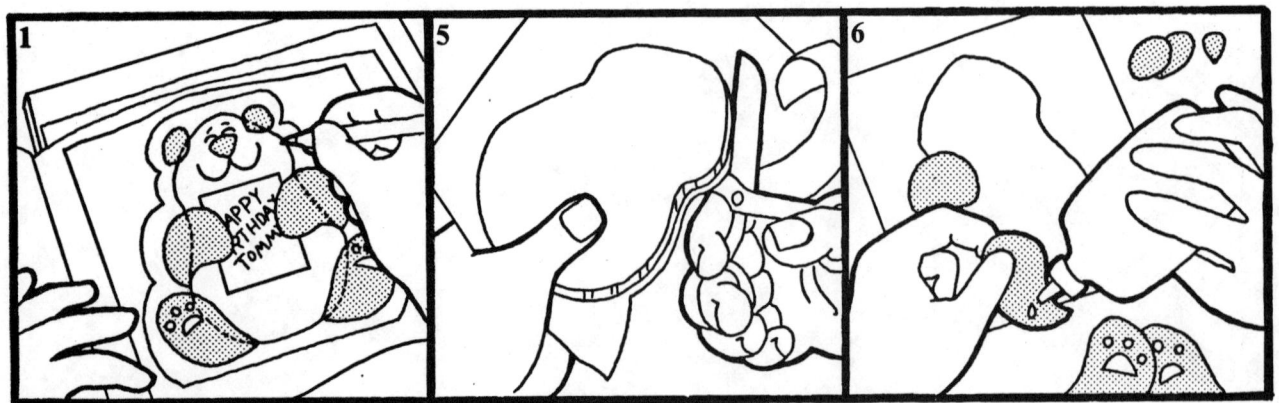

5. Cut out your design material (wrapping, foil, fabrics) for each element—materials and colors are recommended for each card, but you can use any combinations you like. Lay the tracing paper guide on top of the material. Hold the pieces firmly while cutting so they won't shift and cut *both* the tracing paper guide and the design material.

   Hint: If you are making quantities of cards (or the design calls for many of one element), transfer each design element to light cardboard with a pencil and carbon paper (see How to Transfer in Techniques section). Cut out the element and you have a cardboard cutting guide. Now stack layers of your design materials, hold the guide firmly on top, and cut closely around the guide to make many design pieces at one time.

6. When all the design elements have been cut, glue them down on the card paper. The order of gluing is specified for each card design— usually the larger pieces first, the detail pieces last. Position each design piece under its outline on the tracing paper design and then glue. Repeat until your card is complete.

7. When the glue is dry, add your message and refold your card.

FINISHED CARDS

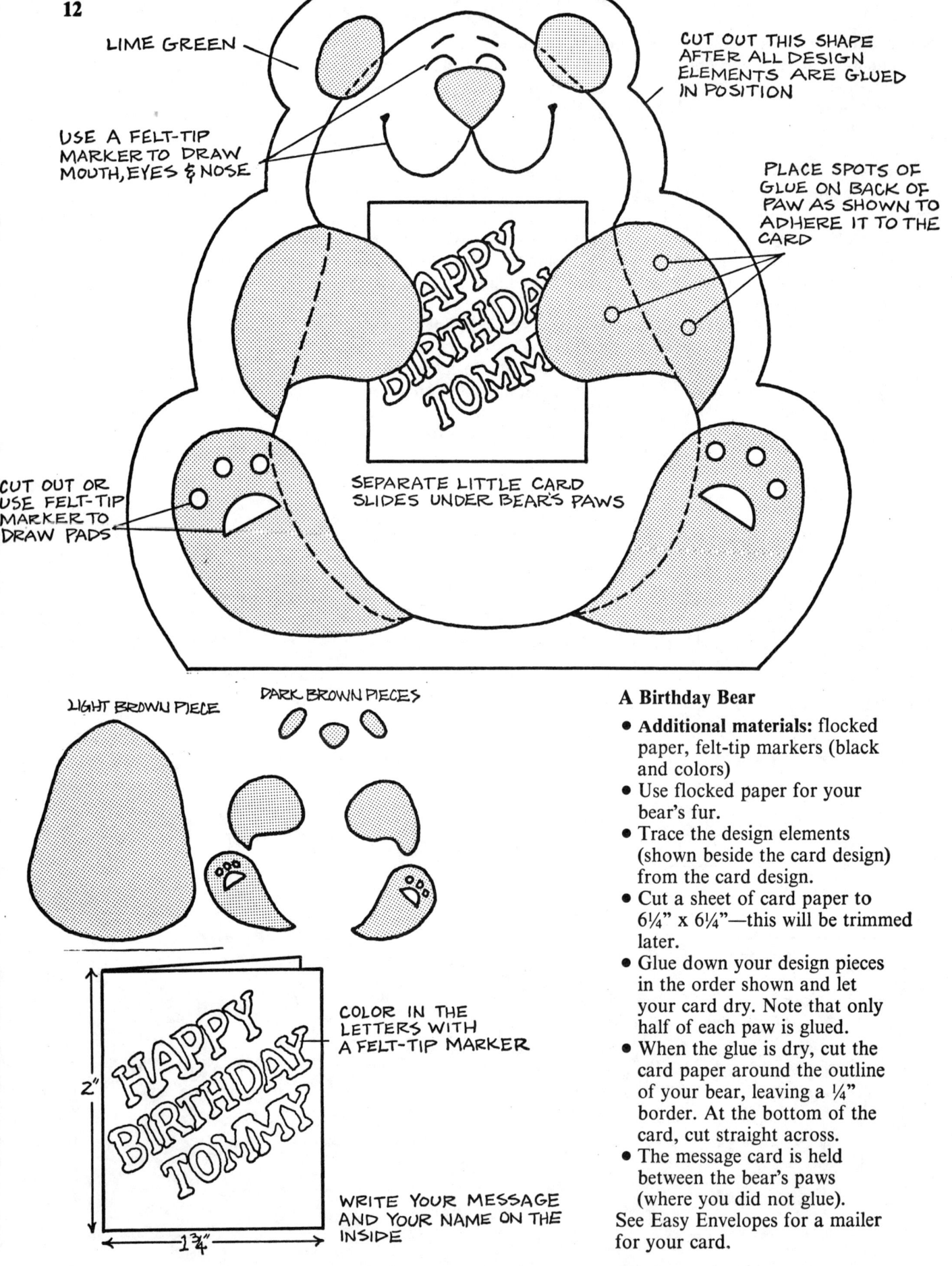

LIME GREEN

CUT OUT THIS SHAPE
AFTER ALL DESIGN
ELEMENTS ARE GLUED
IN POSITION

USE A FELT-TIP
MARKER TO DRAW
MOUTH, EYES & NOSE

PLACE SPOTS OF
GLUE ON BACK OF
PAW AS SHOWN TO
ADHERE IT TO THE
CARD

CUT OUT OR
USE FELT-TIP
MARKER TO
DRAW PADS

SEPARATE LITTLE CARD
SLIDES UNDER BEAR'S PAWS

LIGHT BROWN PIECE

DARK BROWN PIECES

A Birthday Bear

- **Additional materials:** flocked paper, felt-tip markers (black and colors)
- Use flocked paper for your bear's fur.
- Trace the design elements (shown beside the card design) from the card design.
- Cut a sheet of card paper to 6¼" x 6¼"—this will be trimmed later.
- Glue down your design pieces in the order shown and let your card dry. Note that only half of each paw is glued.
- When the glue is dry, cut the card paper around the outline of your bear, leaving a ¼" border. At the bottom of the card, cut straight across.
- The message card is held between the bear's paws (where you did not glue).

See Easy Envelopes for a mailer for your card.

COLOR IN THE
LETTERS WITH
A FELT-TIP MARKER

2"

1¾"

WRITE YOUR MESSAGE
AND YOUR NAME ON THE
INSIDE

A Christmas Winter Card

- **Additional material:** hole punch, gummed stickers
- For an added wintry effect, glue patterned rice paper over your card paper before scoring and folding.
- Cut, score, and fold your paper (unfolded size 4¼" x 10").
- Note that when your card is folded, the fold comes just above the children's mittens.

Your folded card fits into an A6 envelope.

FINISHED CARD FOLDED

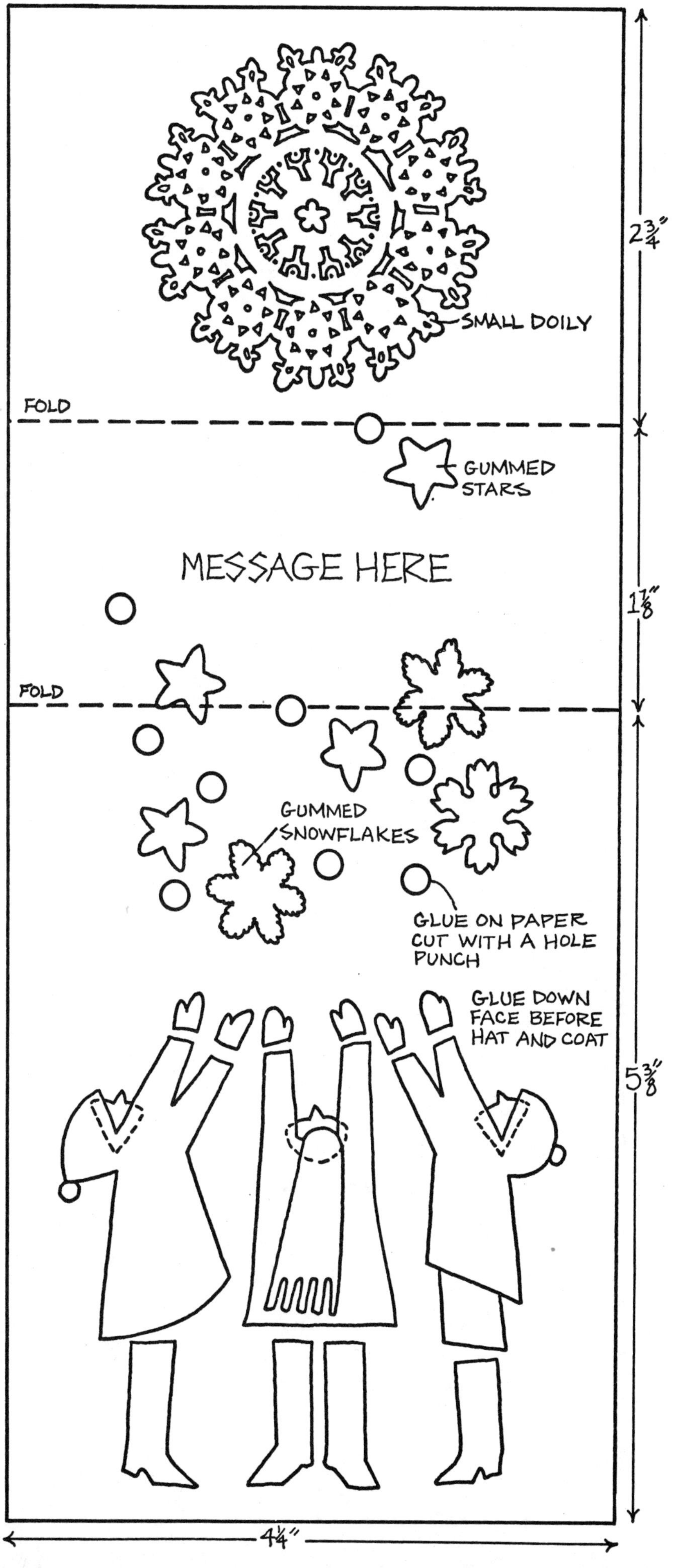

SMALL DOILY

FOLD

GUMMED STARS

MESSAGE HERE

FOLD

GUMMED SNOWFLAKES

GLUE ON PAPER CUT WITH A HOLE PUNCH

GLUE DOWN FACE BEFORE HAT AND COAT

2¾"

1⅞"

5⅜"

4¼"

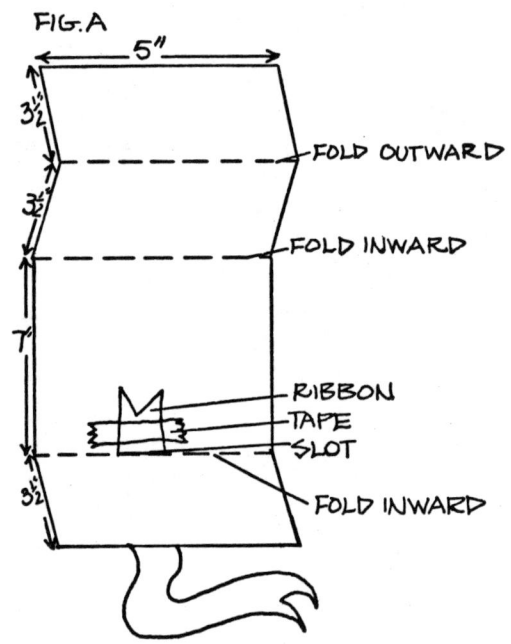

FIG. A

5"

3½"

FOLD OUTWARD

3½"

FOLD INWARD

7"

RIBBON
TAPE
SLOT

3½"

FOLD INWARD

A Money-Gift Card

- **Additional materials:** ribbon, colored paper, scotch tape, money
- Cut, score, and fold your card paper into four panels (fig. A, unfolded size 5" x 17½"). Unfold for the next steps.
- Cut a slot wide enough for the ribbon along the fold line of the bottom panel (fig. A). Tape the end of a 13" ribbon as shown, slip it through the slot, and fold up the panel and glue both sides (fig. B). Now glue the ribbon to the folded panel.
- Cut the hand out of colored paper and glue it to the top panel (fig. C). Then cut a slot along the index finger wide enough for another 13" piece of ribbon.
- Tape this piece of ribbon to the back of the panel under the forefinger.
- Tuck the money in the money-pocket and refold the card (fig. D). The ribbon ties into a bow to keep your card closed (fig. E).

Your card fits into an open-end 5½" x 7½" envelope.

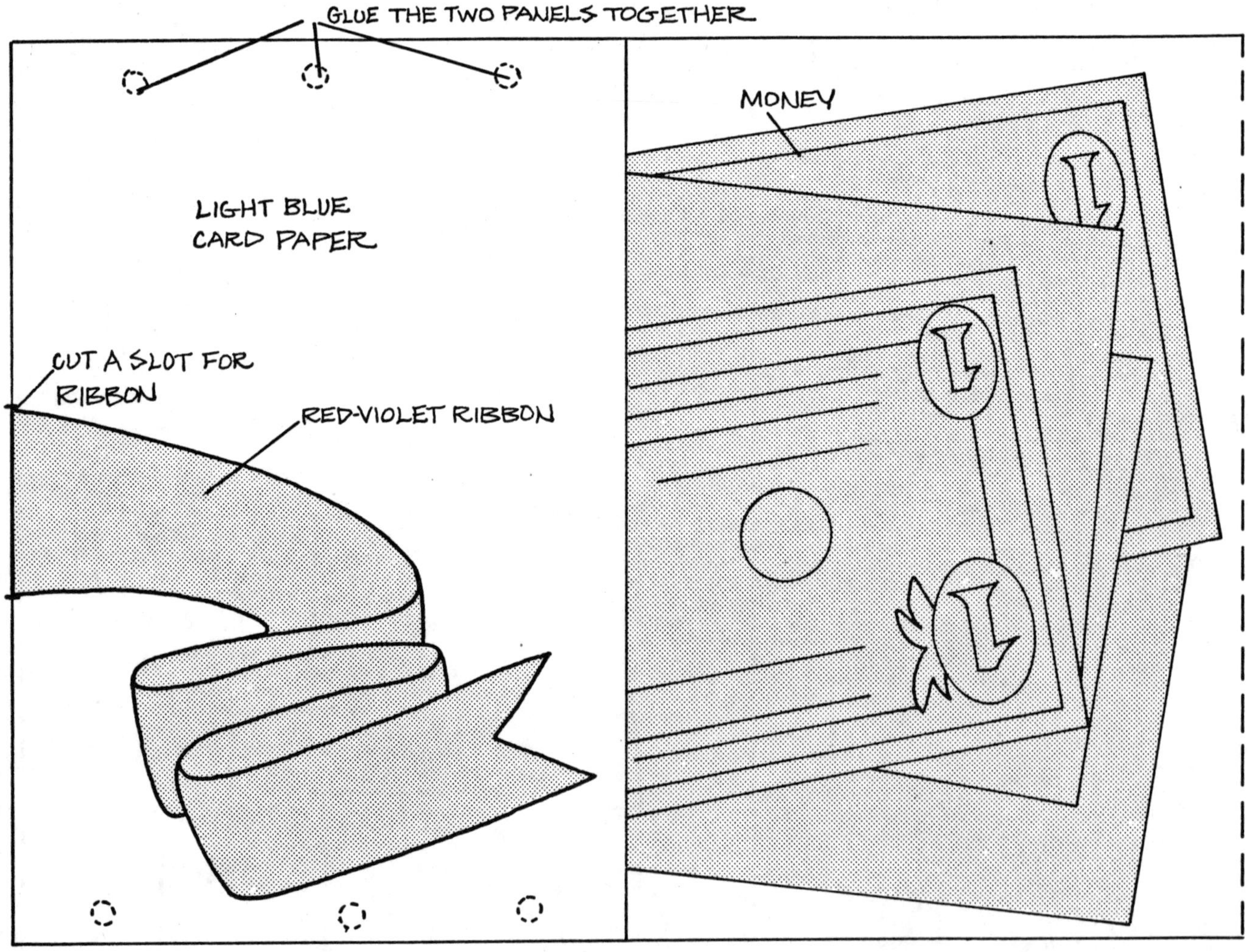

GLUE THE TWO PANELS TOGETHER

LIGHT BLUE
CARD PAPER

CUT A SLOT FOR
RIBBON

RED-VIOLET RIBBON

MONEY

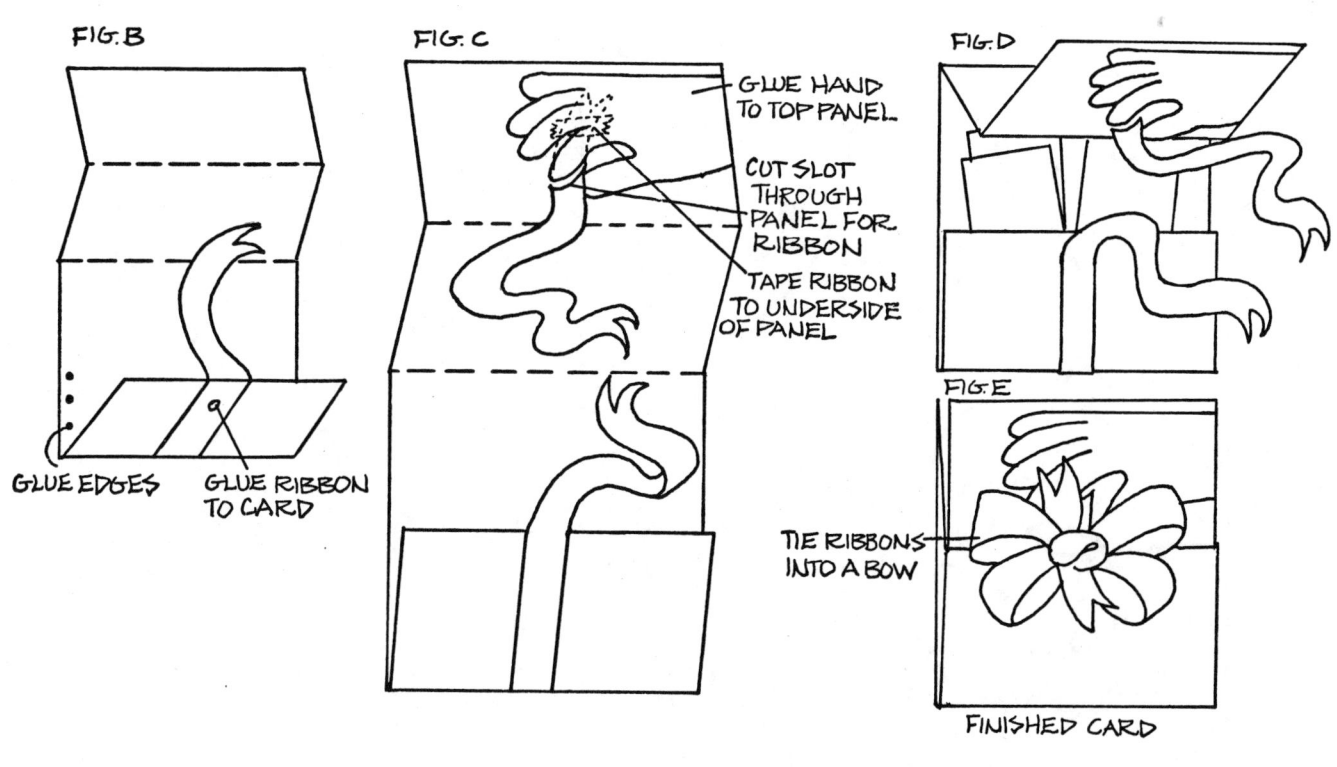

FIG. B

GLUE EDGES   GLUE RIBBON TO CARD

FIG. C

GLUE HAND TO TOP PANEL

CUT SLOT THROUGH PANEL FOR RIBBON

TAPE RIBBON TO UNDERSIDE OF PANEL

FIG. D

FIG. E

TIE RIBBONS INTO A BOW

FINISHED CARD

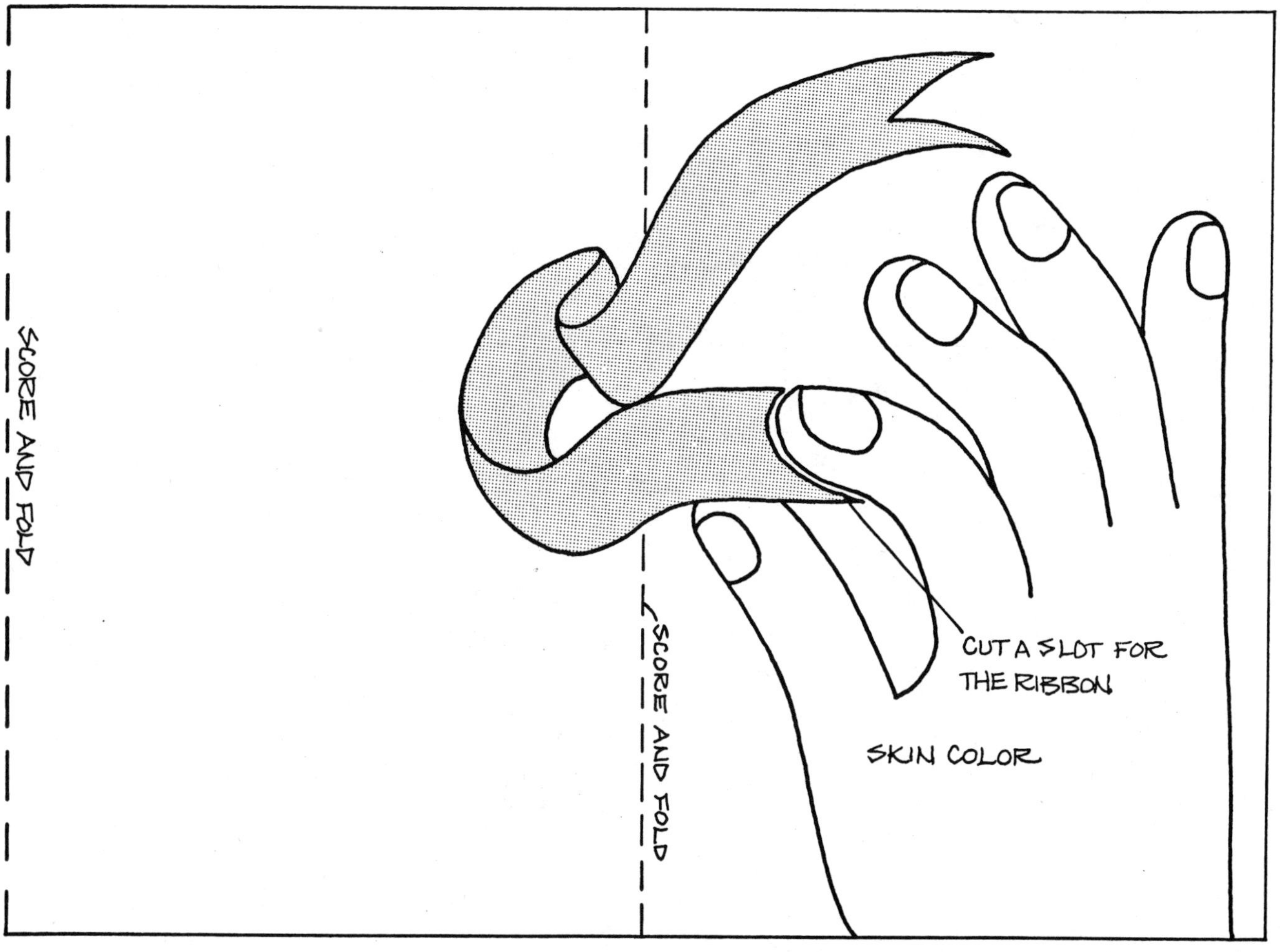

SCORE AND FOLD

SCORE AND FOLD

CUT A SLOT FOR THE RIBBON

SKIN COLOR

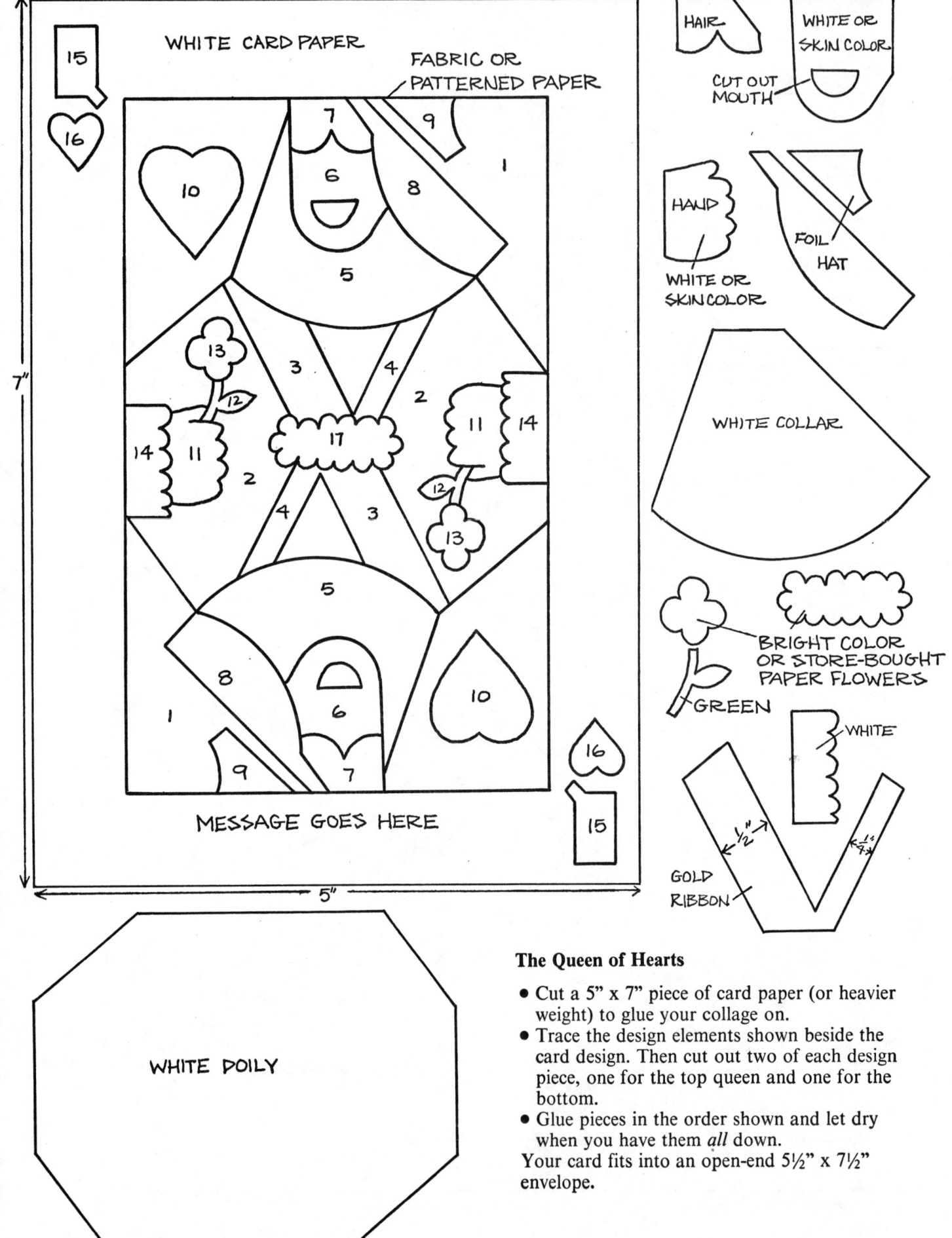

The Queen of Hearts

- Cut a 5" x 7" piece of card paper (or heavier weight) to glue your collage on.
- Trace the design elements shown beside the card design. Then cut out two of each design piece, one for the top queen and one for the bottom.
- Glue pieces in the order shown and let dry when you have them *all* down.

Your card fits into an open-end 5½" x 7½" envelope.

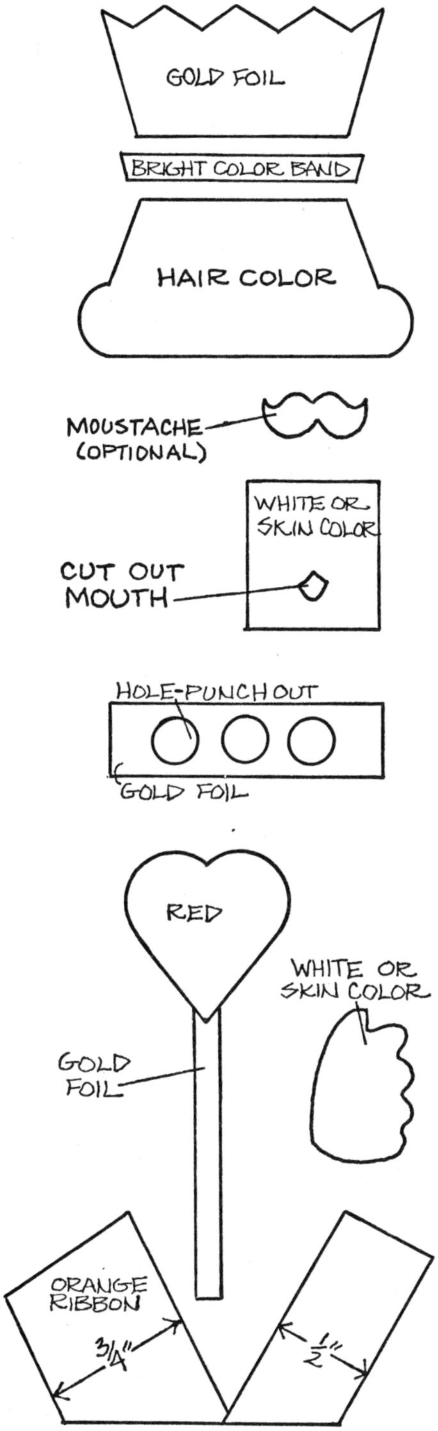

GOLD FOIL

BRIGHT COLOR BAND

HAIR COLOR

MOUSTACHE (OPTIONAL)

CUT OUT MOUTH

WHITE OR SKIN COLOR

HOLE-PUNCH OUT

GOLD FOIL

RED

WHITE OR SKIN COLOR

GOLD FOIL

ORANGE RIBBON

3/4"   1/2"

14

15

BEIGE OR WHITE CARD PAPER

BROWN & GOLD PATTERNED PAPER

8
9
1
12
5   6
7
10
2
3   4
11
13
4   3
11
2
5   6
7
1
9
8
10
12
15
14

7"

5"

MESSAGE GOES HERE

The King of Hearts

- Cut a 5" x 7" piece of card paper (or heavier weight) to glue your collage on.
- Trace the design elements shown beside the card design. Then cut out two of each design piece, one for the top king and one for the bottom.
- Glue pieces in the order shown and let dry when you have them *all* down.

Your card fits into an open-end 5½" x 7½" envelope.

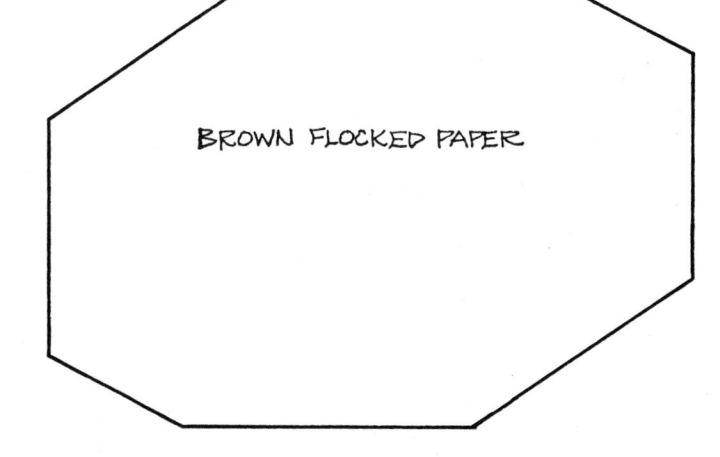

BROWN FLOCKED PAPER

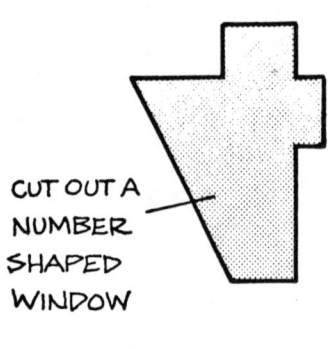

CUT OUT A
NUMBER
SHAPED
WINDOW

WHITE CARD PAPER

- - - SCORE AND FOLD - - -

YOUR MESSAGE
HERE

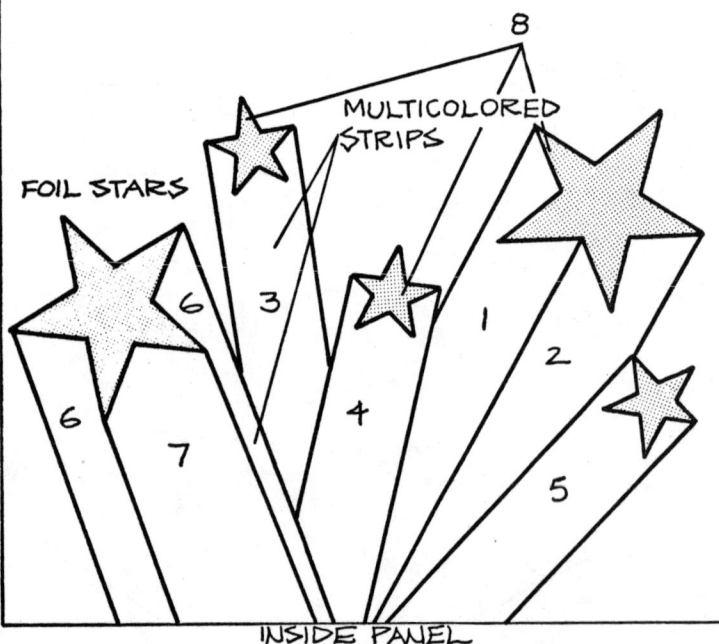

8

MULTICOLORED
STRIPS

FOIL STARS

6

3

1

2

6

4

5

7

INSIDE PANEL

All-Occasion Numbers Card

- Choose your numbers to correspond to the occasion (fig. A), and then trace them to make cutting guides. Use coins to guide your tracing and cutting curves.
- Cut, score, and fold your card paper (unfolded size 4" x 10").
- Cut out a number-shaped window in the front panel of your card using the cutting guides and an X-acto knife.

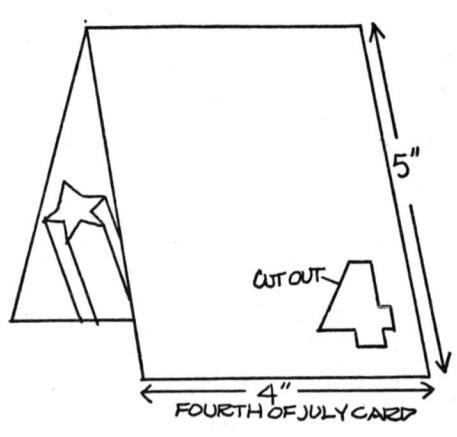

5"

CUT OUT 4

4"

FOURTH OF JULY CARD

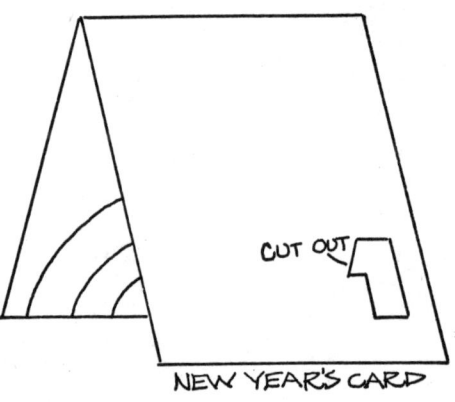

CUT OUT 1

NEW YEAR'S CARD

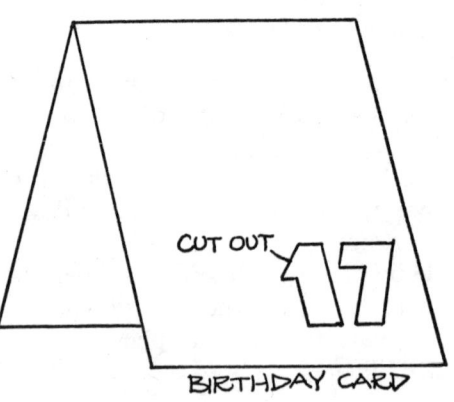

CUT OUT 17

BIRTHDAY CARD

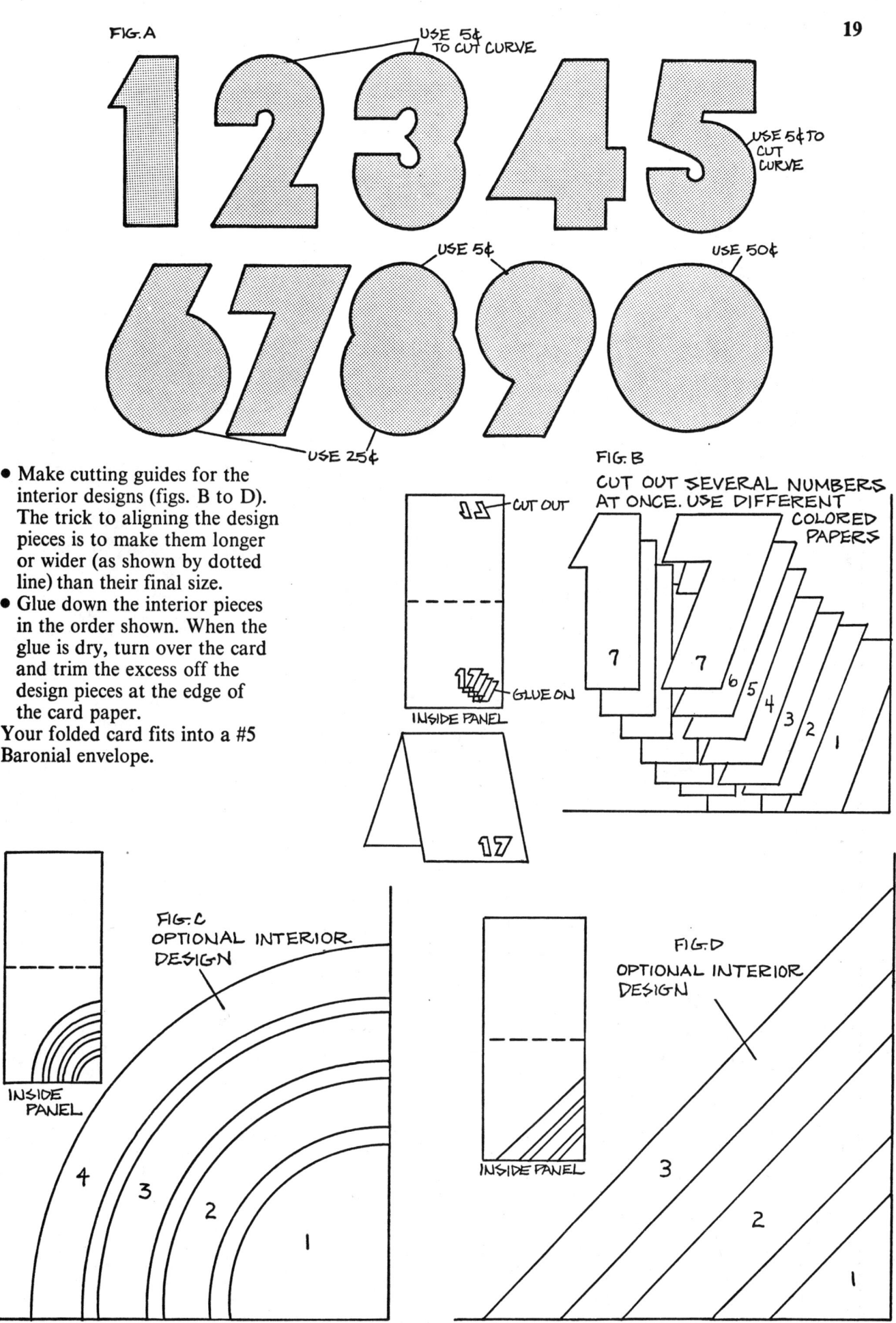

FIG. A

USE 5¢ TO CUT CURVE

USE 5¢ TO CUT CURVE

USE 5¢

USE 50¢

USE 25¢

- Make cutting guides for the interior designs (figs. B to D). The trick to aligning the design pieces is to make them longer or wider (as shown by dotted line) than their final size.
- Glue down the interior pieces in the order shown. When the glue is dry, turn over the card and trim the excess off the design pieces at the edge of the card paper.

Your folded card fits into a #5 Baronial envelope.

CUT OUT

GLUE ON

INSIDE PANEL

17

FIG. B

CUT OUT SEVERAL NUMBERS AT ONCE. USE DIFFERENT COLORED PAPERS

7 7 6 5 4 3 2 1

INSIDE PANEL

FIG. C OPTIONAL INTERIOR DESIGN

4 3 2 1

INSIDE PANEL

FIG. D OPTIONAL INTERIOR DESIGN

3 2 1

20

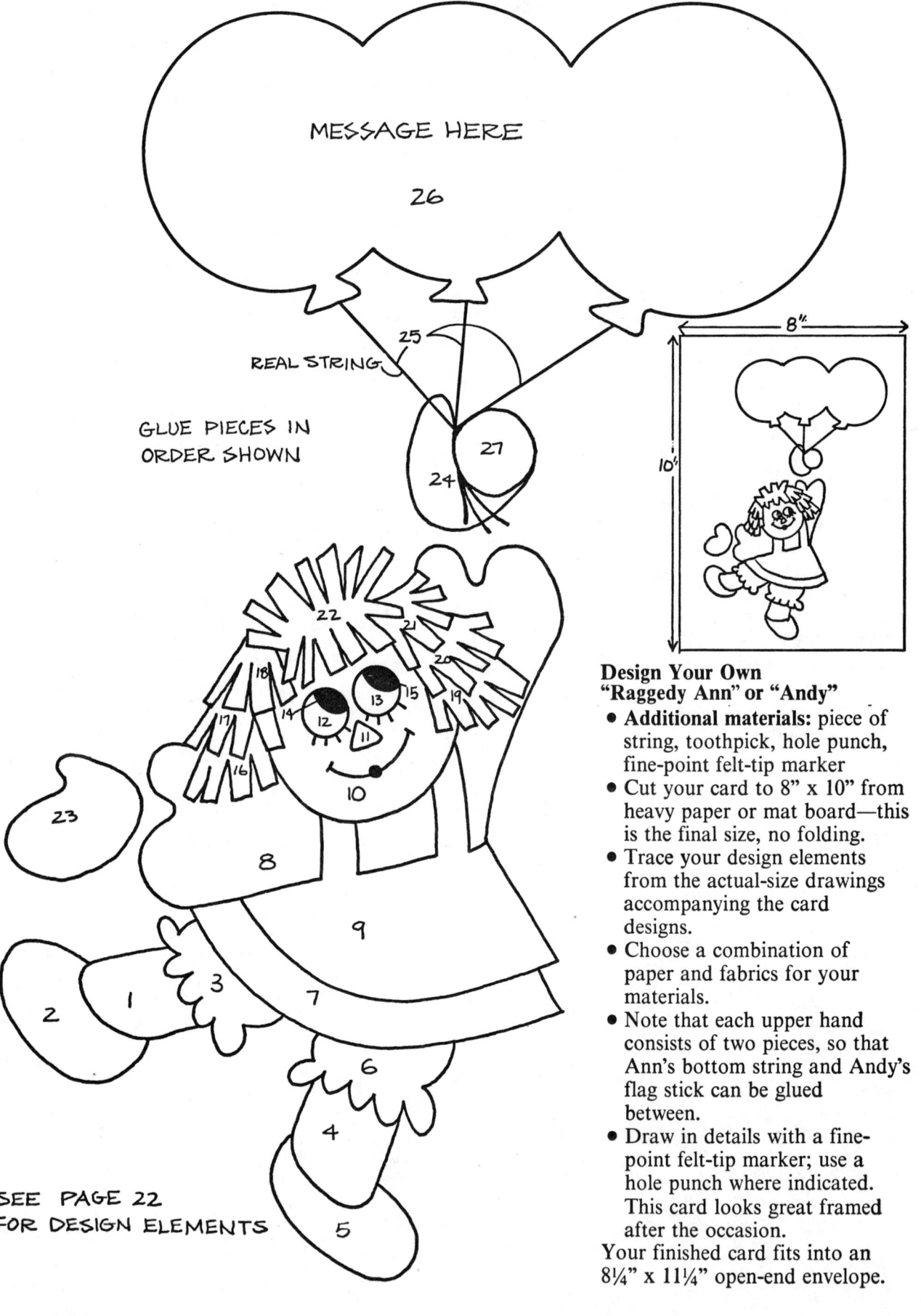

MESSAGE HERE

26

25

REAL STRING

GLUE PIECES IN
ORDER SHOWN

27

24

22

21

18

20

17   14   15   19

12   13

16   11

10

23

8

9

2   1   3   7

6

4

5

SEE PAGE 22
FOR DESIGN ELEMENTS

8"

10"

**Design Your Own
"Raggedy Ann" or "Andy"**

- **Additional materials:** piece of string, toothpick, hole punch, fine-point felt-tip marker
- Cut your card to 8" x 10" from heavy paper or mat board—this is the final size, no folding.
- Trace your design elements from the actual-size drawings accompanying the card designs.
- Choose a combination of paper and fabrics for your materials.
- Note that each upper hand consists of two pieces, so that Ann's bottom string and Andy's flag stick can be glued between.
- Draw in details with a fine-point felt-tip marker; use a hole punch where indicated. This card looks great framed after the occasion.

Your finished card fits into an 8¼" x 11¼" open-end envelope.

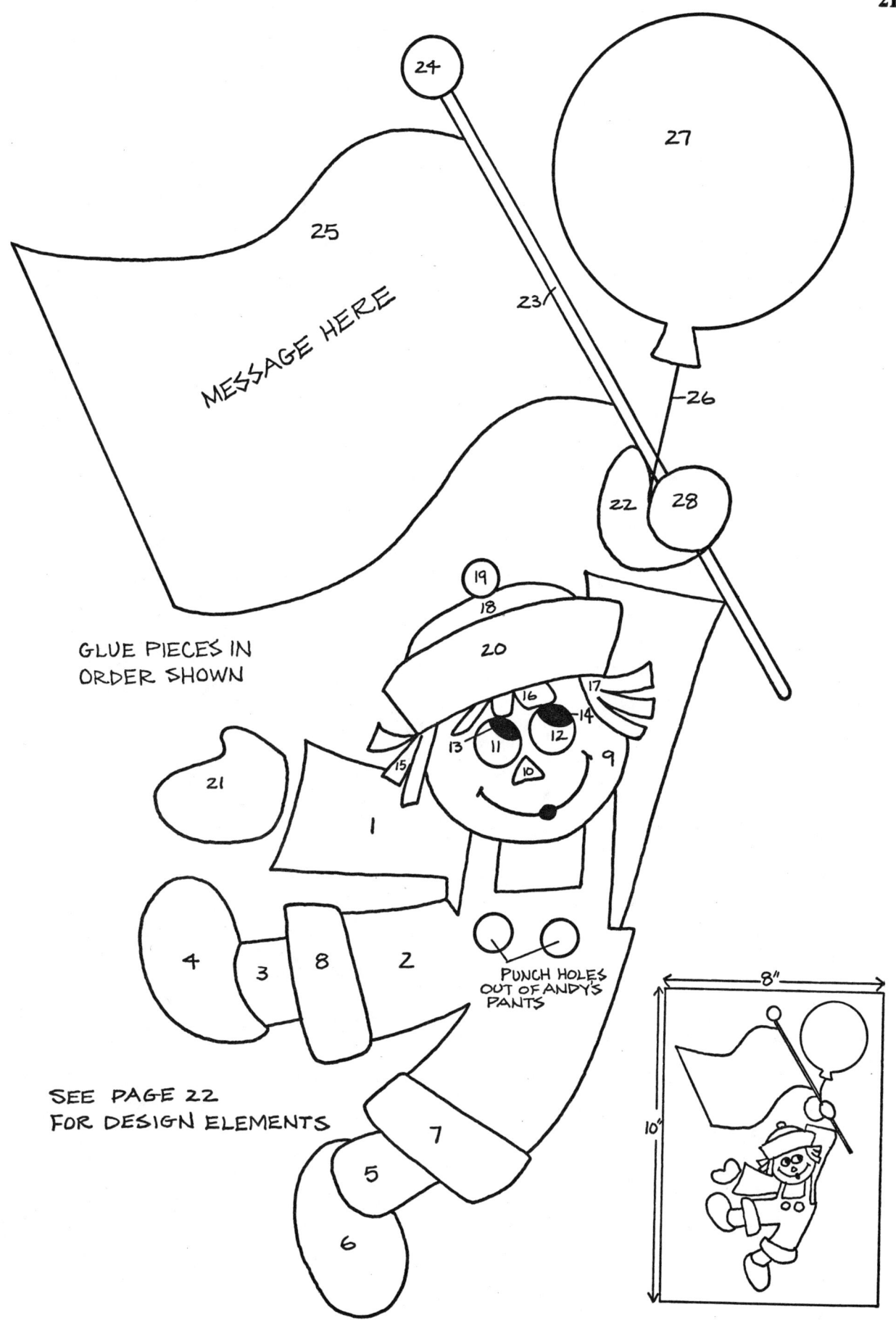

MESSAGE HERE

GLUE PIECES IN
ORDER SHOWN

PUNCH HOLES
OUT OF ANDY'S
PANTS

SEE PAGE 22
FOR DESIGN ELEMENTS

8"

10"

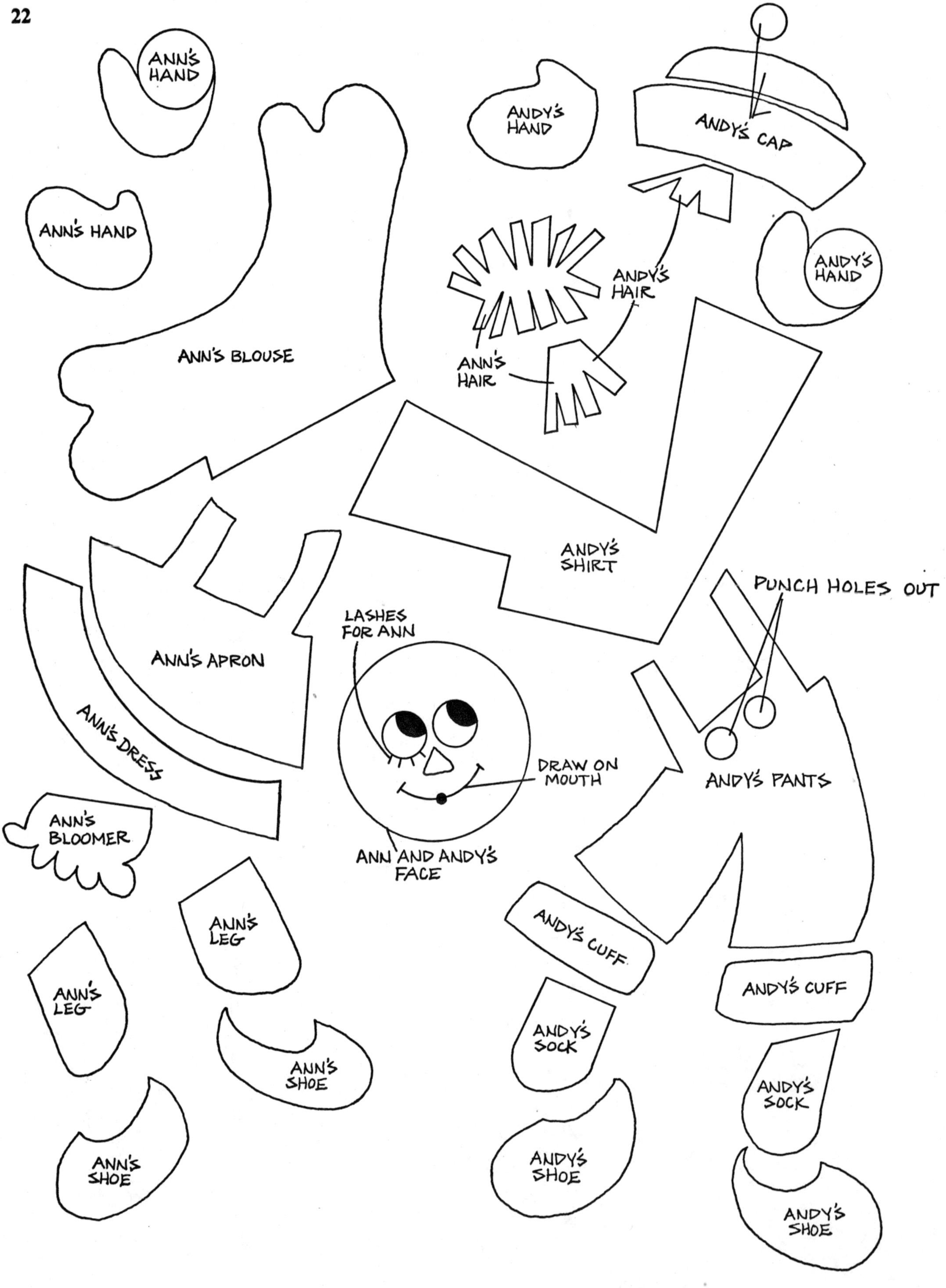

ANN'S HAND

ANN'S HAND

ANDY'S HAND

ANDY'S CAP

ANN'S BLOUSE

ANDY'S HAIR

ANN'S HAIR

ANDY'S HAND

ANDY'S SHIRT

PUNCH HOLES OUT

ANN'S APRON

LASHES FOR ANN

DRAW ON MOUTH

ANDY'S PANTS

ANN'S DRESS

ANN'S BLOOMER

ANN AND ANDY'S FACE

ANDY'S CUFF

ANN'S LEG

ANDY'S CUFF

ANN'S LEG

ANDY'S SOCK

ANN'S SHOE

ANDY'S SOCK

ANN'S SHOE

ANDY'S SHOE

ANDY'S SHOE

A Christmas Wreath

- **Additional materials:** colored paper, hole punch, ribbon
- Make a cardboard cutting guide from the leaf shape (fig. A) so you can cut out many leaves at one time. Use a hole punch to make the berries.
- Cut and score your card (unfolded size 4½" x 7¼"). Score only the two short lines indicated, not across the wreath area. Using a can or jar lid as a guide, lightly pencil the circle shown in figure B and then cut around the upper semicircle between the score lines.
- With the penciled and cut circle as a guide, glue down the holly wreath, overlapping the leaves from the top clockwise. Add the berries. Now top with a bow of ribbon or cut paper (fig. C).

Your folded card fits into an A6 envelope.

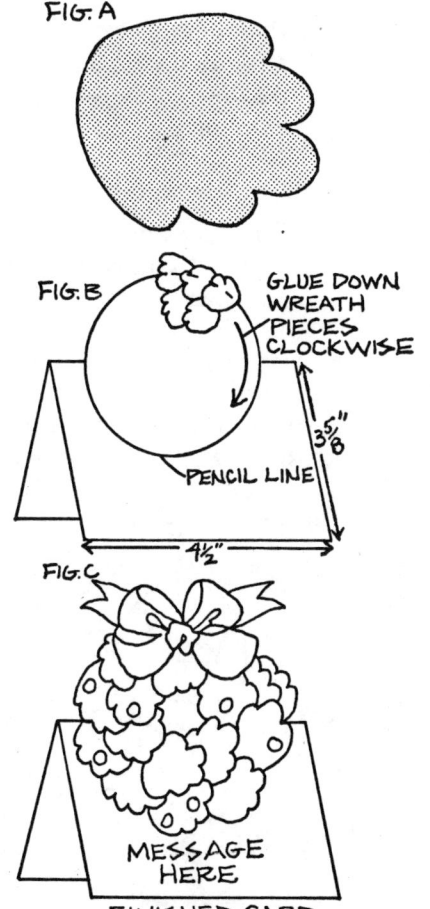

FIG. A

FIG. B

GLUE DOWN WREATH PIECES CLOCKWISE

PENCIL LINE

3⅝"

4½"

FIG. C

MESSAGE HERE

FINISHED CARD

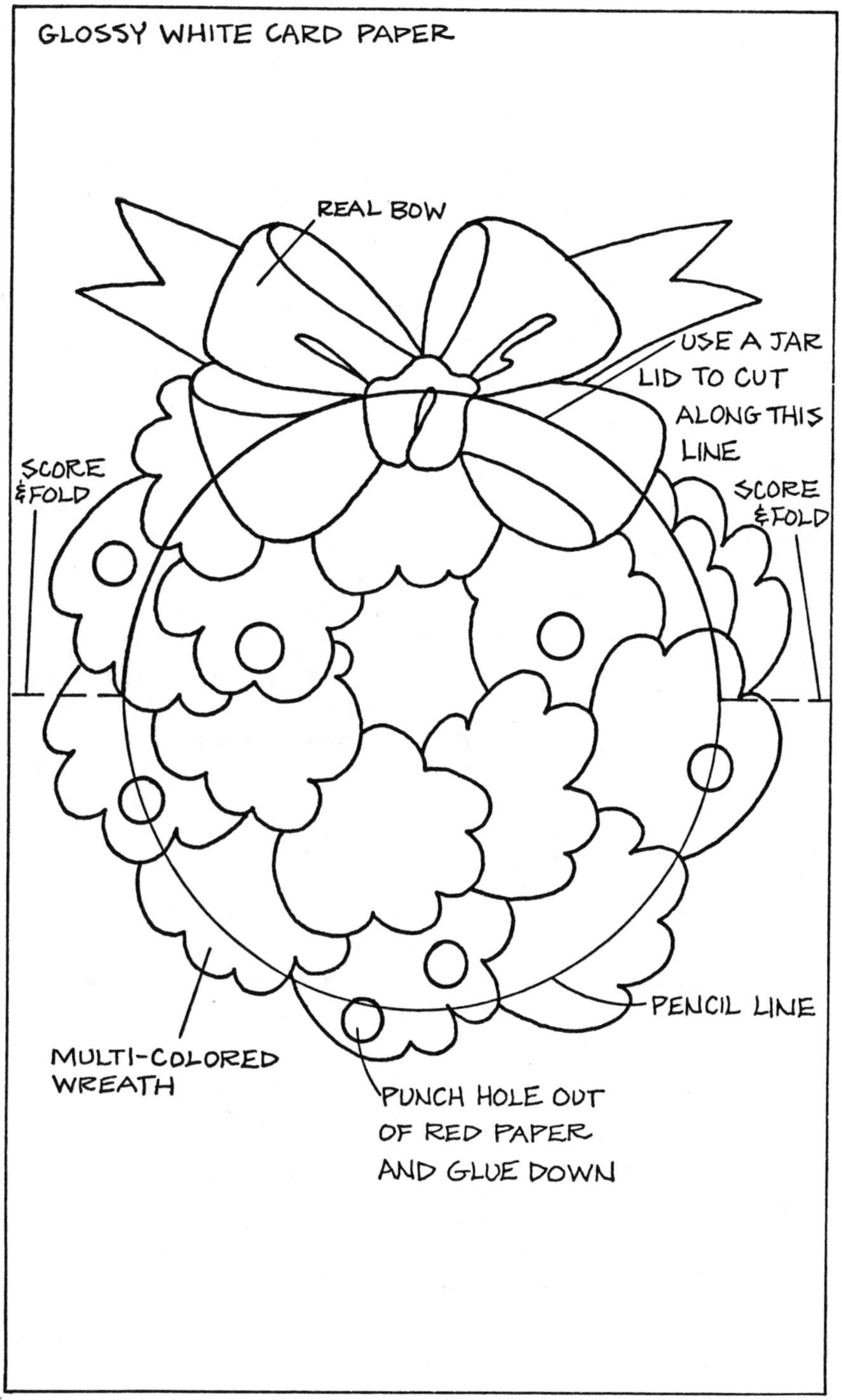

GLOSSY WHITE CARD PAPER

REAL BOW

USE A JAR LID TO CUT ALONG THIS LINE

SCORE & FOLD

SCORE & FOLD

PENCIL LINE

MULTI-COLORED WREATH

PUNCH HOLE OUT OF RED PAPER AND GLUE DOWN

Paper Doily Cards

Appearance: Lacy, delicate.
Skill required: A creative eye for color and design, and a willingness to experiment.
Quantity/Time: One at a time, fairly quick.

MATERIALS	• Recommended card paper: medium- to heavy-weight, white or colored (see All About Paper). Construction paper is not recommended. • Easy Envelopes • Commercially made doilies (white, gold, silver), available at party and five-and-dime stores • Light cardboard • Colored paper, patterned gift wrapping, foil and rice papers, fabric • Foil and printed appliqués (birds, cherubs, butterflies), ribbon, strawflowers • Carbon paper • Tracing paper • White glue or glue stick • Masking Tape
TOOLS	• Sharp pencil • See individual cards for • Scissors additional materials and tools
HOW TO MAKE THE CARD	1. Trace one of the card designs and its rectangular border onto a piece of tracing paper. 2. Cut, score, and fold your card paper. 3. Lightly tape one edge of the traced design to the card paper (now unfolded), using two small pieces of masking tape to make a hinge. The tracing should be positioned properly on the card according to the card design. 4. Now trace each design element as shown in the card design onto its own piece of tracing paper. These are your cutting guides. 5. Cut out your desired doily or design material (paper, gift wrap, fabric) for each element. Hold the pieces firmly while cutting so they

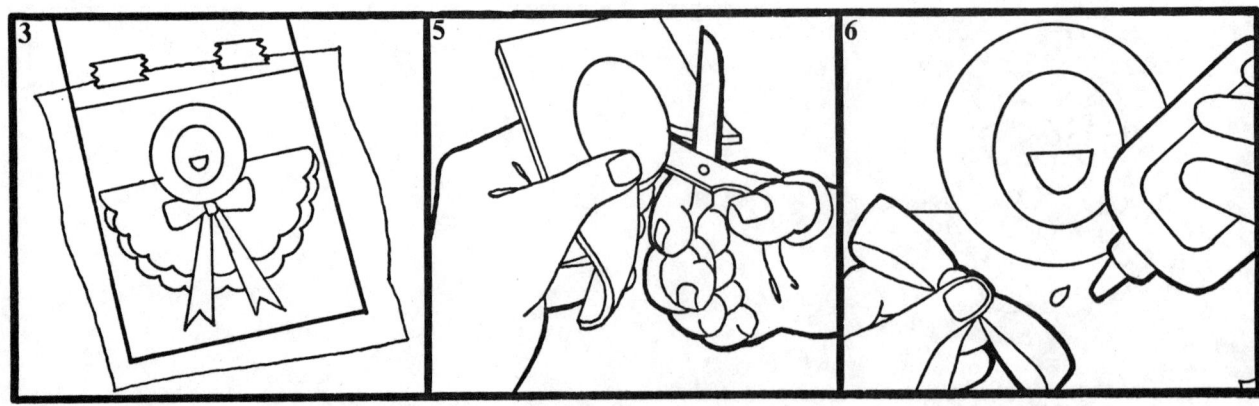

won't shift and cut *both* the tracing paper guide and the doily or design material.

Hint: If you are making quantities of cards, make many design pieces at one time. Transfer each design element to light cardboard with a pencil and carbon paper (see How to Transfer in Techniques section), cut out the element, and you have a cardboard cutting guide. Now stack layers of your design materials, hold the guide firmly on top, and cut closely around the guide.

6. When all the design elements have been cut, glue them down on the card paper. The order of gluing is specified for each card design— usually the larger pieces first. Position each design piece under its outline on the tracing paper and then glue.

7. When all glue has dried, refold your card and send.

VARIATIONS TO TRY AFTER MAKING YOUR FIRST CARD

1. Spatter different-colored paints on the doilies or colored paper before gluing (see Spatter Cards section).
2. Add additional appropriate materials to your card, ribbon, Christmas stickers, dried strawflowers, a small piece of real pine or holly.

Simple Baby Shower or Birth Announcement

- **Additional material:** ribbon
- Glue design pieces and ribbon to front panel of card.
- Follow the order of gluing shown.
- Write your message inside. The unfolded card measures 4" x 10". Folded, it fits into an A2 envelope.

FINISHED CARD

WHITE CARD PAPER
OFF WHITE
SKIN COLOR
CUT OUT THIS SHAPE
PINK OR BLUE RIBBON
GOLD OR WHITE DOILY

FRONT PANEL

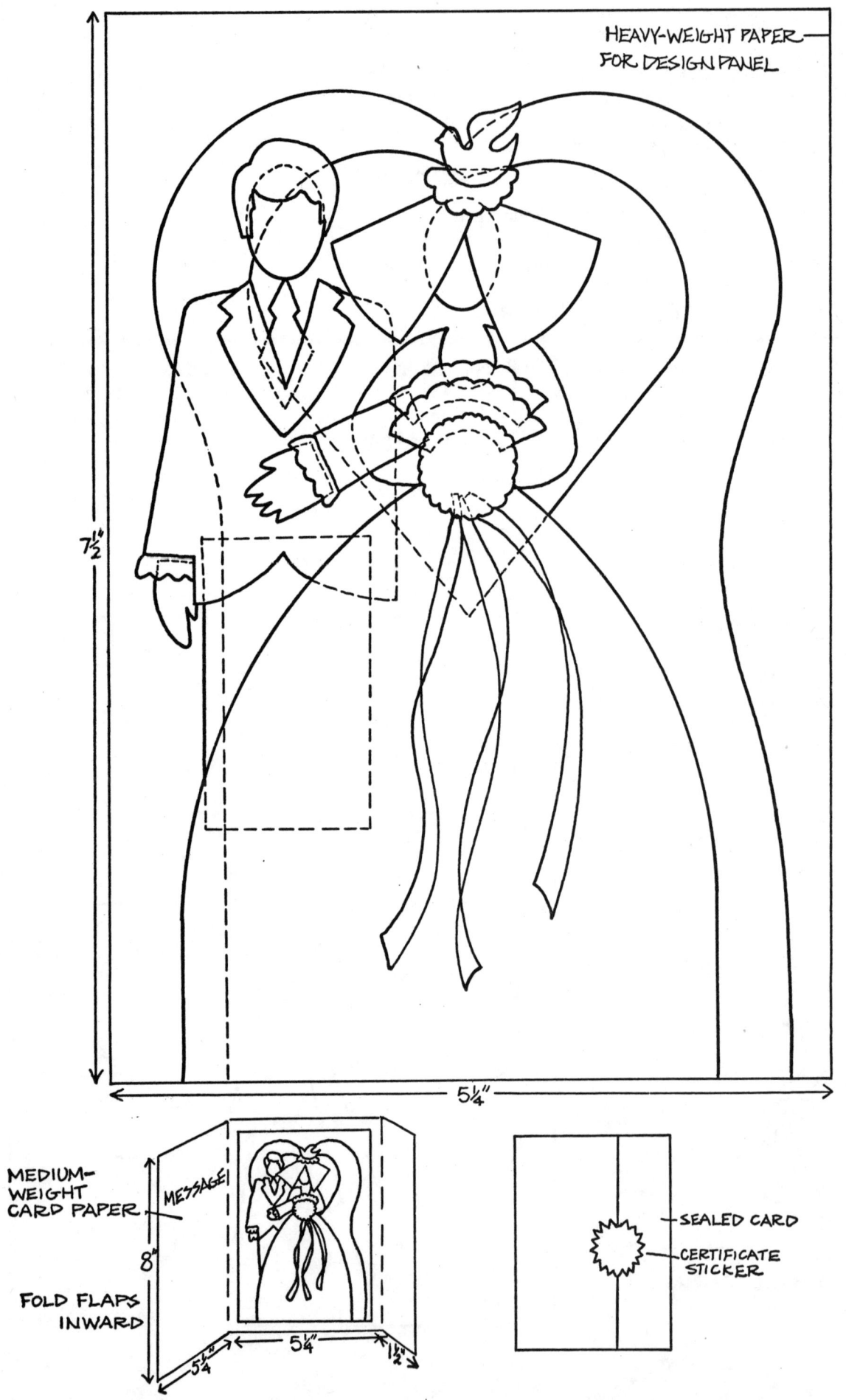

HEAVY-WEIGHT PAPER
FOR DESIGN PANEL

7½"

5¼"

MEDIUM-
WEIGHT
CARD PAPER

MESSAGE!

8"

FOLD FLAPS
INWARD

5¼"

5¼"

½"

SEALED CARD

CERTIFICATE
STICKER

FIG. A

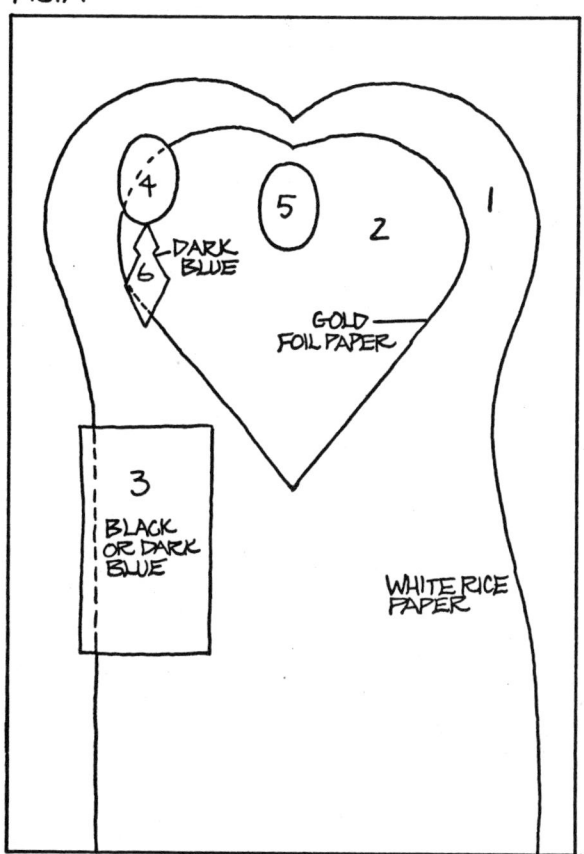

DARK BLUE

GOLD FOIL PAPER

BLACK OR DARK BLUE

WHITE RICE PAPER

FIG. B

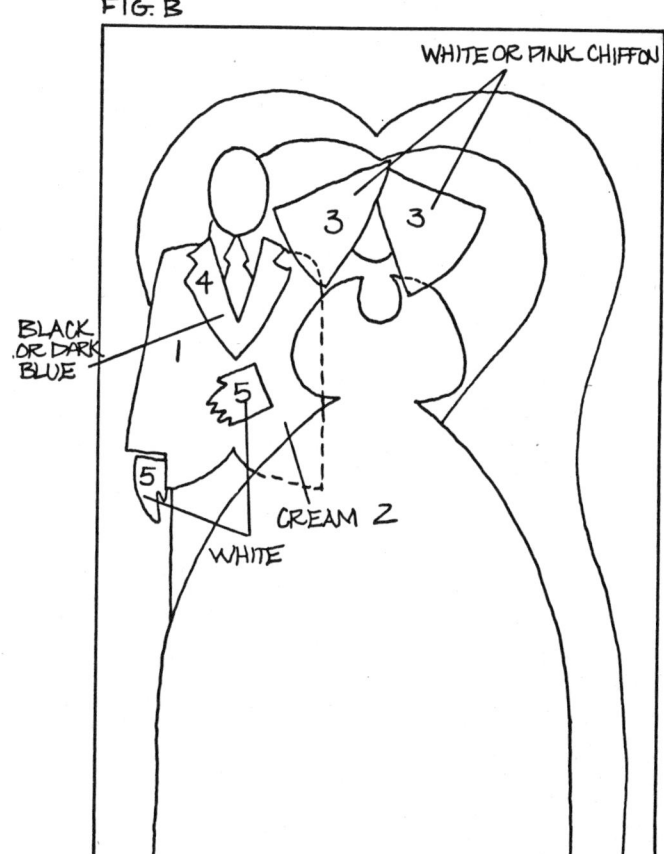

WHITE OR PINK CHIFFON

BLACK OR DARK BLUE

CREAM 2

WHITE

Bride-and-Groom Wedding Card

- **Additional material:** gummed stickers
- Trace the solid lines of the design for your hinged tracing paper. Make your cutting guides by tracing each of the design elements (shown in figures A to C) from the card design.
- Cut a panel of heavy-weight paper, perhaps covered with lighter weight patterned paper. The panel should be about an inch longer than its trimmed size (5¼"x7½"), large enough for both design and hinge.
- Glue the design pieces on the panel, following the order of gluing shown in figures A to C.
- Fig. B: Make her gown (2) by first gluing a doily or rice paper on top of gold or silver foil or wrapping paper and then cutting them out as one piece.
- Fig. C: Glue only the tips of the ribbons (4) at the bride's waist. Her bouquet can be put together with ready-made fabric flowers or bits of colored paper glued onto layers of cutout doilies (5, 6, 7). The bird and nest for her crown are foil appliqués (ready-made or cutout) and are glued on last.
- When all glue has dried, trim the design panel to size.
- Cut, score, and fold the card paper (unfolded size 8"x12"). Mount the design panel on the card paper as shown.

Your finished card is a self-mailer. Seal with a gold sticker.

FIG. C

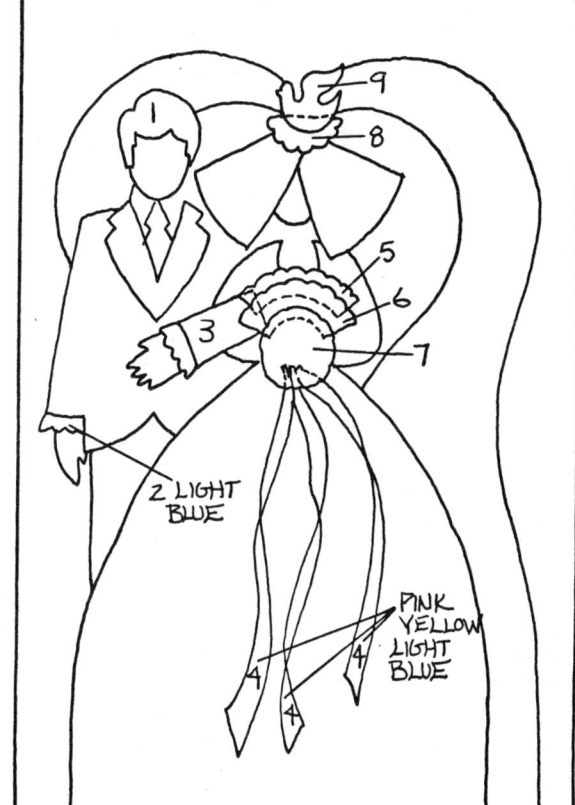

2 LIGHT BLUE

PINK YELLOW LIGHT BLUE

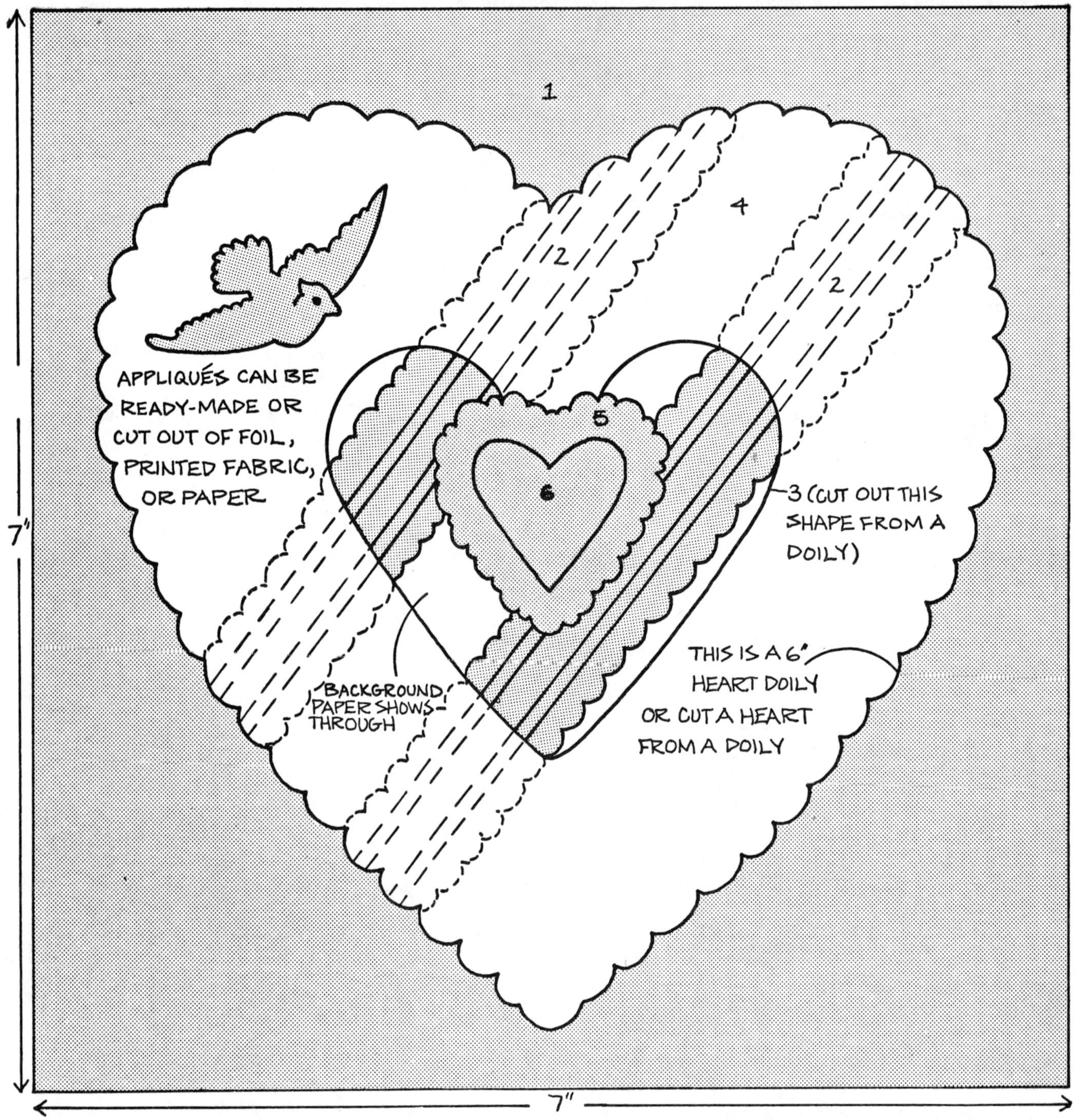

1

4

2

2

APPLIQUÉS CAN BE
READY-MADE OR
CUT OUT OF FOIL,
PRINTED FABRIC,
OR PAPER

5

6

3 (CUT OUT THIS
SHAPE FROM A
DOILY)

BACKGROUND
PAPER SHOWS
THROUGH

THIS IS A 6"
HEART DOILY
OR CUT A HEART
FROM A DOILY

7"

7"

YOUR
MESSAGE
HERE

8"

8"

8"

Valentine's Day, Mother's Day, and Wedding Card

- The design pieces will go on a panel of heavy-weight paper that has been covered with rice paper or patterned paper. The panel should be about an inch longer than its trimmed size (7" x 7"), large enough for both design and hinge.
- Follow the order of gluing shown.
- Cut, score, and fold the card paper (unfolded size 8" x 16").
- When the glue is dry, trim the panel to size and mount on the card paper as shown.

The folded card measures 8" x 8". See Easy Envelopes for a mailer.

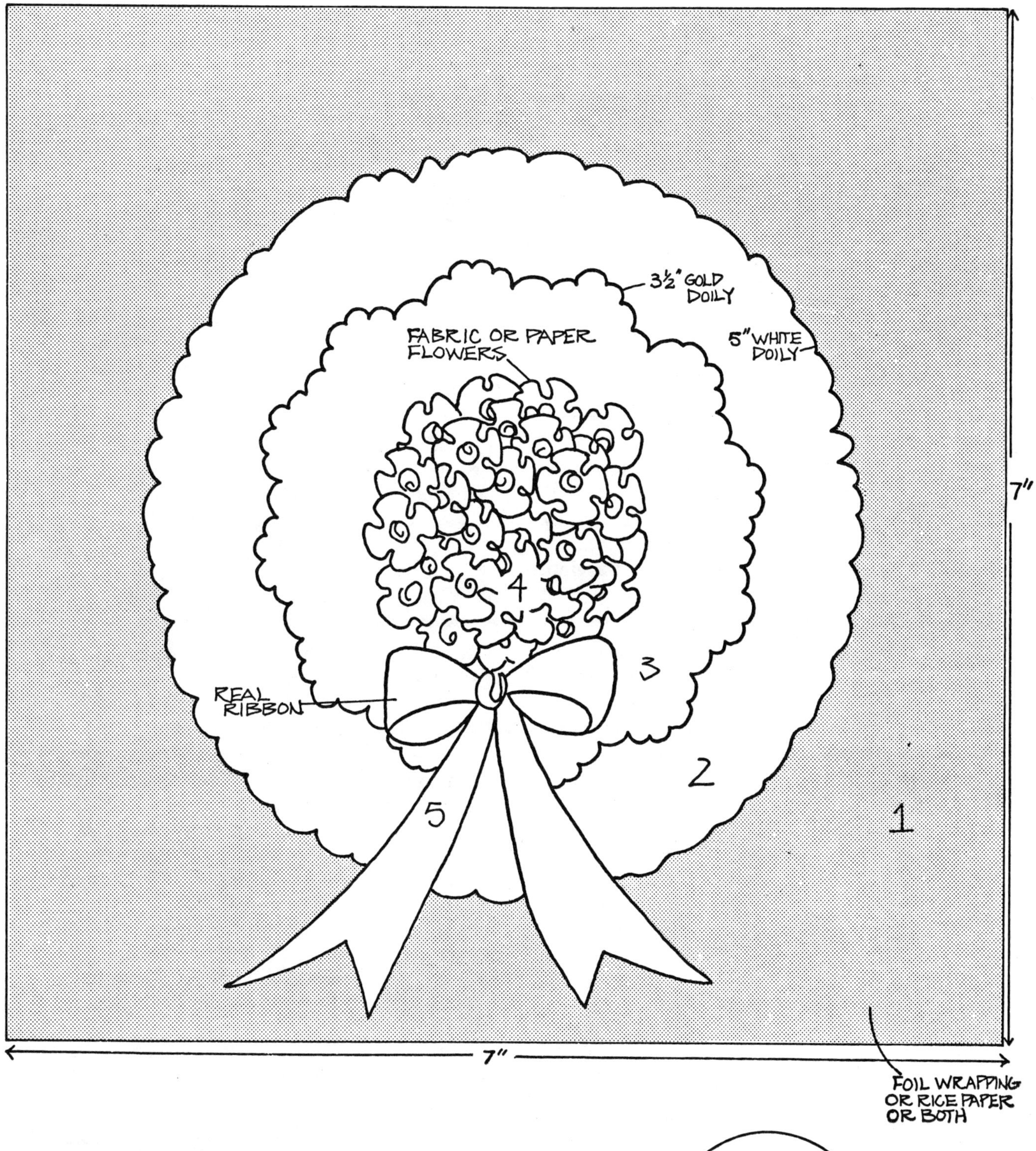

3½" GOLD DOILY

FABRIC OR PAPER FLOWERS

5" WHITE DOILY

4

3

2

1

REAL RIBBON

5

7"

7"

FOIL WRAPPING OR RICE PAPER OR BOTH

No-Cutting Bouquet Card

- **Additional material:** ribbon
- Cut a panel of heavy-weight paper to 7" x 7" and cover with patterned paper or rice paper.
- No tracing paper needed here, just glue pieces in order shown. The ribbon (5) is glued beneath the flowers and then tied in a bow or cut into streamers.
- Let the glue dry, trim, and write your message. If you can part with this card, see Pinwheel Envelope in Easy Envelopes.

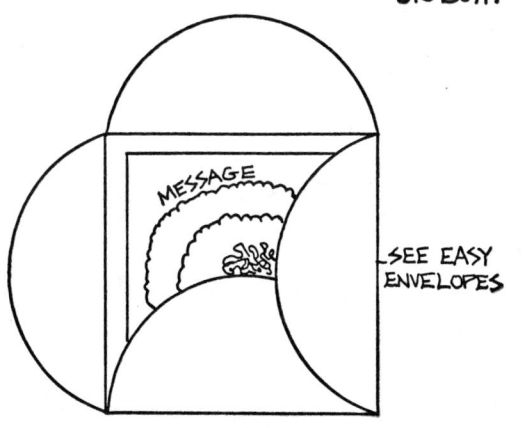

MESSAGE

SEE EASY ENVELOPES

Letter Cutout Cards

Appearance: Simple, bold statement. The card is the message.
Skill required: A good hand with cutting tools.
Quantity/Time: Multiple cards. Up to three or four at a time can be made fairly quickly.

MATERIALS	
• Recommended card paper: medium-weight, heavy enough for card to stand up (see All About Paper) • Easy Envelopes	• Assorted colored papers, foils, gift wrapping, and fabrics • Light cardboard • Tracing paper • Carbon paper • White glue or glue stick

TOOLS	
• Sharp pencil • Scissors or an X-acto knife • Ruler • Back side of a breadboard, or	heavy cardboard (to protect your table when cutting) • See individual cards for additional materials and tools

HOW TO MAKE THE CARD

1. Cover the card design with tracing paper and transfer the letters to light cardboard with a sharp pencil and carbon paper (see How to Transfer in Techniques section). Use a ruler to keep your lines straight.
2. Cut the letters out of the cardboard (a ruler and X-acto knife will give you straight cuts and a 1 lb. coffee can will help you with the curves). These cardboard letters are your cutting guides.
3. Trim your cutout material (fabric, paper, foil) to a workable size, a bit larger than the guide. Then, holding the guide and material firmly together, cut closely around the guide to make the letter cutouts. Repeat for each guide.
   Hint: If you need more than one of the same letter or are making quantities of cards, stack layers of your materials and cut out several

at once. Don't let the layers slip, and make sure you cut through all of them.
4. Glue the letter cutouts to the card paper as shown in the card design.
5. When the glue has dried, cut, score, and fold your card.

---

1. Spatter the card paper before you glue on the letters (see Spatter Cards section).
2. Cut your letters out of old photos or magazine illustrations.
3. If the design is cut out as one word, use card paper as your cutout material and just fold and tuck the word into an envelope as is.
4. Cut your one word out of card paper, glue a different color paper over each letter, and let glue dry. Then turn card over and cut away excess paper. Fold and mail.
5. Glue bright wrapping paper onto the card paper before adding the letter cutouts.

**VARIATIONS TO TRY
AFTER MAKING
YOUR FIRST CARD**

FINISHED CARDS

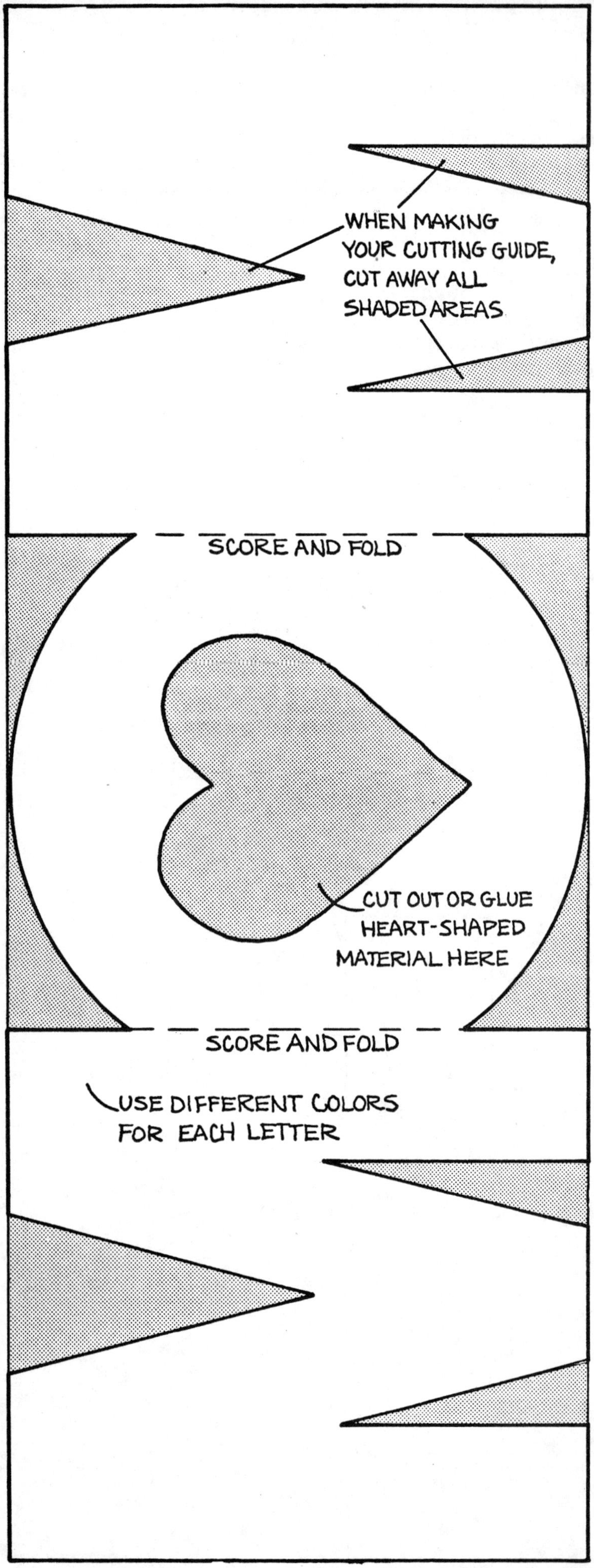

WHEN MAKING
YOUR CUTTING GUIDE,
CUT AWAY ALL
SHADED AREAS

SCORE AND FOLD

CUT OUT OR GLUE
HEART-SHAPED
MATERIAL HERE

SCORE AND FOLD

USE DIFFERENT COLORS
FOR EACH LETTER

Mother's Day Card

- Make one cutting guide for "M" and one for "O."
- Choose cutout materials that mean something to her: her favorite section of the paper, magazine pages, duplicate family photos.
- Cut out both "M"s at the same time. Leave a window for the heart or cut it out of a different material (velvet, lace, doily) and glue on.
- Cut your card paper to size (4"x10¼"), lightly mark where to fold, and glue down the letters.

When the glue is dry, write your message and then score and fold your card (fig. A, 4"x4"). See Easy Envelopes for a mailer. Another heart on the envelope makes a nice, final touch.

Recommended Variations: #3 and #4

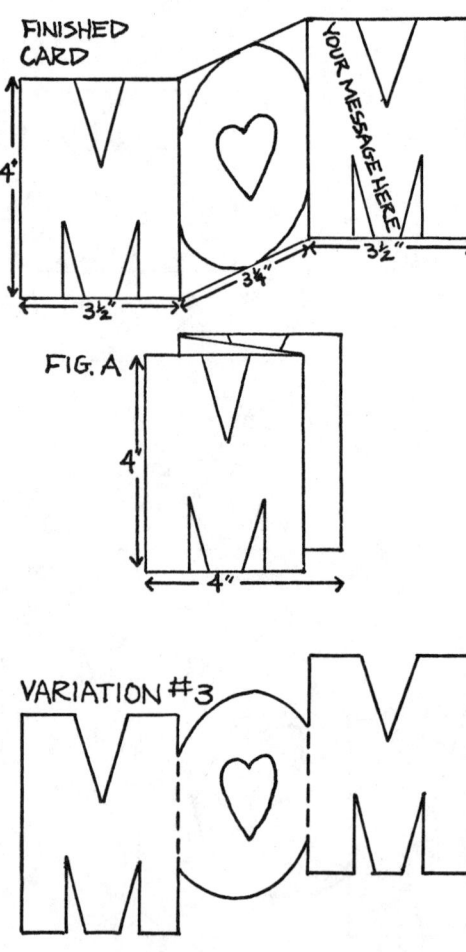

FINISHED CARD

YOUR MESSAGE HERE

4"

3½"   3¼"   3½"

FIG. A

4"

4"

VARIATION #3

Father's Day Card

- **Additional material:** gummed stickers
- Make one cutting guide for "D" and one for "A."
- Choose cutout materials that mean something to him: his favorite section of the paper, magazine pages, duplicate family photos.
- Cut out both "D"s at the same time.
- Cut your card paper to size (4"x16¾"), score, and fold.
- Glue the letters as shown in figures A to C. When the glue is dry, trim away excess card paper around the curve of the last "D."

Write your message, and seal.

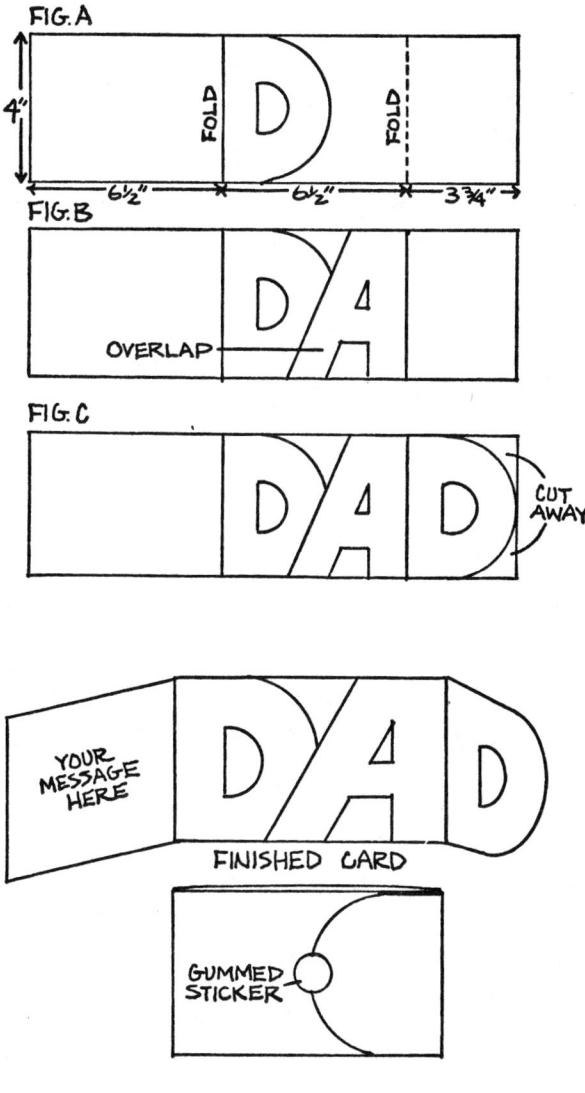

FIG. A

4"

FOLD   D   FOLD

6½"   6½"   3¾"

FIG. B

D A

OVERLAP

FIG. C

D A D   CUT AWAY

YOUR MESSAGE HERE   D A D

FINISHED CARD

GUMMED STICKER

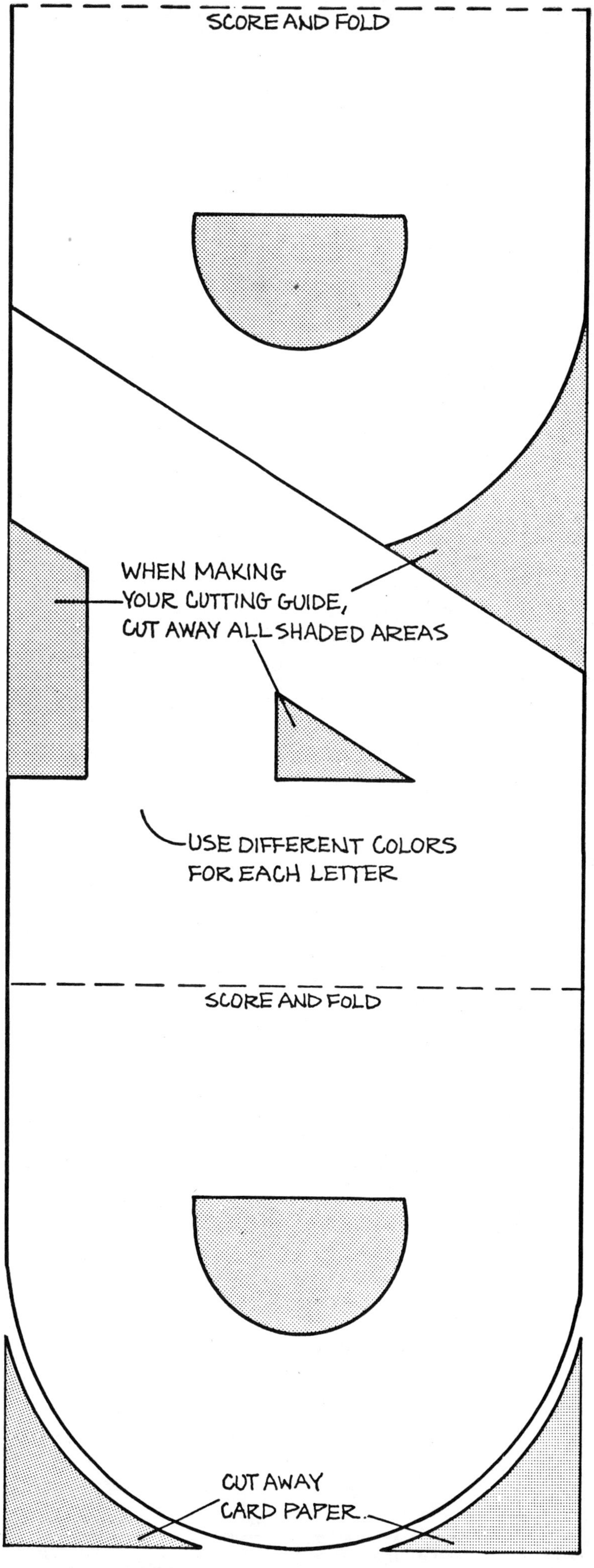

SCORE AND FOLD

WHEN MAKING YOUR CUTTING GUIDE, CUT AWAY ALL SHADED AREAS

USE DIFFERENT COLORS FOR EACH LETTER

SCORE AND FOLD

CUT AWAY CARD PAPER.

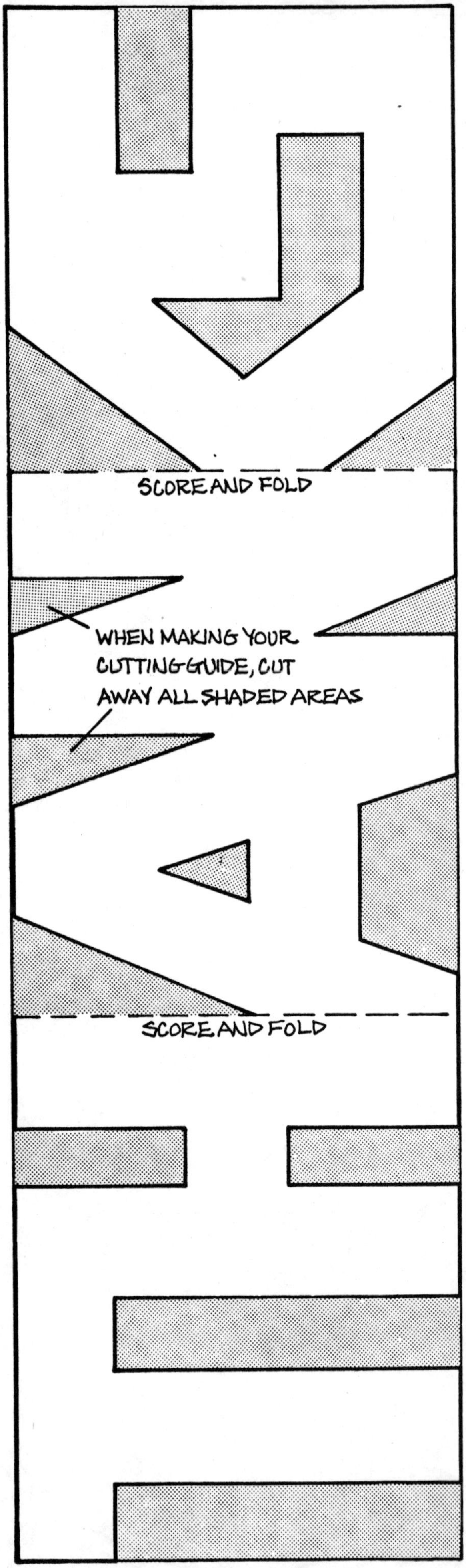
SCORE AND FOLD
WHEN MAKING YOUR CUTTING GUIDE, CUT AWAY ALL SHADED AREAS
SCORE AND FOLD

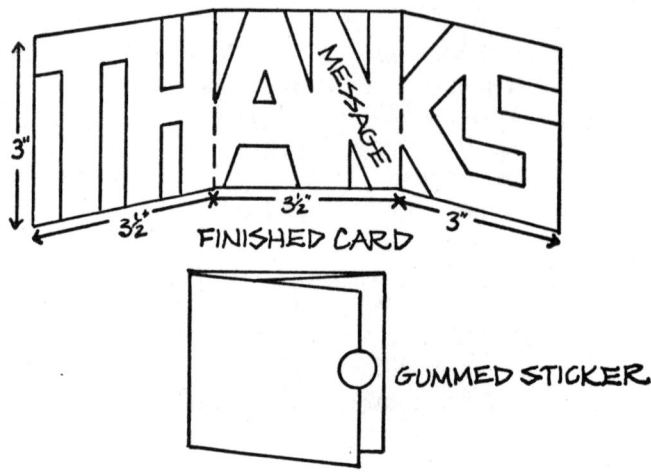

THANKS
MESSAGE
3"
3½"
3½"
3"
FINISHED CARD

GUMMED STICKER

A Thank You

- **Additional materials:** gummed stickers
- Make one cutting guide for the whole word. Use a ruler when tracing and cutting.
- Choose cutout color to contrast with card paper.
- Glue the "THANKS" to your card paper. When dry, cut the card to size (3"x10"), score, and fold.

No envelope is necessary. Seal with a sticker.

Recommended Variation: #3 (folded size 3"x3½", see Easy Envelopes)

VARIATION #3
CUT OUT
THANKS
FOLD
FOLD
HEAVY PAPER

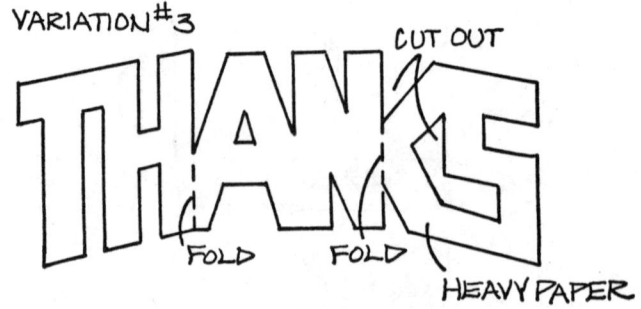

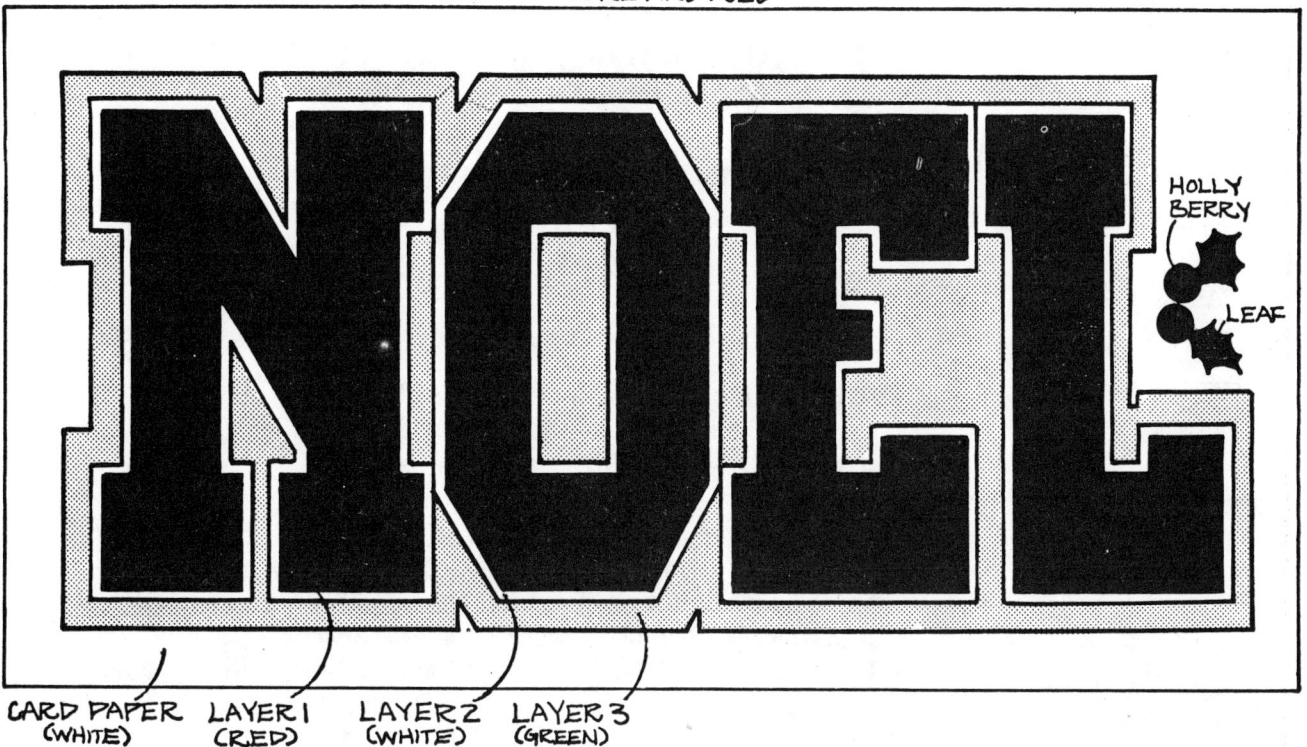

CARD PAPER (WHITE)   LAYER 1 (RED)   LAYER 2 (WHITE)   LAYER 3 (GREEN)

HOLLY BERRY

LEAF

Noel! Noel! Noel!

- **Additional material:** hole punch
- Make your cutting guides from the black letters (layer 1) in the card design.
- Use medium-weight paper as your cutout material for all layers.
- Cut out the letters (layer 1) and glue them individually on a different color paper (layer 2, fig. A). Let glue set between each step.
- Cut along the outside of the letters, leaving about $1/16$" border (fig. B), and then glue the two-layered letters spelling "NOEL" to another paper (layer 3, fig. C).
- Cut around the outside of the *whole* word, leaving about $1/8$" border (fig. D). Use a ruler whenever possible when cutting.
- Cut the card paper to size (7"x7"), score, and fold. Now glue the three-layered "NOEL" centered on the front panel.
- Glue down the berries and holly. A hole punch and red paper will make the berries; a few snips of the scissors and green paper will give you the holly.

The finished, folded card will fit a Monarch-size envelope.

Variation: A simpler version. Cut three layers of paper at one time for each letter and then glue them down overlapping as in figure E.

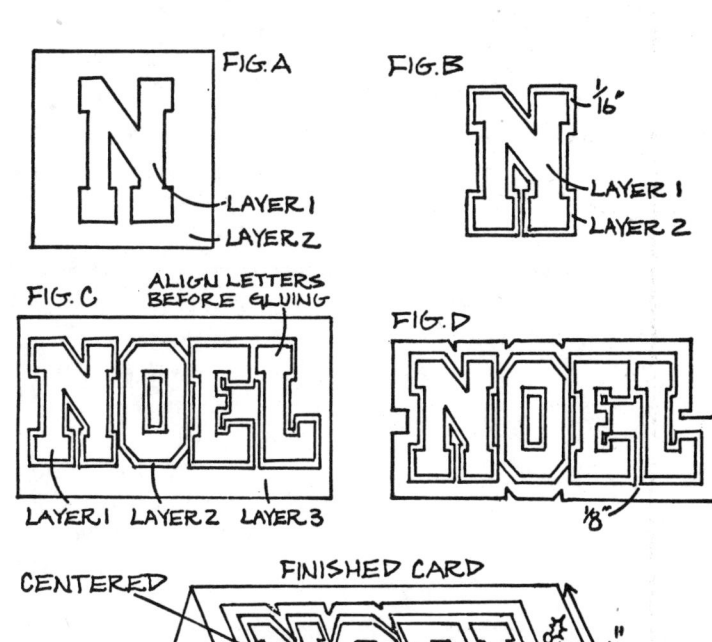

FIG. A

LAYER 1
LAYER 2

FIG. B

$1/16$"
LAYER 1
LAYER 2

FIG. C

ALIGN LETTERS BEFORE GLUING

LAYER 1   LAYER 2   LAYER 3

FIG. D

$1/8$"

CENTERED

FINISHED CARD

$3\frac{1}{2}$"

7"

MESSAGE GOES ON THE INSIDE

VARIATION FIG. E

Embossed Cards

Appearance: A very elegant look. A simple design raised on the surface of the card.

Skill required: Needs careful cutting of the cardboard guide.

Quantity/Time: Once you make your guide, you can make up to thirty cards very quickly.

MATERIALS	
• Recommended paper: water-color paper, colored blotter paper or medium weight cover paper, (see All About Paper)	• Heavy cardboard for embossing guide (smooth illustration board, boxboard or non-corrugated cardboard, or posterboard)
• Easy Envelopes	• Emory board or fine sandpaper
• White glue	• Tracing paper
• Masking tape	• Carbon paper

TOOLS	
• Sharp pencil	• Hammer
• X-acto knife (with extra blades)	• Straight pin
• Back side of a breadboard, or heavy cardboard (to protect your table when cutting)	• See individual cards for additional materials and tools

HOW TO MAKE THE CARD

1. Cover the card design with tracing paper and transfer it to the heavy cardboard with a pencil and carbon paper (see How to Transfer in Techniques section)—be sure to include the border around the design. The cardboard should be an inch or two larger than the folded card size.
2. Cut out the embossing guide (use a new blade in the X-acto knife for best cutting). Try to make your cuts straight down, not on a slant, and save both the cutouts and the resulting stencil. After cutting, gently sand the edges of both cutouts and stencil until smooth.

   Hint: Thinner board (posterboard) is easier to cut, but the thicker board (illustration board) will produce a deeper impression in the

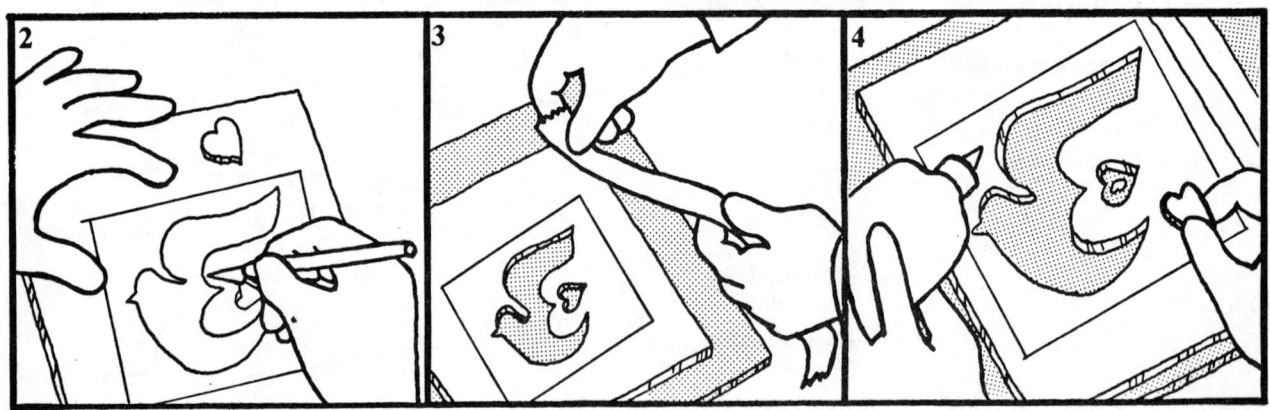

card. When cutting thicker board, make two cuttings—a shallow one to outline the design, and then a deep one to separate the cutout.

3. Place the stencil on another piece of heavy cardboard (the base-board), which should be an inch or two larger than the stencil. Now join the hinge side of the stencil (indicated on the card design) to the baseboard with masking tape, to make a hinge.

4. Replace the cutouts in the stencil and glue them to the baseboard. After the glue dries you should be able to work the hinge and have the stencil fit over the glued-down cutouts perfectly.

5. To make a centering guide for your card paper, poke holes through the stencil (two holes are indicated on the card design) with a pin or the tip of your X-acto knife. Be sure to push all the way into the baseboard. Now lift the stencil and lay a strip of masking tape along the baseboard connecting the two holes. To make the holes easy to see, mark on the tape with a pen where the pin holes are.

6. Cut your card paper to size and line it up along the masking tape edge and between the pin hole marks. Check the card design for the proper edge of the paper to align with the tape.

7. Lower the stencil and trap the paper firmly between the cutouts and the stencil.

8. Tap around the edges of the design with a hammer. Tap lightly to avoid tearing the paper.

9. Lift up the stencil and look at the paper. If the design is not raised from the surface, lower the stencil and continue tapping. If the surface is raised, the paper is embossed and can be removed, scored, and folded.

10. You can easily make large quantities of the same card with one embossing guide. Just center each piece of card paper and tap out the design.

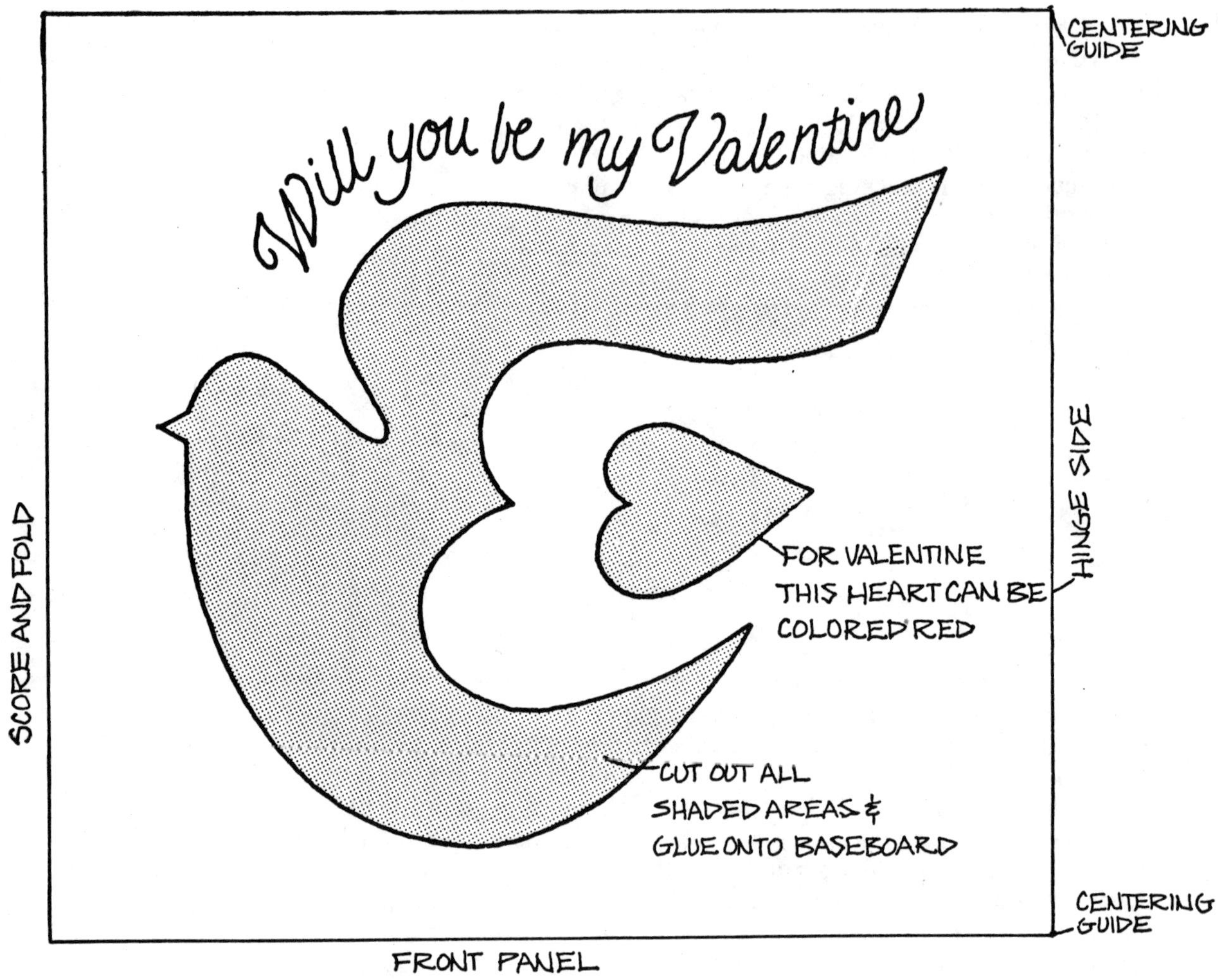

Will you be my Valentine

CENTERING GUIDE

HINGE SIDE

SCORE AND FOLD

FOR VALENTINE THIS HEART CAN BE COLORED RED

CUT OUT ALL SHADED AREAS & GLUE ONTO BASEBOARD

CENTERING GUIDE

FRONT PANEL

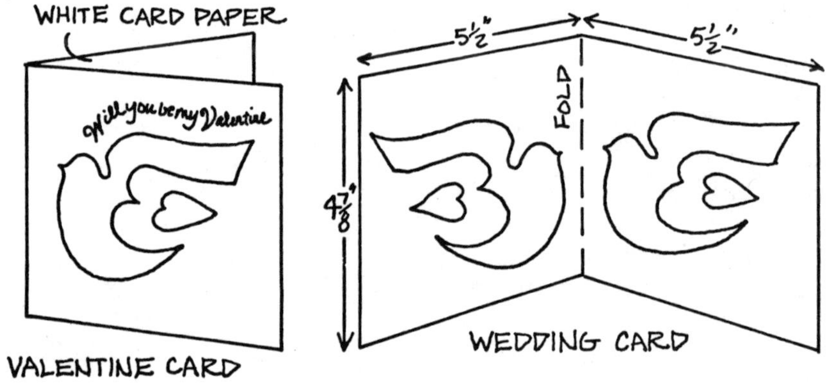

WHITE CARD PAPER

Will you be my Valentine

VALENTINE CARD

5½"   5½"

FOLD

4⅞"

WEDDING CARD

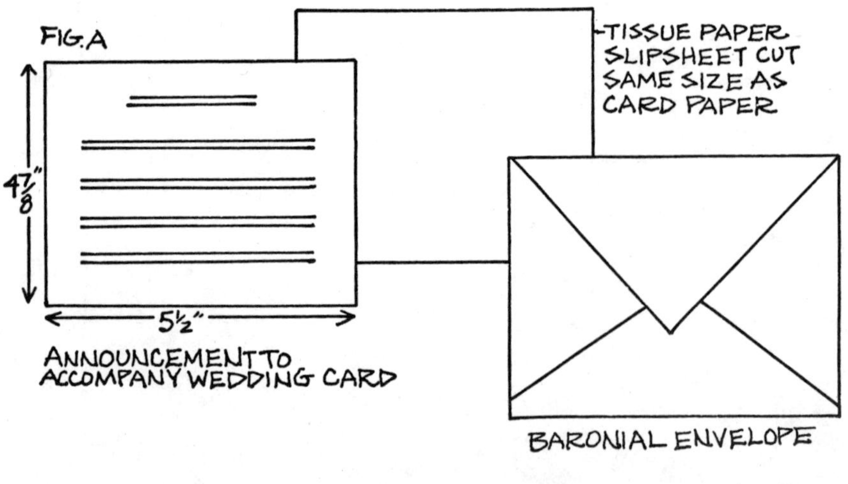

FIG. A

4⅞"

5½"

ANNOUNCEMENT TO ACCOMPANY WEDDING CARD

TISSUE PAPER SLIPSHEET CUT SAME SIZE AS CARD PAPER

BARONIAL ENVELOPE

Wedding or Valentine's Dove

- **Additional materials:** felt-tip marker, colored paper, card-weight paper, tissue paper
- Emboss only the front panel for the Valentine's Day card. The heart can be colored using a felt-tip marker or cut-out paper.
- For a wedding card emboss the entire card. The trick is to score and fold the card paper first and then emboss the folded card layers. This will give you a dove on the front, and a pair of doves when the card is opened.
- Cut an announcement card and tissue (fig. A) to accompany the wedding card.

Each card unfolded measures 4⅞"x11". When folded, your card fits into a #6 Baronial envelope.

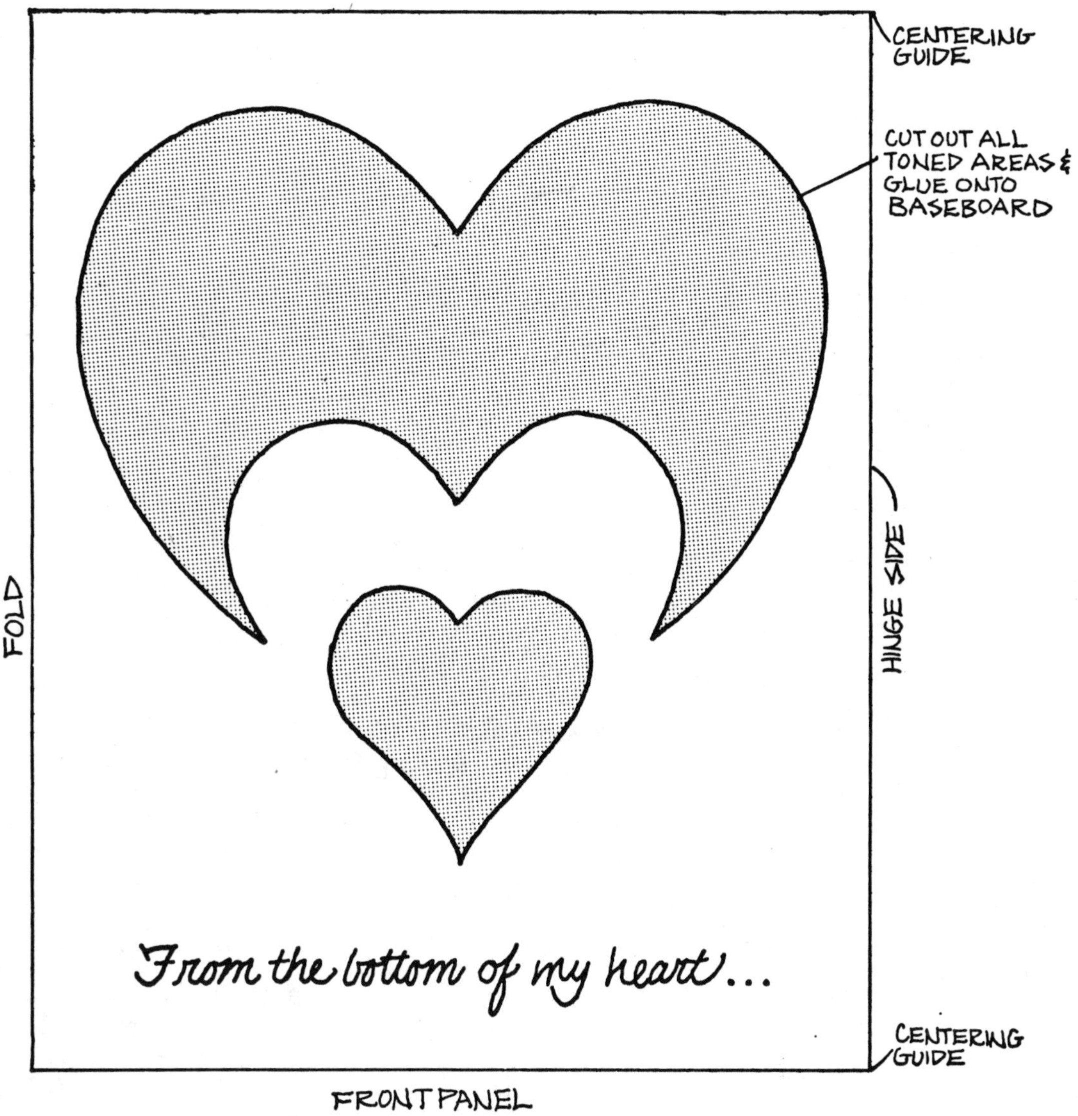

CENTERING GUIDE

CUT OUT ALL TONED AREAS & GLUE ONTO BASEBOARD

FOLD

HINGE SIDE

From the bottom of my heart...

CENTERING GUIDE

FRONT PANEL

WHITE CARD PAPER

5½"

4½"

FINISHED CARD

A6 ENVELOPE

All Occasions Heart

- **Additional materials:** felt-tip marker, colored paper
- Add color to the smaller heart with a felt-tip marker or cut paper.
  The unfolded card measures 5½"x9". When folded, your card fits into an A6 envelope.

Variation: Use the stencil of the smaller heart to cut out a window in the card paper. Leave the window open, or mount a photograph on the inside of the card to show through.

VARIATION

FOLD

CUTOUT

be my Valentine

Love Judy

PHOTO

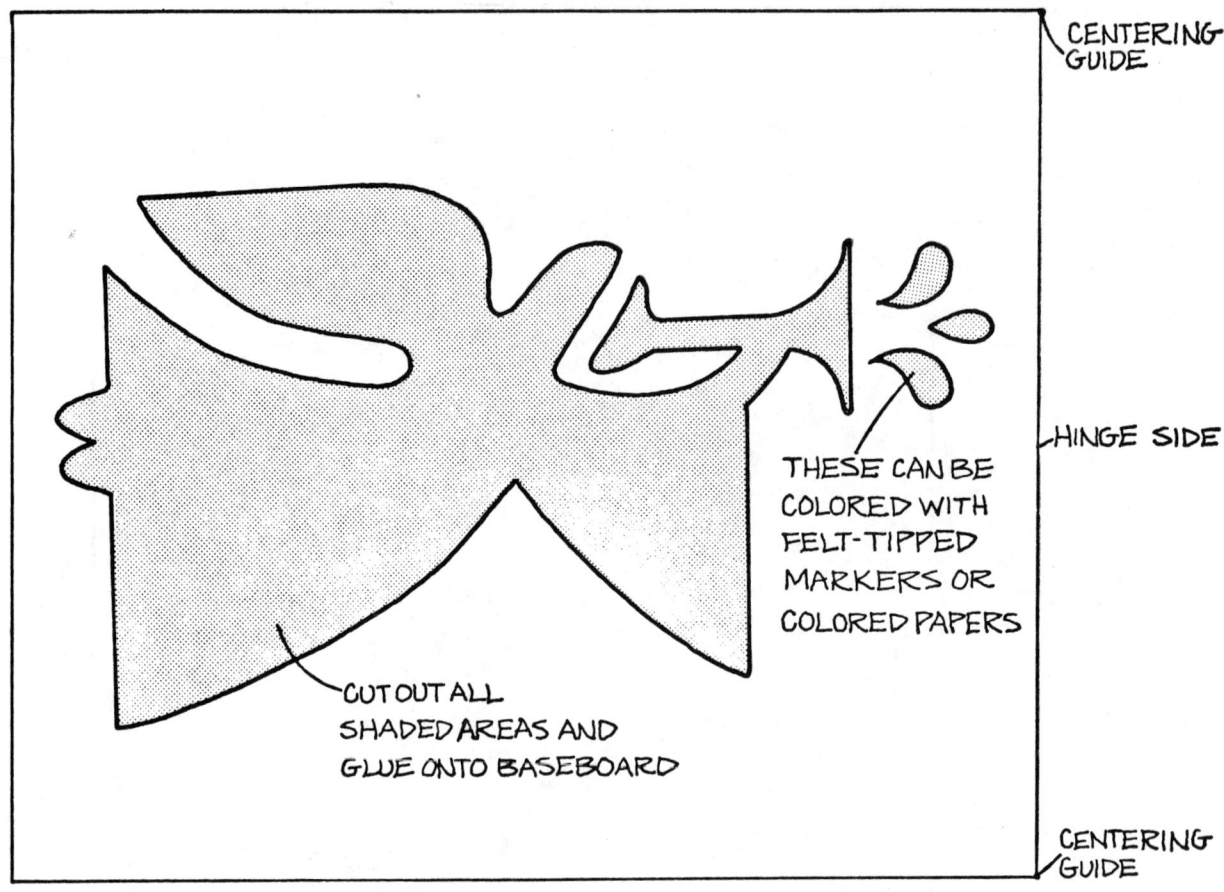

SCORE AND FOLD

CENTERING GUIDE

HINGE SIDE

THESE CAN BE COLORED WITH FELT-TIPPED MARKERS OR COLORED PAPERS

CUT OUT ALL SHADED AREAS AND GLUE ONTO BASEBOARD

CENTERING GUIDE

FRONT PANEL

A Christmas Angel

● These cuts need care, so change X-acto blades often. The unfolded card measures 5½" x 9". When folded, your card is 4½" x 5½" and fits into an A6 envelope.

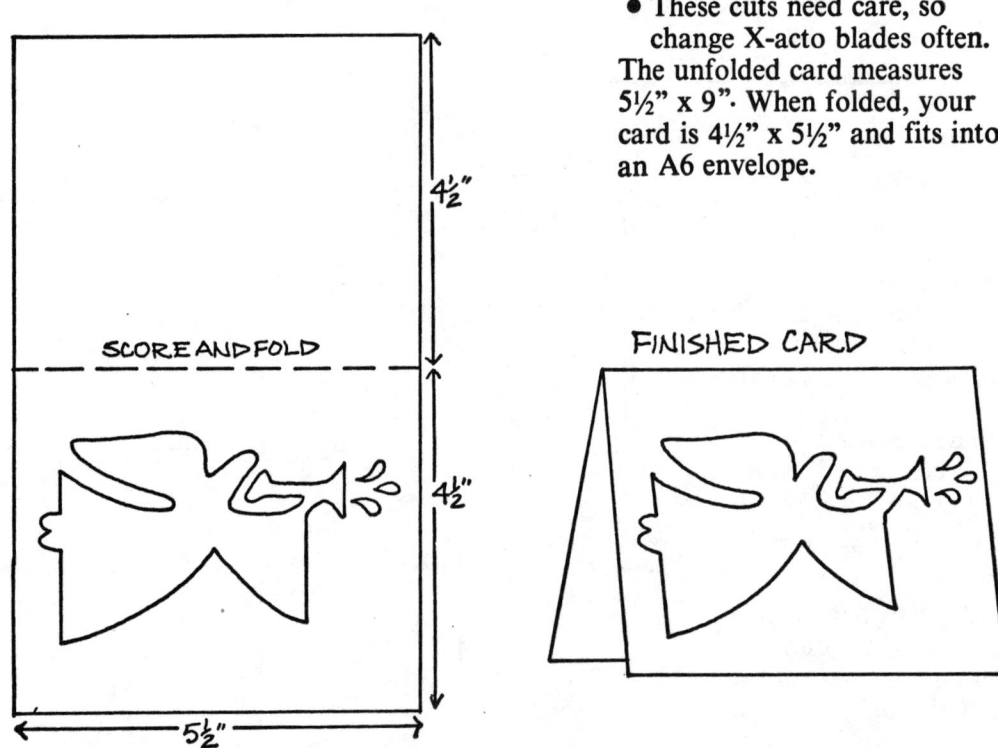

4½"

SCORE AND FOLD

4½"

5½"

FINISHED CARD

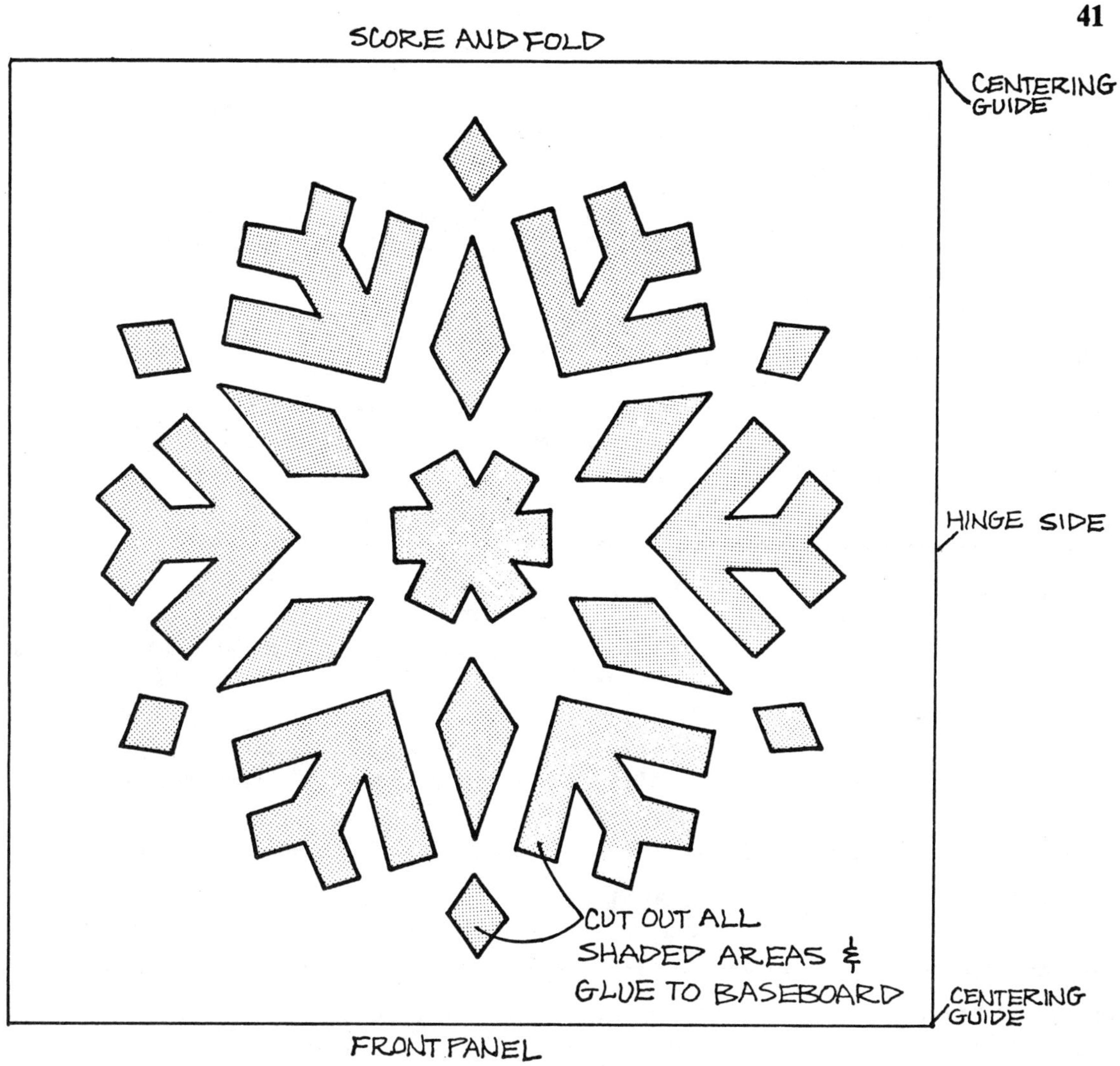

SCORE AND FOLD

CENTERING GUIDE

HINGE SIDE

CUT OUT ALL
SHADED AREAS &
GLUE TO BASEBOARD

CENTERING GUIDE

FRONT PANEL

White Christmas

● Cut precisely and you will
have a masterpiece. Change
X-acto blades often.
The unfolded card measures
5" x 10". When folded, your
card is 5" x 5" and fits the
Pinwheel Envelope described in
Easy Envelopes.

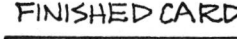

FINISHED CARD

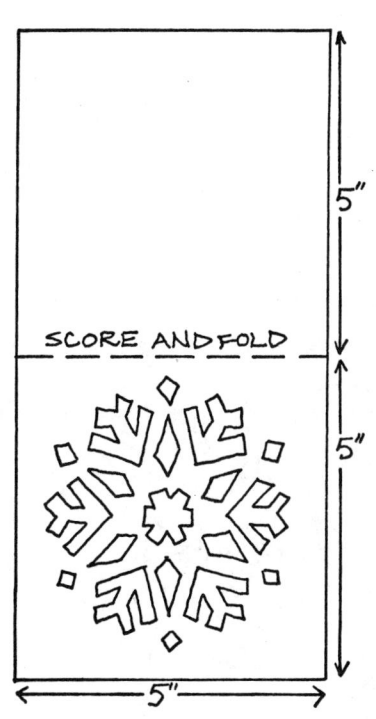

5"

SCORE AND FOLD

5"

5"

Good Luck! from the O'Brian's

Pop-Up & Cutout Cards

Appearance: Slightly "animated," fully dimensional cards.
Skill required: Lots of careful folding, cutting, and positioning of card parts.
Quantity/Time: Must be made one at a time. Moderately slow.

MATERIALS	• Recommended card paper: medium-weight, colored or coated cover paper (see All About Paper) • Easy Envelopes • Assorted colored papers (any weight), leftover gift wrapping, foils, fabrics	• Light cardboard • Back side of a breadboard, or heavy cardboard (to protect your table when cutting) • Tracing paper • Carbon paper • White glue or glue stick
TOOLS	• Sharp pencil • Scissors or X-acto knife	• See individual cards for additional materials and tools

HOW TO MAKE THE CARD

1. Cover the card design page with tracing paper and transfer the design elements to the light cardboard with a pencil and carbon paper (see How to Transfer in Techniques section). Note that sometimes you will take the design elements from the card design and sometimes from full-size drawings accompanying the card design.
2. Cut each design shape out of the light cardboard. These cardboard cutouts are your guides to cutting the design pieces out of the various papers and fabrics.
3. Starting with your design material (papers, foils, fabrics) a bit larger than your guide, lay the cutting guide on the material, hold the pieces firmly together, and then cut all around the guide. The

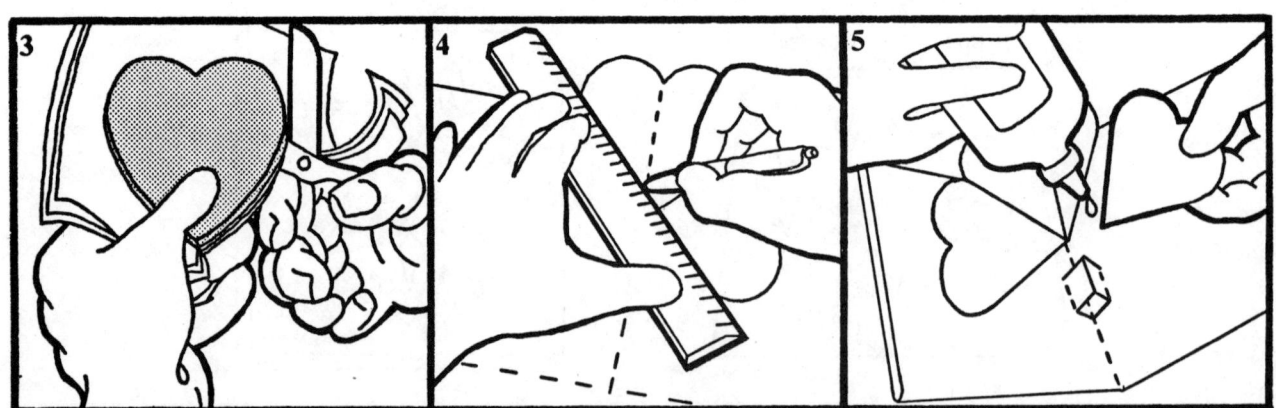

design material now has the shape of the design element. Repeat for each cutting guide.

Hint: If you are making quantities of cards, or many of one design shape, stack your materials and cut out several at one time. Take care that the layers of materials do not shift while you are cutting.

4. Cut, score, and fold your card paper as shown in the card design.
5. Glue the design elements together, as shown. Let dry.
6. Now glue the completed design to the card paper, let the glue dry, and refold.

---

1. Spatter *on* the inside design instead of cutting it *out*. You can use the remaining paper cut away from the main design element as the stencil for spattering (see Spatter Cards section).
2. Before you glue on the completed design (step 6), spatter the card paper to add color and texture.

VARIATIONS TO TRY AFTER MAKING YOUR FIRST CARD

FINISHED CARDS

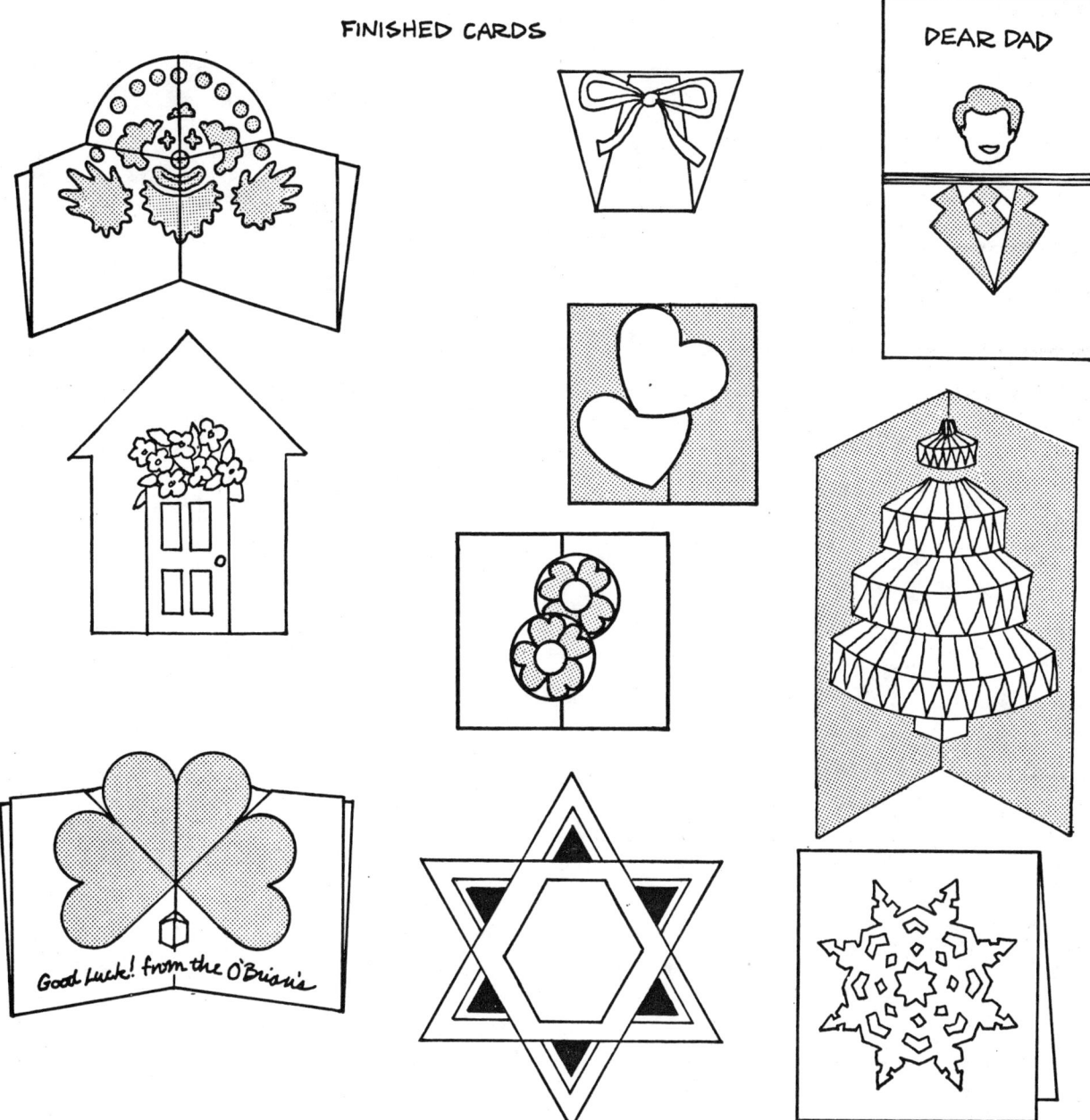

44

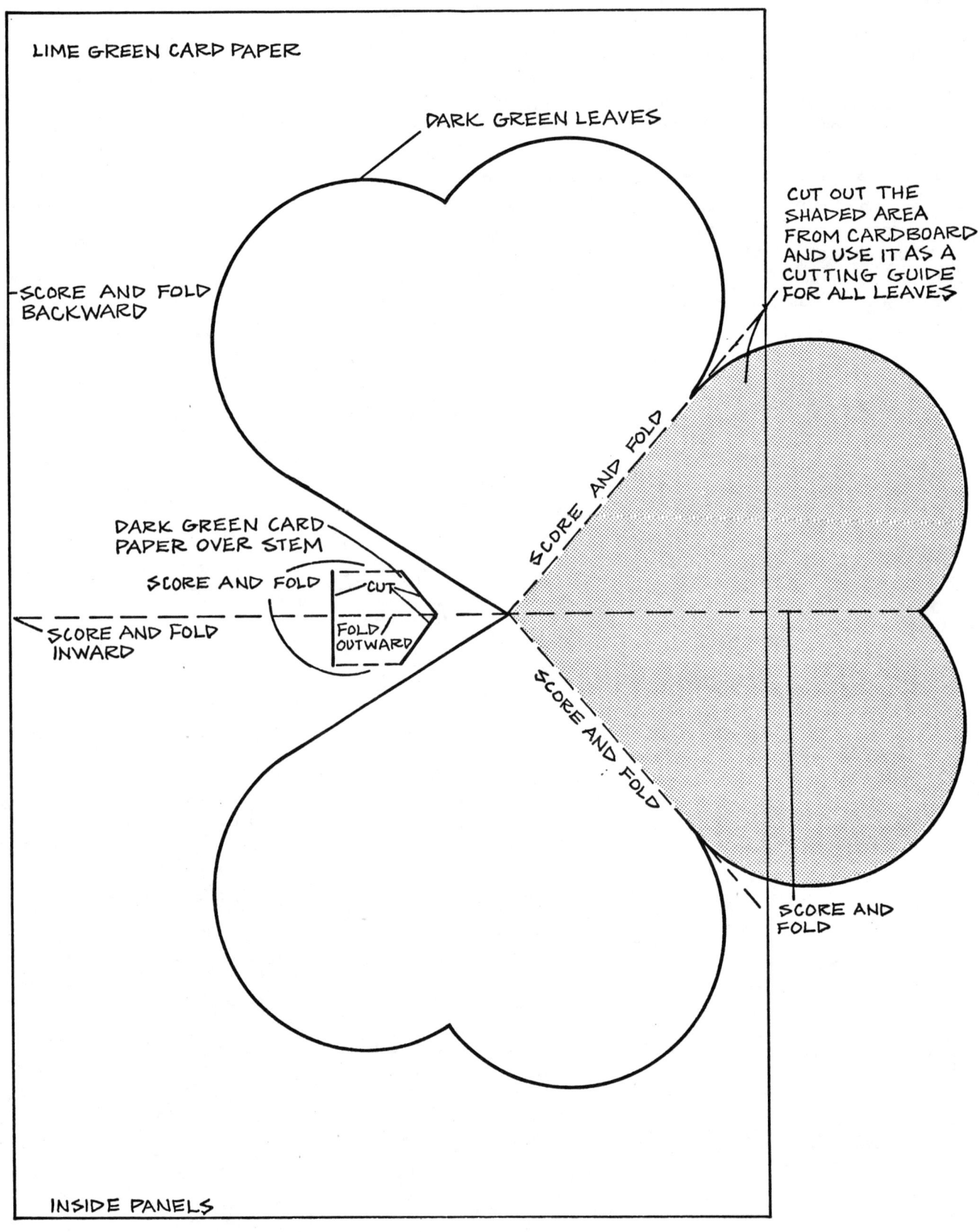

LIME GREEN CARD PAPER

DARK GREEN LEAVES

SCORE AND FOLD
BACKWARD

CUT OUT THE
SHADED AREA
FROM CARDBOARD
AND USE IT AS A
CUTTING GUIDE
FOR ALL LEAVES

SCORE AND FOLD

DARK GREEN CARD
PAPER OVER STEM

SCORE AND FOLD

CUT

FOLD
OUTWARD

SCORE AND FOLD
INWARD

SCORE AND FOLD

SCORE AND
FOLD

INSIDE PANELS

For Saint Patrick's Day

- **Additional material:** gummed stickers
- Score and fold an 8½" x 11" piece of card paper in quarters (figs. A and B). Reopen one fold.
- Cut out one cardboard cutting-guide leaf, using the center leaf as your guide. Then cut all three leaves at one time from dark green paper.
- For the leaves: fold one leaf in half and glue to the card (fig. C). To do this accurately, place your card paper on top of the card design illustration with the edges and center fold lines aligned. Position the cutout folded leaf over the card paper and the illustration, so that the fold lines and outline of the cutout leaf and illustrated leaf match. Now glue. Note that the the bottom layer of card paper remains untouched in all of these steps.
- Score the card paper along the straight edges of the leaf to the top of the paper (fig. D). Fold the paper and leaf towards you and pinch along the scored lines (fig. E). This is vital to obtain the right pop-up action. Now glue on the other two leaves.
- For the stem: Make three short cuts for the top and bottom of the stem, as shown (fig. F), cutting through only one layer of paper. Lift up the stem and fold the center of it out, so that when the card is folded it is popped out.
- Write your message inside and fold your card (fig. G).

Your finished card is a self-mailer. Seal with a gummed sticker.

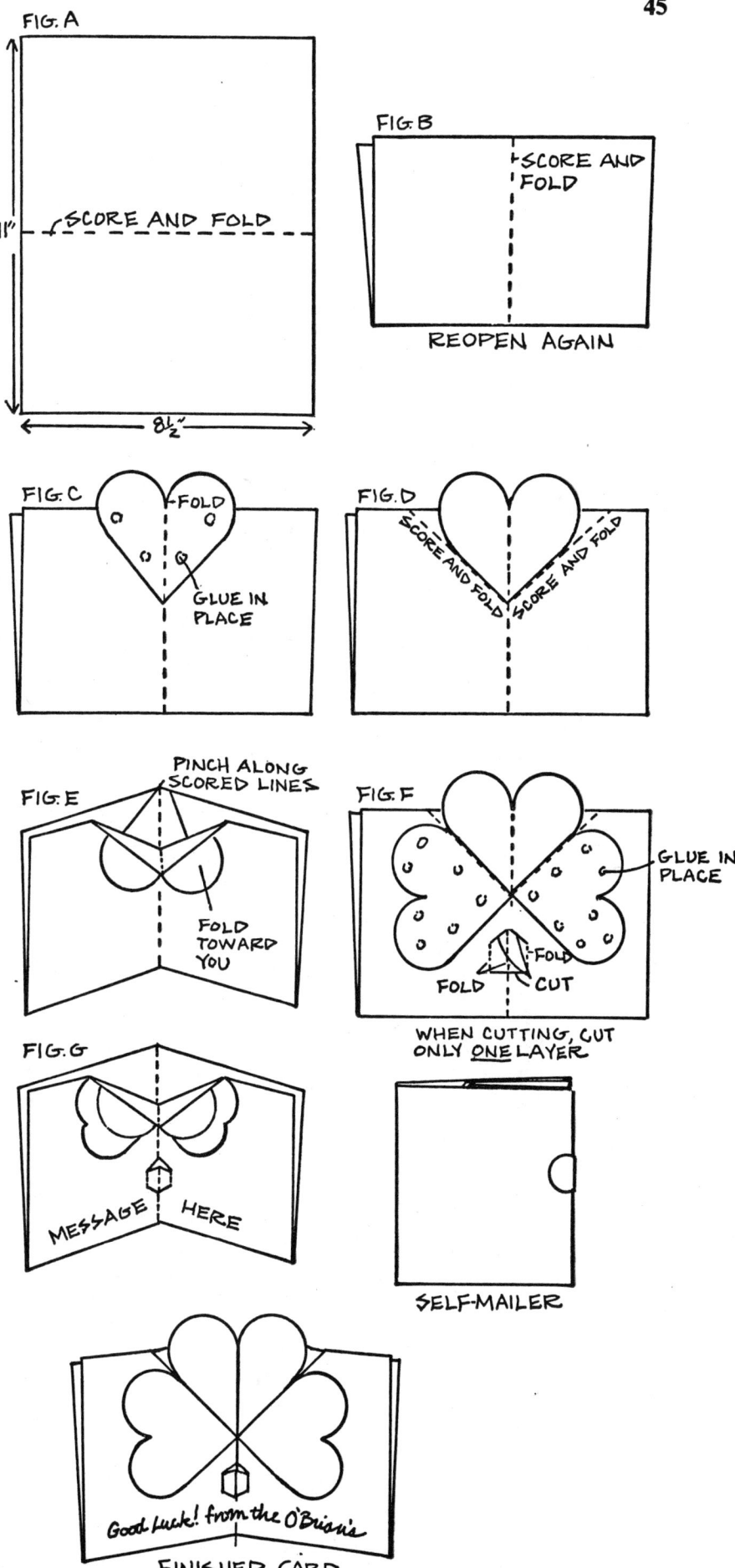

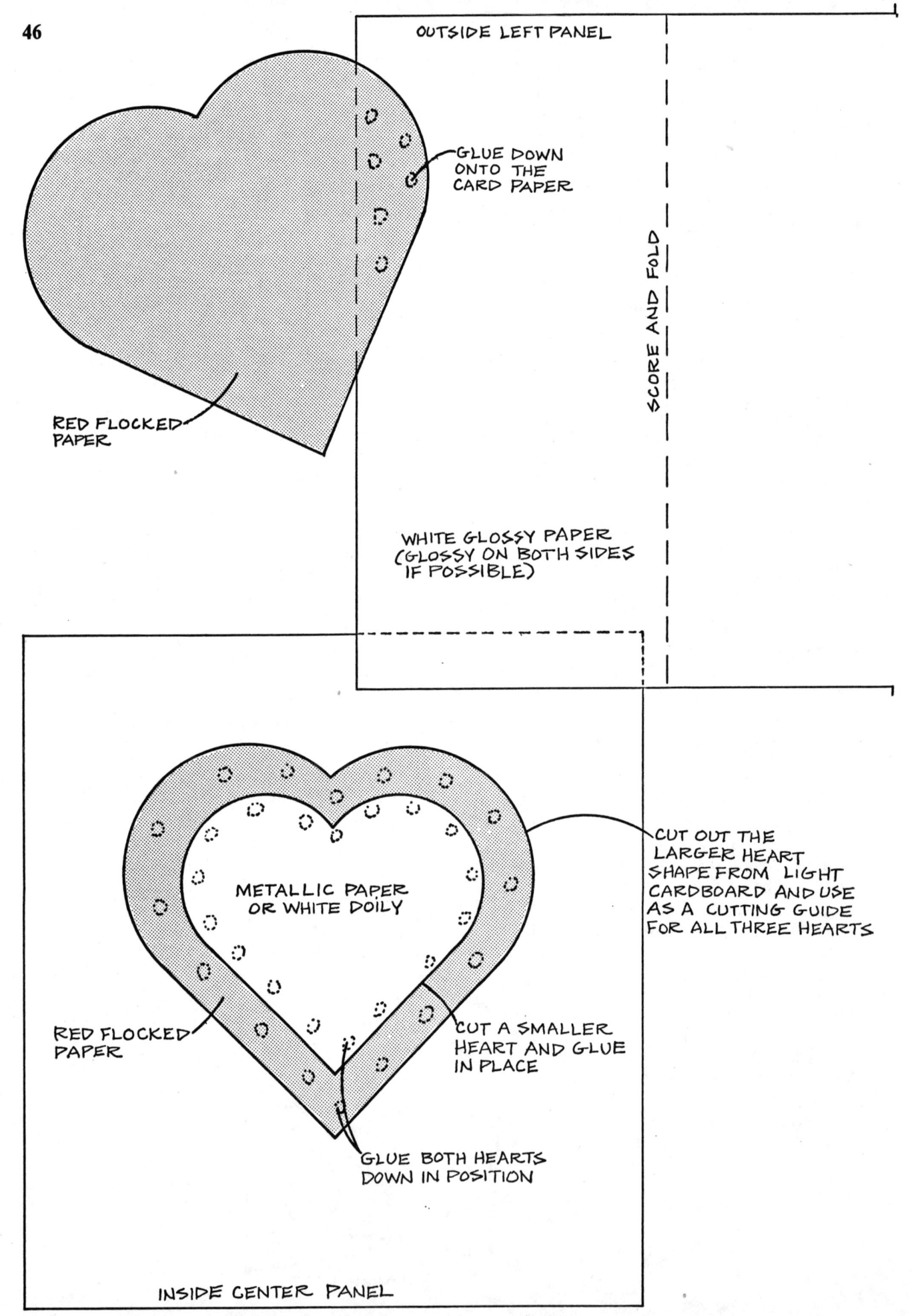

46

OUTSIDE LEFT PANEL

GLUE DOWN
ONTO THE
CARD PAPER

SCORE AND FOLD

RED FLOCKED
PAPER

WHITE GLOSSY PAPER
(GLOSSY ON BOTH SIDES
IF POSSIBLE)

CUT OUT THE
LARGER HEART
SHAPE FROM LIGHT
CARDBOARD AND USE
AS A CUTTING GUIDE
FOR ALL THREE HEARTS

METALLIC PAPER
OR WHITE DOILY

CUT A SMALLER
HEART AND GLUE
IN PLACE

RED FLOCKED
PAPER

GLUE BOTH HEARTS
DOWN IN POSITION

INSIDE CENTER PANEL

OUTSIDE RIGHT PANEL

SCORE AND FOLD

GLUE DOWN ONTO THE CARD PAPER

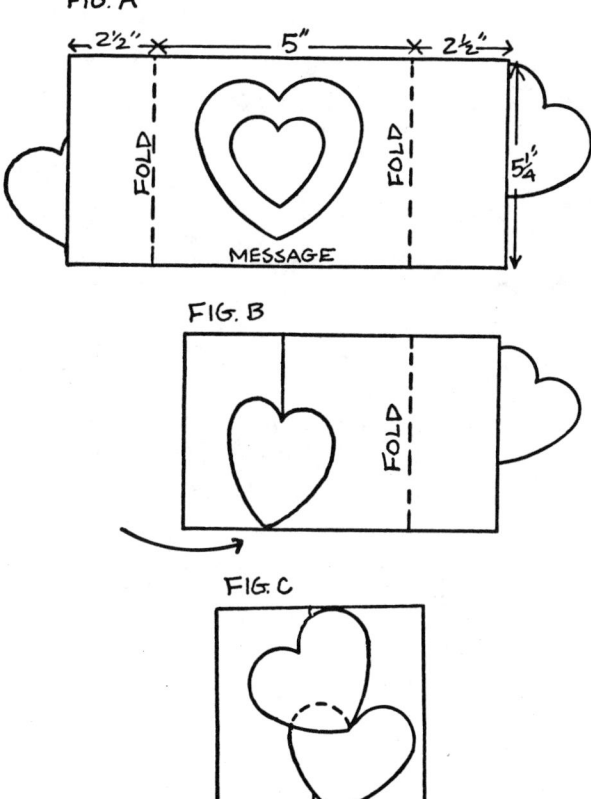

FIG. A

← 2½" → FOLD ← 5" → FOLD ← 2½" →

5¼"

MESSAGE

FIG. B

FOLD

FIG. C

FINISHED CARD

Valentine's Day, Mother's Day, or Father's Day

- Use the larger of the inside hearts as the cutting guide for the two hearts on the outside panels. These outside hearts should be cut out of medium-weight paper, heavy enough to keep the card shut when folded.
- Cut, score, and fold your card (unfolded size 5¼" x 10"). Unfold for the next steps.
- To make sure the outside hearts interlock, place your card paper outside-up on top of the outside-card illustration, aligned at the edges. Lay the cutout left heart in position over the illustrated heart and your card paper, and glue as shown. Repeat with the right heart.
- When the glue is dry, turn the card over and glue the two inside-panel hearts in place.
- Refold your card as shown in figures A, B, and C—the hearts will interlock.

You can send your card as a self-mailer, or make an envelope for it (see Easy Envelopes).

ORANGE CARD PAPER

SCORE AND FOLD

CUT A SLIT
ALONG FLOWER

GLUE DOWN ONTO
THE CARD PAPER

OUTSIDE LEFT PANEL

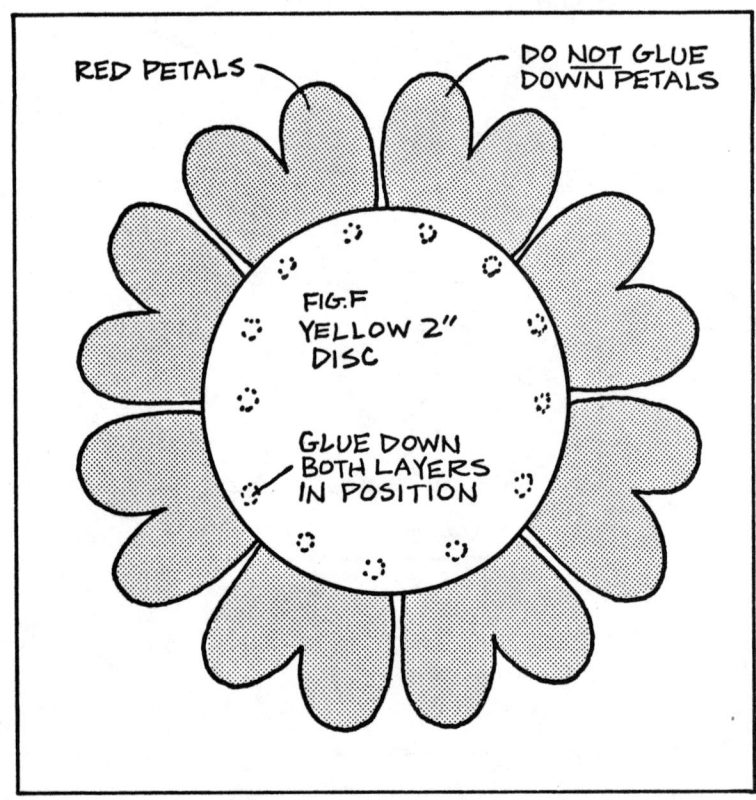

RED PETALS

DO NOT GLUE
DOWN PETALS

FIG.F
YELLOW 2"
DISC

GLUE DOWN
BOTH LAYERS
IN POSITION

INSIDE CENTER PANEL

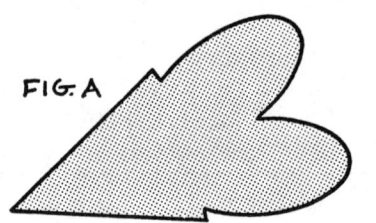

FIG. A

CENTER FLOWER CUTTING GUIDE

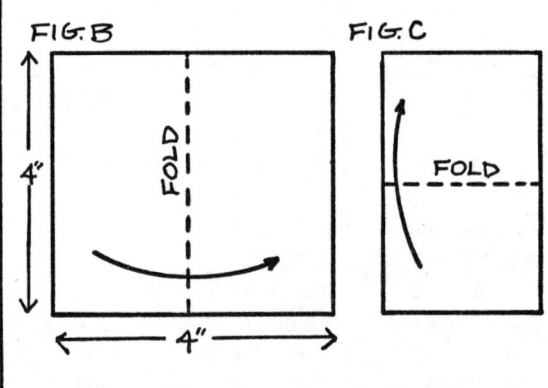

FIG.B

4"

FOLD

4"

FIG.C

FOLD

FIG.D

FOLD

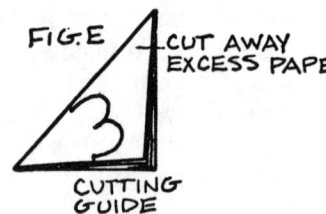

FIG.E

CUT AWAY
EXCESS PAPER

CUTTING
GUIDE

49

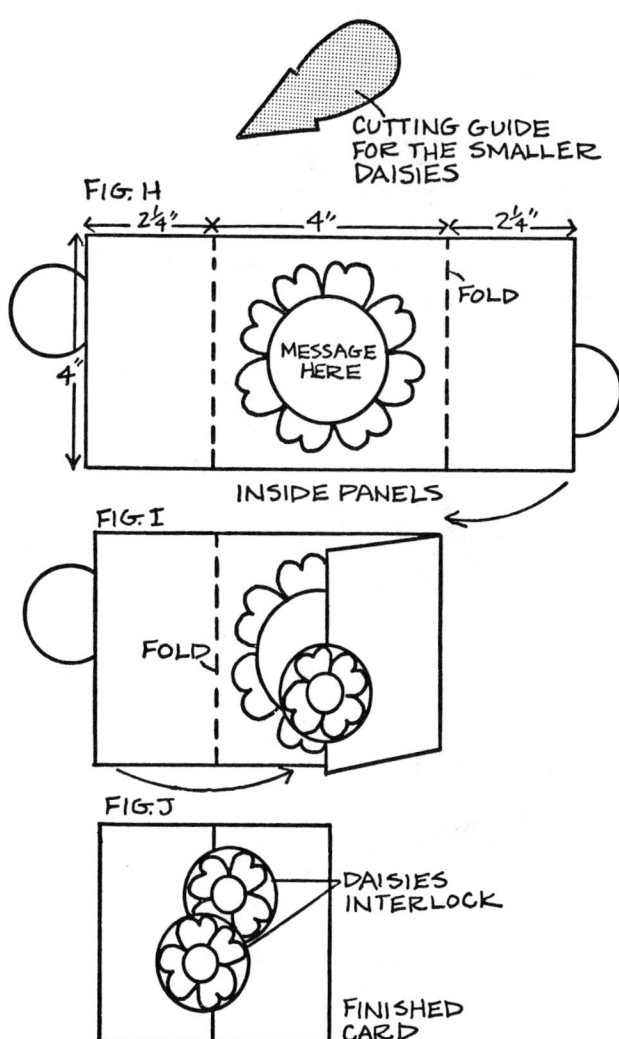

YELLOW 2" DISC

RED PETALS

ORANGE 1" DISC

GLUE DOWN ONTO THE CARD PAPER

FIG. G
GLUE DOWN THESE TWO LAYERS TO THE 2" DISC BEFORE GLUING DOWN TO YOUR CARD PAPER

SCORE AND FOLD

OUTSIDE RIGHT PANEL

All-Purpose or Get Well Card

- For the large daisy: Make a cutting guide from figure A. Cut a 4" square piece of lightweight colored paper and fold according to figures B, C, and D—be sure to follow the illustrations, otherwise your petals will not unfold as one piece. Place your cutting guide as indicated in figure E and cut away excess paper. Now unfold the cutout and glue a 2" disc of colored paper in the center (fig. F). Fold up the petals slightly and set aside to dry.
- For the small daisies: Make two. Fold and cut the petals as you did for the large daisy. Unfold, glue them each onto a 2" disc of colored paper, and glue a 1" disc of paper over the center (fig. G). Let dry.
- Cut, score, and fold your card paper (unfolded size 4" x 8½").
- To position the smaller daisies correctly, place your card outside-up on top of the outside-card illustration, aligned at the edges. Lay the cutout left daisy in position over the illustrated daisy and your card paper, and glue as shown. Repeat for the right daisy.
- When the glue is dry, cut a 1" slit along the top of the left flower.
- Turn the card over and glue the large daisy in place in the center panel. Let dry.
- Refold your card as shown in figures H, I, and J—the two daisies will interlock.

You can send your card as a self-mailer, or make an envelope for it (see Easy Envelopes).

CUTTING GUIDE FOR THE SMALLER DAISIES

FIG. H
2¼" 4" 2¼"
FOLD
4"
MESSAGE HERE
INSIDE PANELS

FIG. I
FOLD

FIG. J
DAISIES INTERLOCK
FINISHED CARD

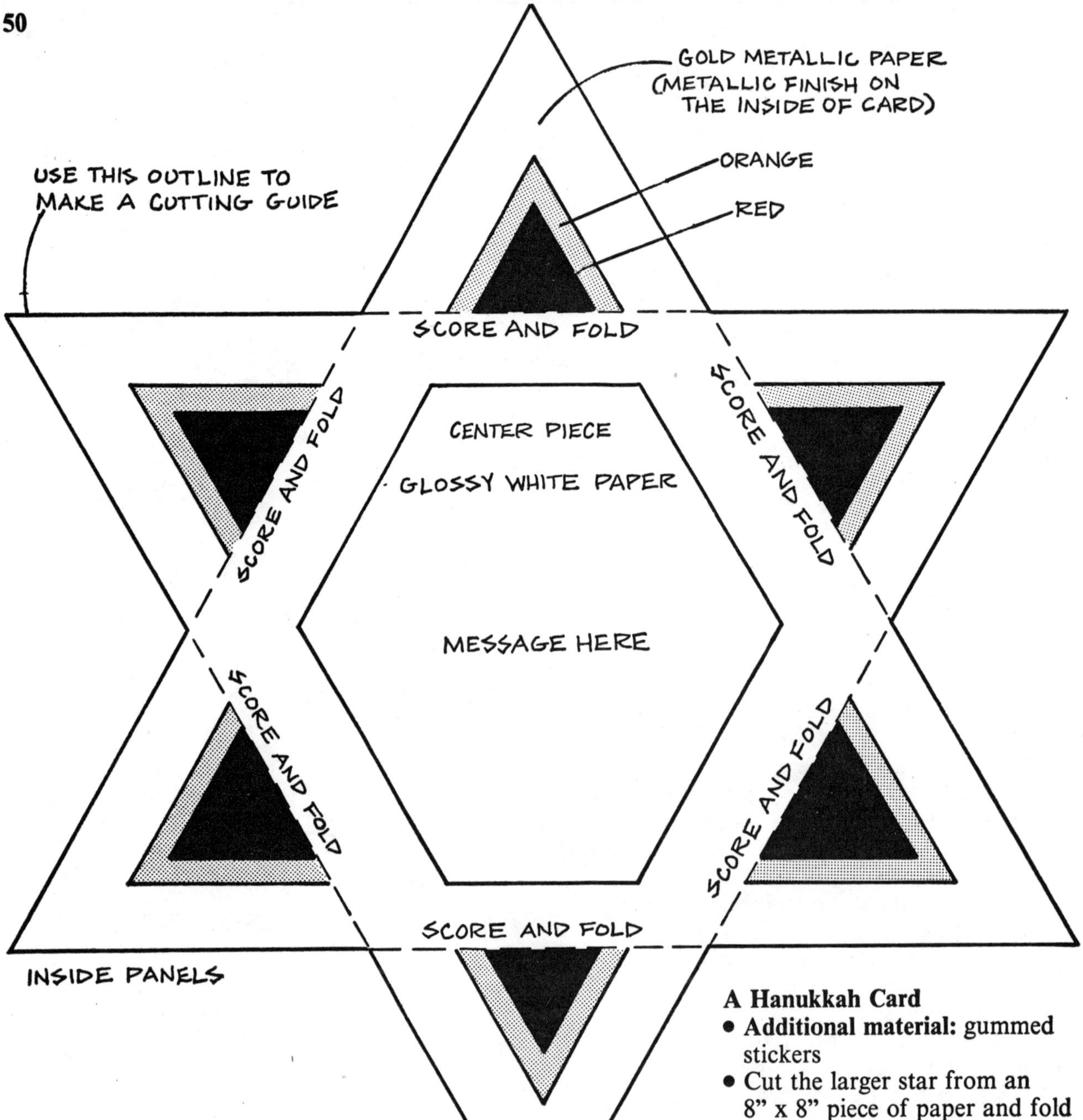

GOLD METALLIC PAPER
(METALLIC FINISH ON
THE INSIDE OF CARD)

ORANGE

RED

USE THIS OUTLINE TO
MAKE A CUTTING GUIDE

SCORE AND FOLD

SCORE AND FOLD

SCORE AND FOLD

CENTER PIECE

GLOSSY WHITE PAPER

MESSAGE HERE

SCORE AND FOLD

SCORE AND FOLD

SCORE AND FOLD

INSIDE PANELS

FIG. A

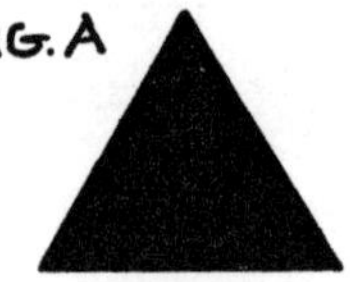

FIG. B

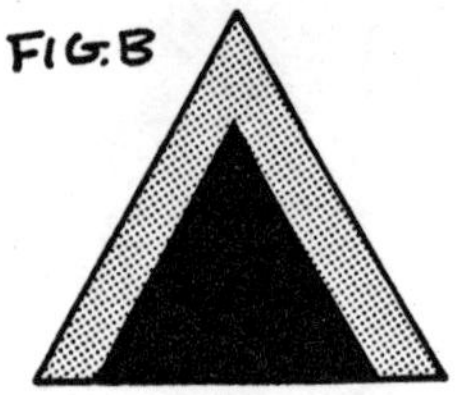

FIG. C

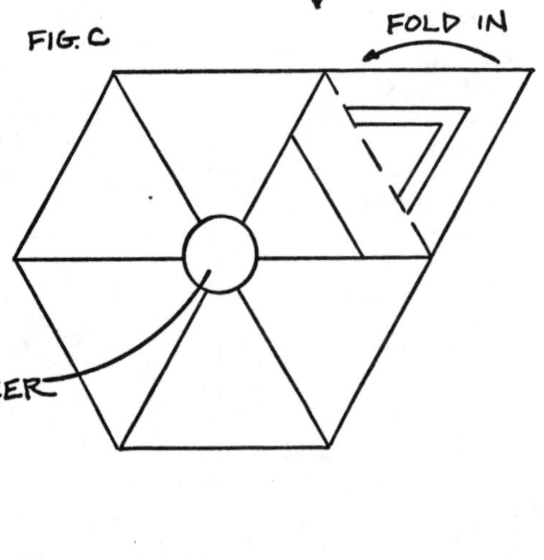

FOLD IN

GUMMED STICKER

A Hanukkah Card
- **Additional material:** gummed stickers
- Cut the larger star from an 8" x 8" piece of paper and fold along the six lines indicated.
- Cut out and glue the center piece to your card.
- Now make cutting guides for the triangle elements in figures A and B and cut out six of each.
- Glue the smaller triangle onto the larger one (fig. B) and then glue the double triangles onto the star points of your card, as shown.
- Let the glue dry and then fold your card (fig. C).

You can seal your finished card with a sticker and make an envelope to send it in (see Easy Envelopes).

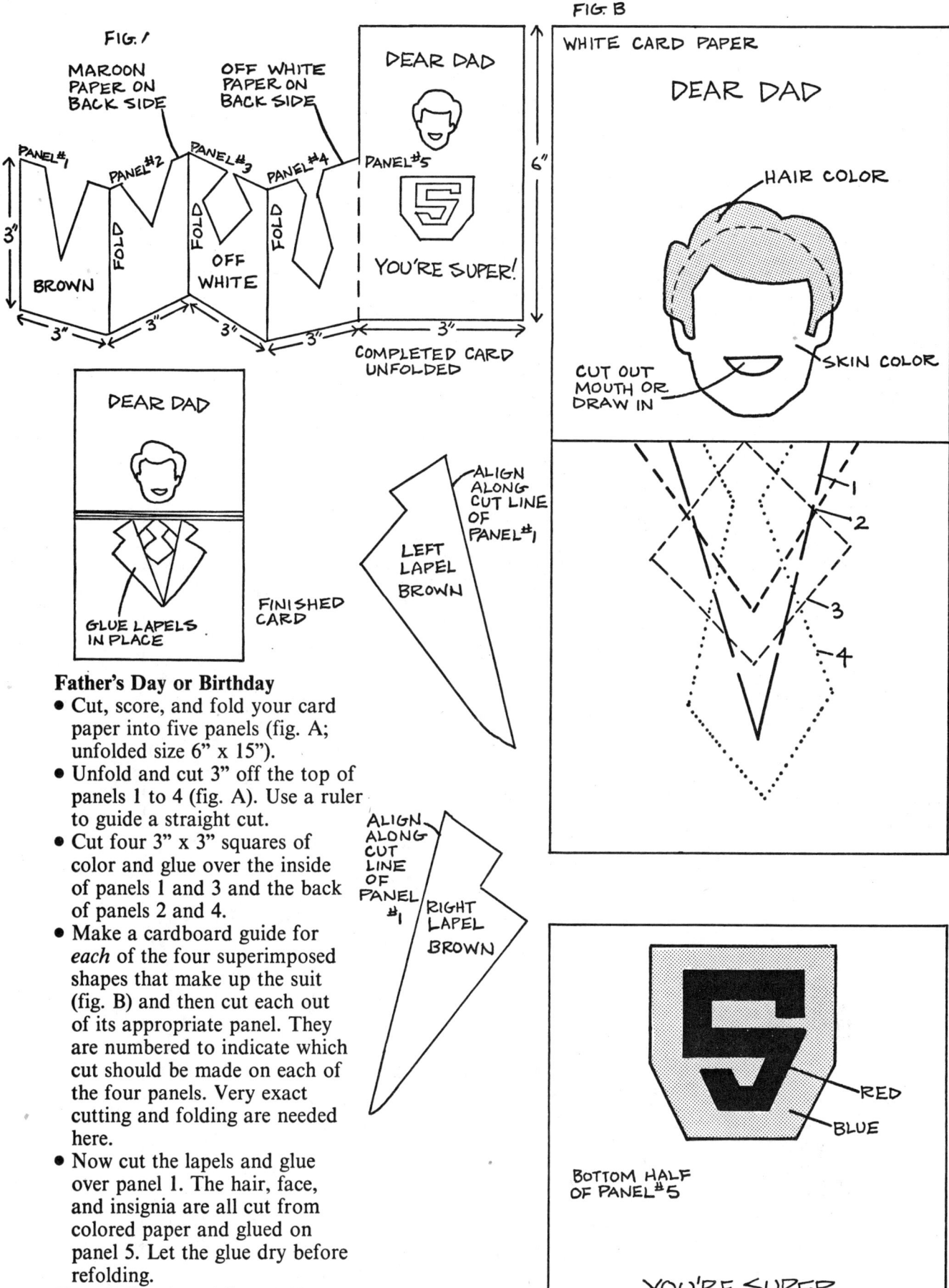

FIG. 1

MAROON PAPER ON BACK SIDE

OFF WHITE PAPER ON BACK SIDE

PANEL #1
PANEL #2
PANEL #3
PANEL #4
PANEL #5

FOLD
FOLD
FOLD

3"

BROWN

OFF WHITE

3" 3" 3" 3" 3"

DEAR DAD

YOU'RE SUPER!

COMPLETED CARD UNFOLDED

FIG. B

WHITE CARD PAPER

DEAR DAD

6"

HAIR COLOR

SKIN COLOR

CUT OUT MOUTH OR DRAW IN

1
2
3
4

DEAR DAD

GLUE LAPELS IN PLACE

FINISHED CARD

ALIGN ALONG CUT LINE OF PANEL #1

LEFT LAPEL BROWN

ALIGN ALONG CUT LINE OF PANEL #1

RIGHT LAPEL BROWN

RED

BLUE

BOTTOM HALF OF PANEL #5

YOU'RE SUPER

Father's Day or Birthday

- Cut, score, and fold your card paper into five panels (fig. A; unfolded size 6" x 15").
- Unfold and cut 3" off the top of panels 1 to 4 (fig. A). Use a ruler to guide a straight cut.
- Cut four 3" x 3" squares of color and glue over the inside of panels 1 and 3 and the back of panels 2 and 4.
- Make a cardboard guide for *each* of the four superimposed shapes that make up the suit (fig. B) and then cut each out of its appropriate panel. They are numbered to indicate which cut should be made on each of the four panels. Very exact cutting and folding are needed here.
- Now cut the lapels and glue over panel 1. The hair, face, and insignia are all cut from colored paper and glued on panel 5. Let the glue dry before refolding.

Your finished card fits a #6¾ envelope.

52

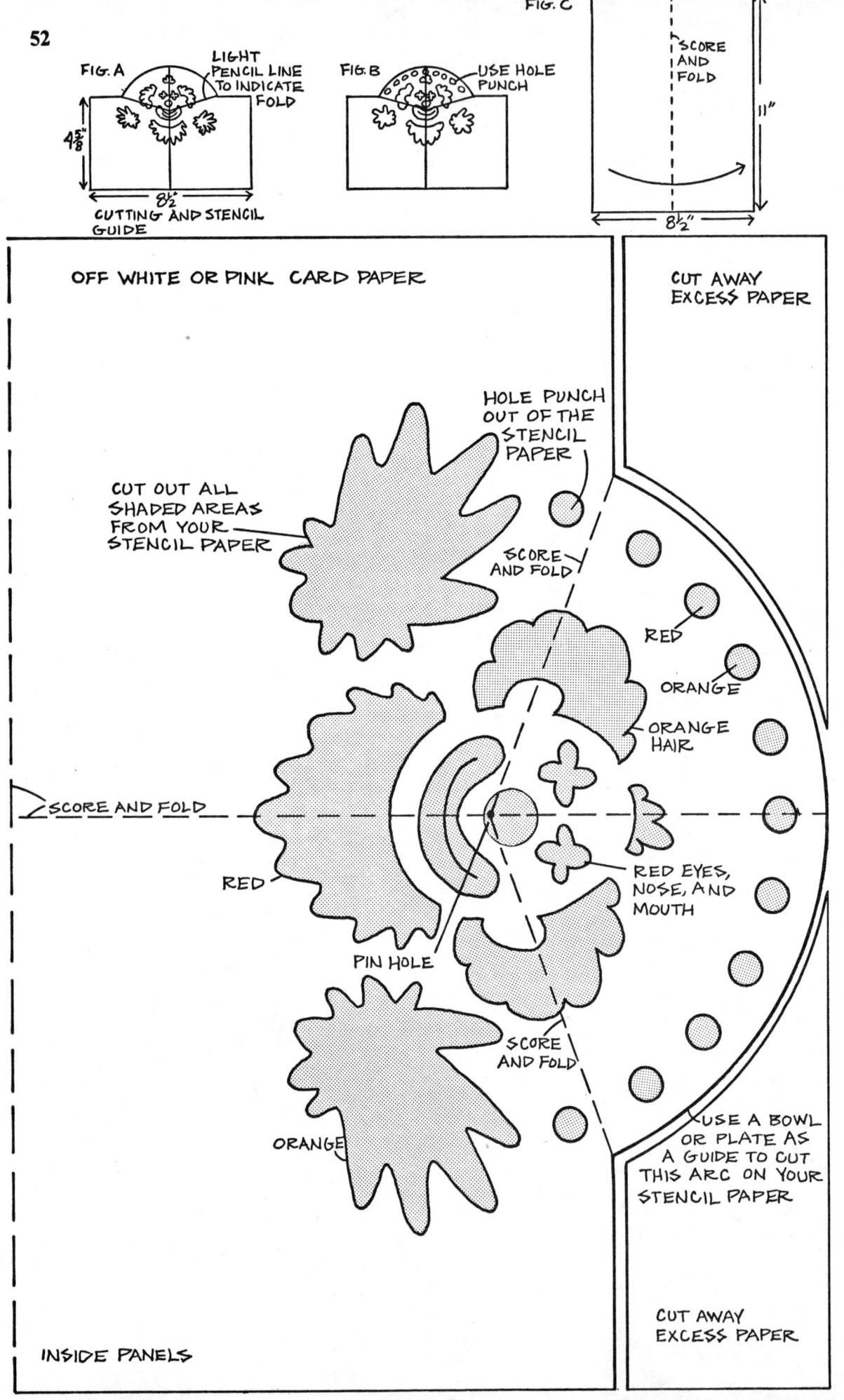

FIG. A

LIGHT PENCIL LINE TO INDICATE FOLD

4⅝"

8½"

CUTTING AND STENCIL GUIDE

FIG. B

USE HOLE PUNCH

FIG. C

SCORE AND FOLD

11"

8½"

OFF WHITE OR PINK CARD PAPER

CUT AWAY EXCESS PAPER

HOLE PUNCH OUT OF THE STENCIL PAPER

CUT OUT ALL SHADED AREAS FROM YOUR STENCIL PAPER

SCORE AND FOLD

RED

ORANGE

ORANGE HAIR

SCORE AND FOLD

RED

RED EYES, NOSE, AND MOUTH

PIN HOLE

SCORE AND FOLD

ORANGE

USE A BOWL OR PLATE AS A GUIDE TO CUT THIS ARC ON YOUR STENCIL PAPER

CUT AWAY EXCESS PAPER

INSIDE PANELS

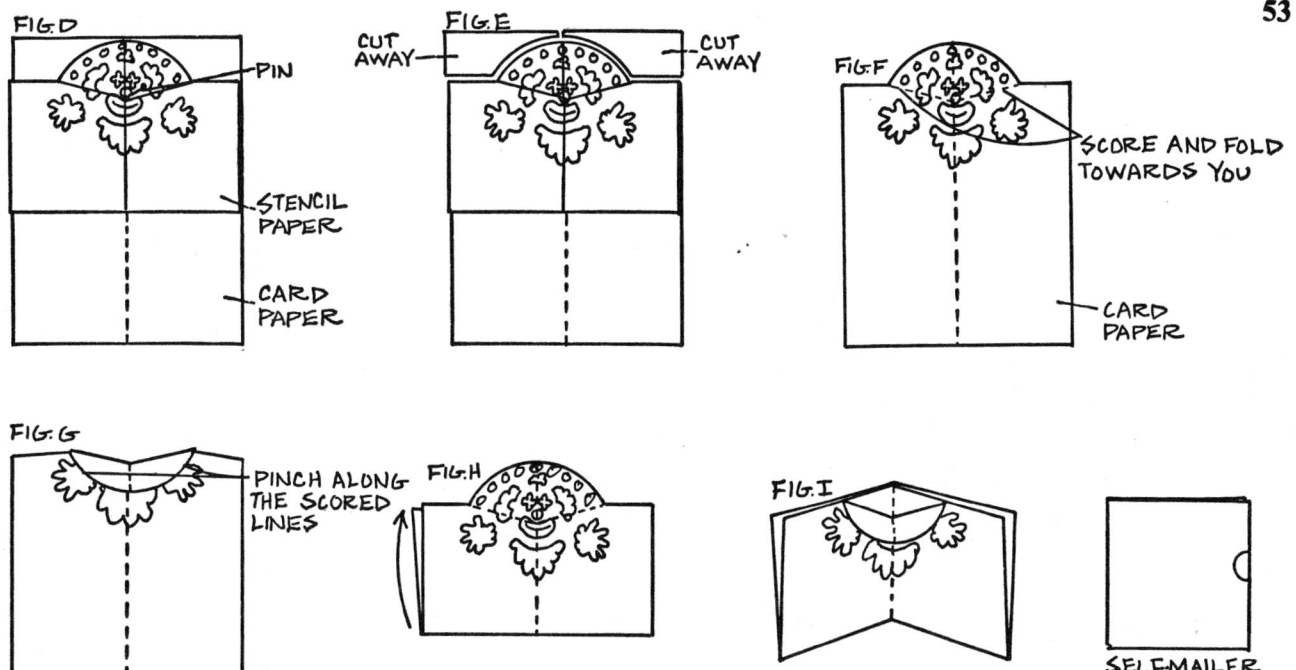

Juggling Clown Birthday Party Invitation

- **Additional materials:** hole punch, stenciling materials, straight pin, gummed stickers
- Read the general instructions in the Stencil Cards section to learn the stenciling technique.
- Transfer the clown design to stencil paper. Mark the pinhole and pencil in all folded lines (these should be erased later). Cut the arch across the top of the paper, around the edges, as shown (fig. A), and then cut away all shaded areas (fig. B). Set your stencil aside.
- Fold your 8½" x 11" card paper lengthwise and open again (fig. C). Align the top edge of of the card paper with the top of the stencil paper arch (fig. D) and match the centerfolds. Push a straight pin through the pinhole mark, through both the stencil and card paper. (A corrugated cardboard base below your card paper will keep the pin from slipping.) Now cut around the arch and the top left and right sides of the card (fig. E).
- Stencil your design. Then remove both stencil and pin and let the colors dry.
- To fold: Use the pinhole as the meeting point and score along the fold marks shown (fig. F). Lift up the card and pinch along the scored lines (fig. G). Fold the bottom half of the card underneath the top (fig. H). Now fold the card closed, bending the arch inward (fig. I).

Your juggling clown is a self-mailer. Seal with a gummed sticker.

Variation: Carry your card theme to napkins and name tags with felt-tip markers (fig. J)

FINISHED CARD

NAME TAG OR PLACE CARD

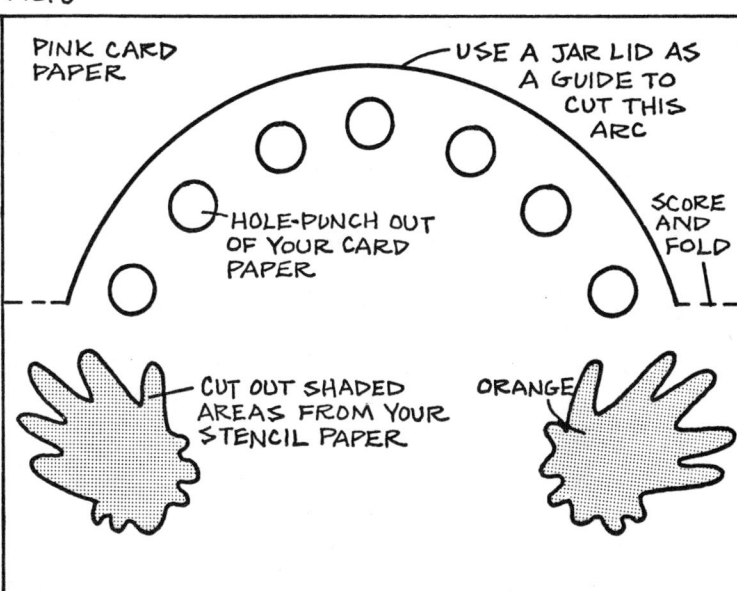

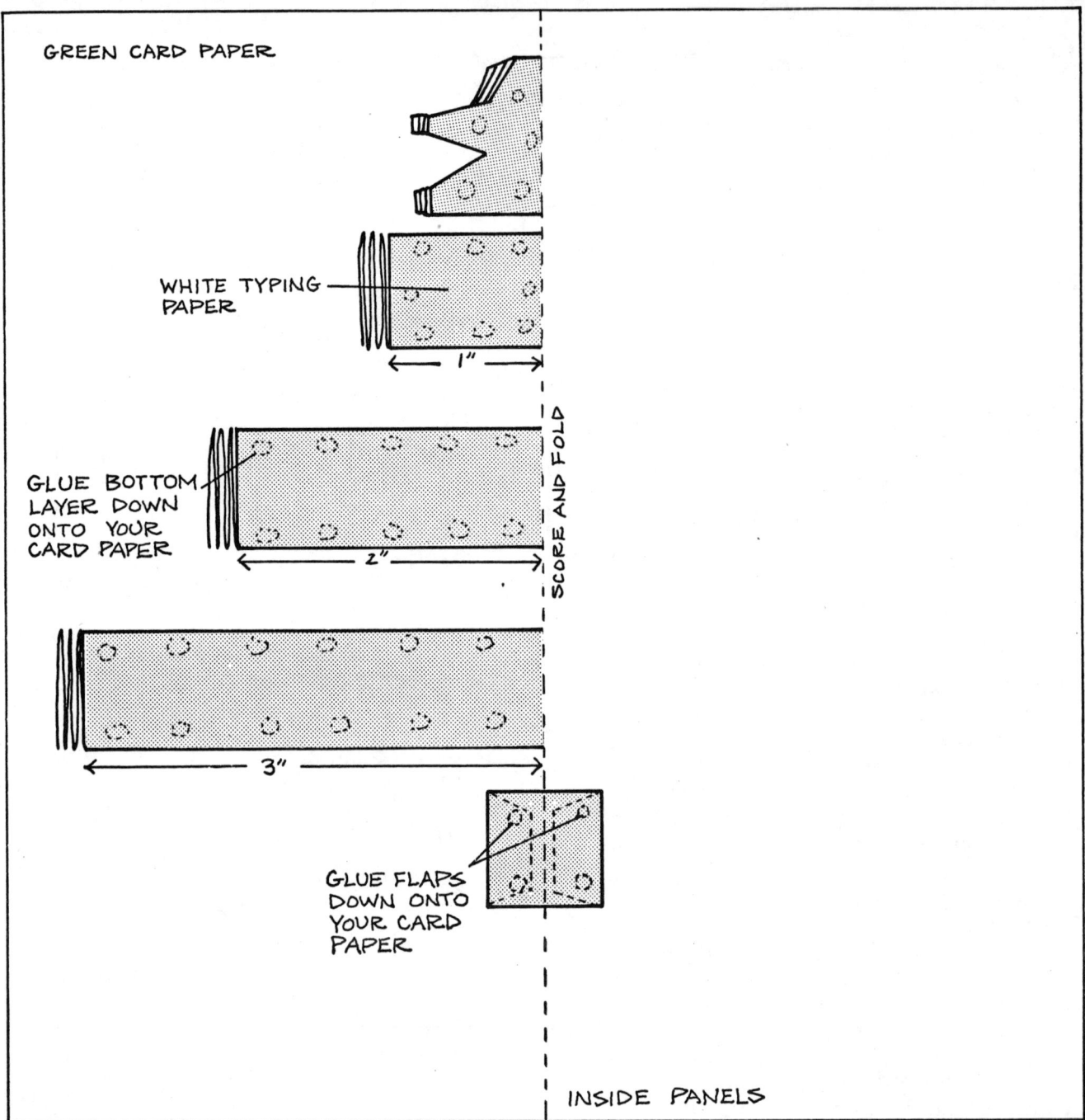

GREEN CARD PAPER

WHITE TYPING PAPER

1"

GLUE BOTTOM LAYER DOWN ONTO YOUR CARD PAPER

2"

SCORE AND FOLD

3"

GLUE FLAPS DOWN ONTO YOUR CARD PAPER

INSIDE PANELS

A Christmas Tree Greeting Card
- **Additional material:** typing paper
- Cut, score, and fold your card paper, as shown (unfolded size 7" x 7").
- Use 8½" x 11" typing paper (or other paper of comparable weight) for the tree. Fold along the 8½" width in an accordion fold, with each fold approximately ¾" wide. Trim off any excess that won't make a complete fold. Keep folded flat as you cut off a 3" piece, a 2" piece, a 1" piece (fig. A), and set aside. The remaining paper is for the treetop ornament.
- Make a cardboard cutting guide of the tree ornament, as shown (fig. A). Cut it out of the remaining accordion-folded paper. Follow the cutting lines exactly, leaving two edges uncut—otherwise your cutout will fall into pieces

instead of folding into a star. Cut the tree base from another small piece of typing paper (fig. B).
- To glue the tree: Open up your card paper. Pencil in lightly where each of the five parts (star, branches, base) should go, using the main illustration as a guide. Begin with the left side of the card and place glue on one side of the accordion-folded pieces. Lay the pieces—one at a time—in position, glue-side down, along the edge of the centerfold line. Then glue the tree base in position. Now place glue on the free side (fig. C) of the accordion-folded pieces and carefully close the card (fig. D). Put under a heavy book to dry. When the glue is dry, open your card to see that the tree is in place.

Your finished and folded card fits into a Monarch-size envelope.

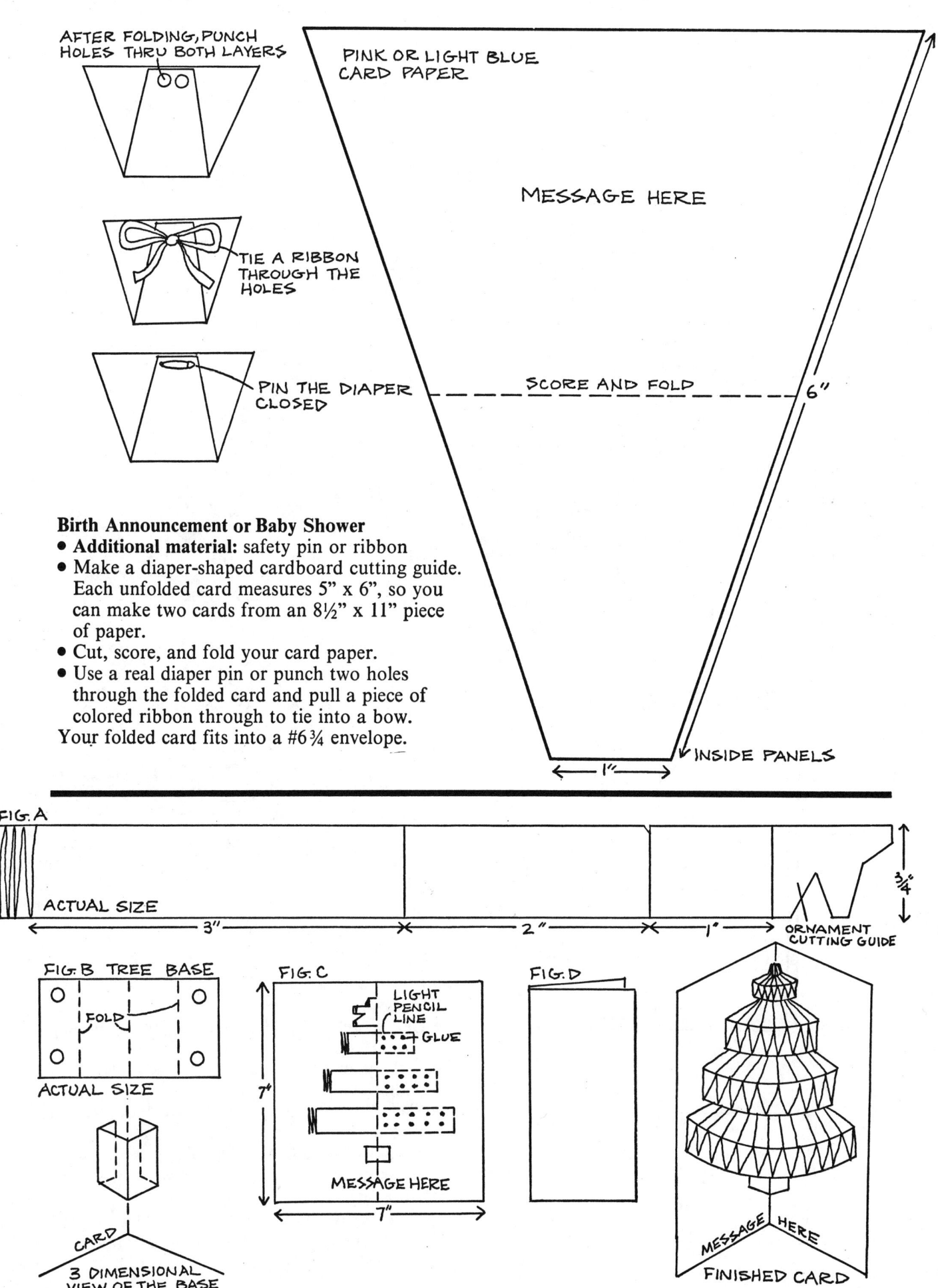

AFTER FOLDING, PUNCH HOLES THRU BOTH LAYERS

PINK OR LIGHT BLUE CARD PAPER

MESSAGE HERE

TIE A RIBBON THROUGH THE HOLES

SCORE AND FOLD — — — 6"

PIN THE DIAPER CLOSED

INSIDE PANELS

1"

Birth Announcement or Baby Shower
- **Additional material:** safety pin or ribbon
- Make a diaper-shaped cardboard cutting guide. Each unfolded card measures 5" x 6", so you can make two cards from an 8½" x 11" piece of paper.
- Cut, score, and fold your card paper.
- Use a real diaper pin or punch two holes through the folded card and pull a piece of colored ribbon through to tie into a bow. Your folded card fits into a #6¾ envelope.

FIG. A
ACTUAL SIZE
3" — 2" — 1"
ORNAMENT CUTTING GUIDE
¾"

FIG. B TREE BASE
FOLD
ACTUAL SIZE
CARD
3 DIMENSIONAL VIEW OF THE BASE

FIG. C
LIGHT PENCIL LINE
GLUE
7"
MESSAGE HERE
7"

FIG. D

MESSAGE HERE
FINISHED CARD

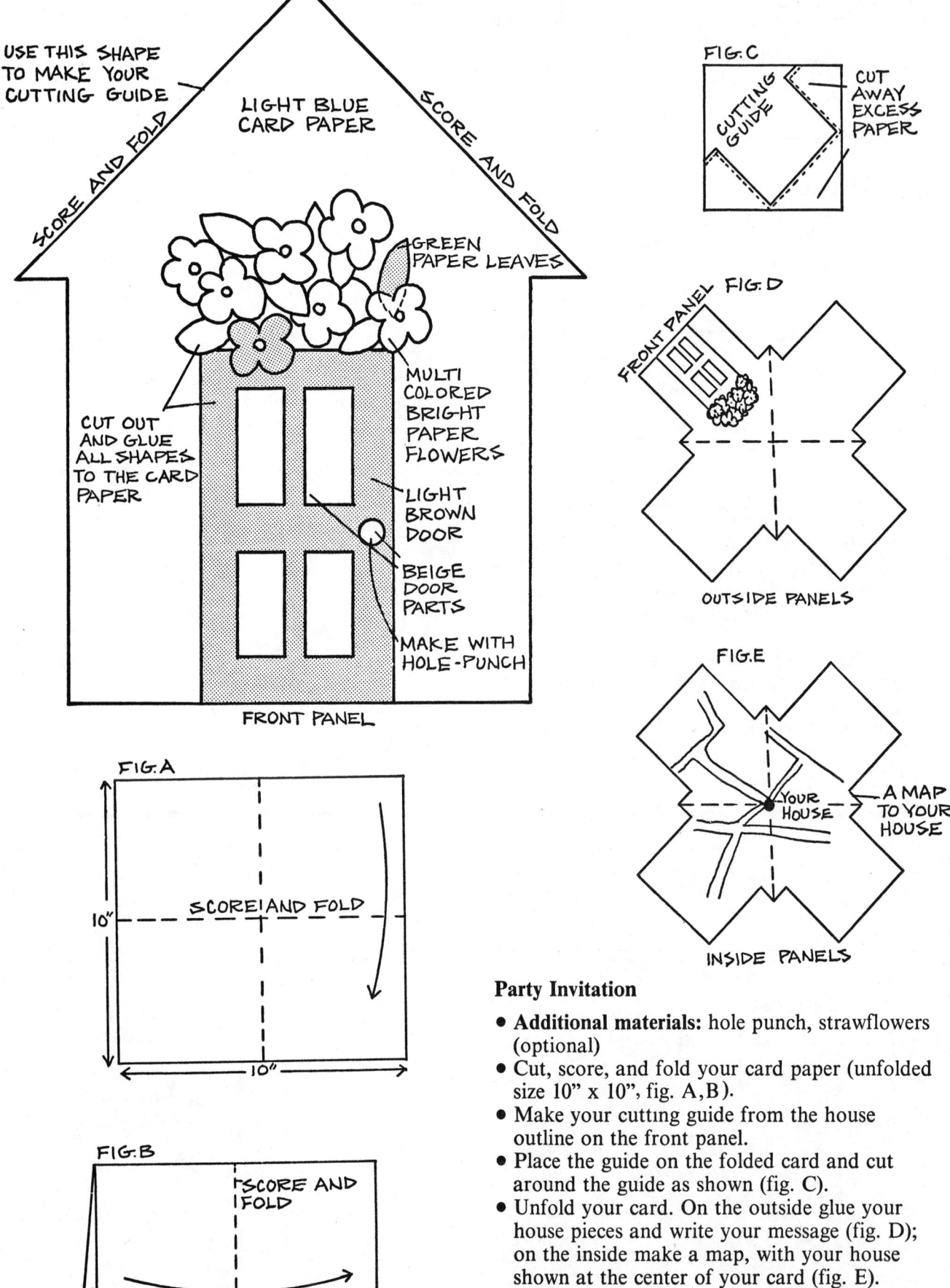

USE THIS SHAPE TO MAKE YOUR CUTTING GUIDE

LIGHT BLUE CARD PAPER

SCORE AND FOLD

SCORE AND FOLD

GREEN PAPER LEAVES

MULTI COLORED BRIGHT PAPER FLOWERS

CUT OUT AND GLUE ALL SHAPES TO THE CARD PAPER

LIGHT BROWN DOOR

BEIGE DOOR PARTS

MAKE WITH HOLE-PUNCH

FRONT PANEL

FIG. C

CUTTING GUIDE

CUT AWAY EXCESS PAPER

FRONT PANEL FIG. D

OUTSIDE PANELS

FIG. E

YOUR HOUSE

A MAP TO YOUR HOUSE

INSIDE PANELS

FIG. A

10"

SCORE AND FOLD

10"

FIG. B

SCORE AND FOLD

Party Invitation

- **Additional materials:** hole punch, strawflowers (optional)
- Cut, score, and fold your card paper (unfolded size 10" x 10", fig. A,B).
- Make your cutting guide from the house outline on the front panel.
- Place the guide on the folded card and cut around the guide as shown (fig. C).
- Unfold your card. On the outside glue your house pieces and write your message (fig. D); on the inside make a map, with your house shown at the center of your card (fig. E).

Your refolded card fits into an A2 envelope.

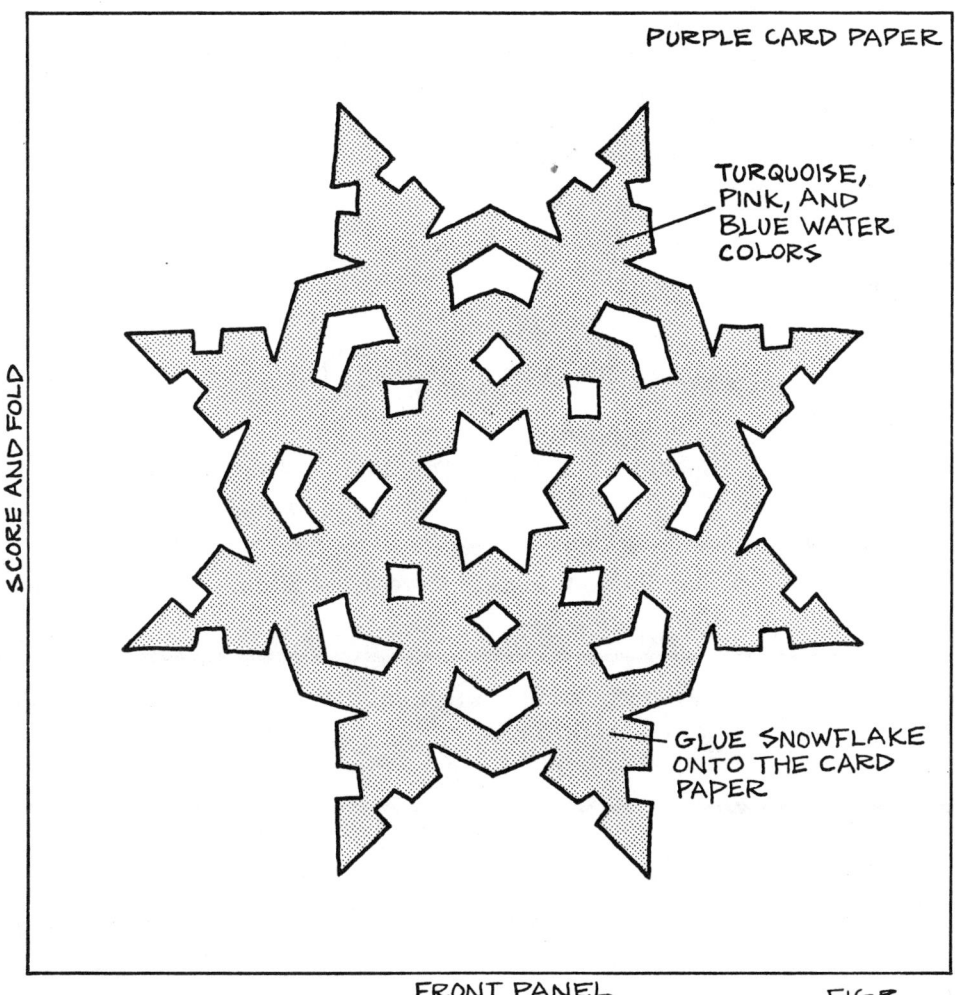

PURPLE CARD PAPER

TURQUOISE, PINK, AND BLUE WATER COLORS

SCORE AND FOLD

GLUE SNOWFLAKE ONTO THE CARD PAPER

FRONT PANEL

A Snowflake

- **Additional materials:** blotter paper or plain rice paper, liquid watercolors or food coloring, paper towels, clothes iron.
- Make a cutting guide from figure A.
- Cut and fold a 5" x 5" piece of blotter paper or rice paper (figs. B, C, D)—follow the illustrations exactly so the snowflake will come out in one piece.
- Lay your cutting guide over the folded paper and cut away excess as shown (fig. E).
- While the card is still folded, place drops of high intensity watercolors (like Dr. Ph. Martin's, see Glossary) or undiluted food coloring on the edges of the snowflake. The colors will be instantly absorbed by the paper. Blot up the excess.
- Now carefully unfold the snowflake and place it between two pieces of paper toweling. Press lightly with a warm iron to eliminate fold marks and to dry out your snowflake.
- Cut, score, and fold your card paper (unfolded size 5" x 10"). Glue the snowflake to the front panel, using glue stick for best results.

To make your own envelope see Easy Envelopes.

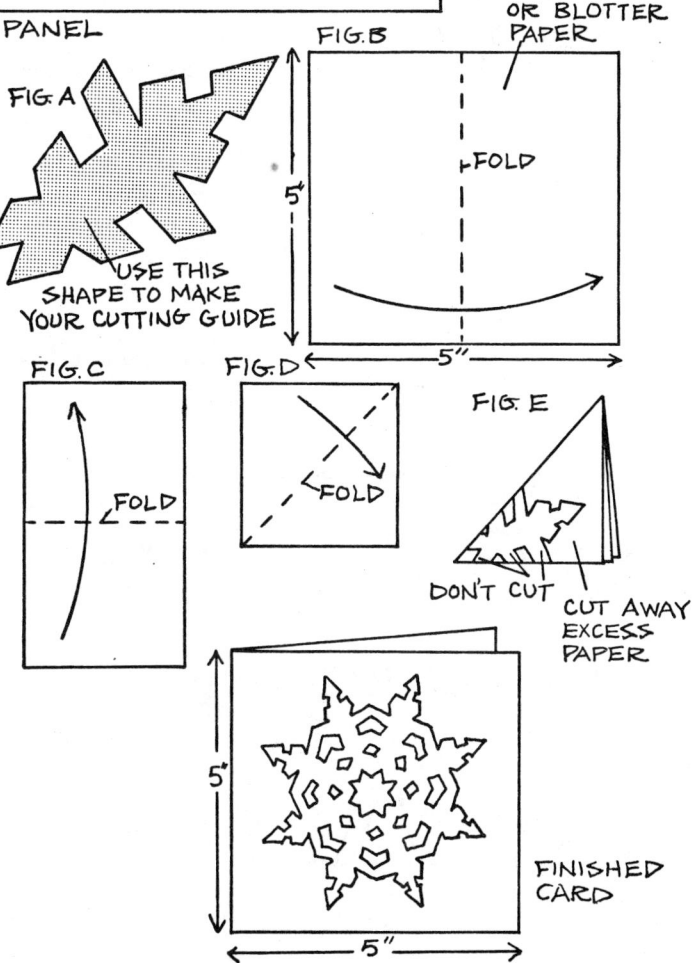

RICE PAPER OR BLOTTER PAPER

FIG. A

USE THIS SHAPE TO MAKE YOUR CUTTING GUIDE

FIG. B

FOLD

5'

5"

FIG. C

FOLD

FIG. D

FOLD

FIG. E

DON'T CUT

CUT AWAY EXCESS PAPER

FINISHED CARD

5'

5"

Photo Greeting Cards

Appearance: A photo you have taken in a card frame you make yourself.
Skill required: Very little.
Quantity/Time: Once you have your photo and duplicates, the frames take little time to make.

MATERIALS	• **Film for your camera (several rolls)**	• **See individual cards for additional materials and tools**
TOOLS	• **Camera (a small automatic camera works fine)** • **Tripod (for shooting indoors)**	• **Shutter-release cable (optional)** • **Clip-on floodlight shade (indoors)** • **Blue photo flood bulb (indoors)**
MISCELLANEOUS	• **A friend to press the shutter release**	

HOW TO TAKE YOUR PHOTO

Your photo card will only be as good as the photos you take. Here are some hints to help you take good quality pictures.

1. Take advantage of natural light. Soft shadows look better, so shoot outdoor photos on an overcast day if possible. Early morning and late afternoon light is preferable to high noon.

2. When shooting indoors, avoid using a built-in flash. Its high intensity flattens features and causes "red-eye." If you use a flash, place a handkerchief or paper tissue over it to soften the light.

3. The best way to shoot a picture indoors is to purchase a blue photo flood bulb and a clip-on shade (regular incandescent lighting with color film will look very orange). To soften or eliminate problem shadows, reflect the light from a white wall, sheet, or board. Hold your light at various heights and angles until you find the most

flattering light for your subject, then clip your light onto some object to hold it in that position.

4. Keep the background simple. A wall, a tall plain fence, or a large bush will provide an interesting nondistracting background.
   Hint: Avoid patterned wallpaper, hanging lamps, and pictures in the background. When outdoors, watch out for neighbors' cars, stray dogs, and telephone poles that appear to be growing out of the subject's head or shoulders.

5. Think natural. Dress your subjects in casual clothes so they will feel at ease. The smiles will come easier. Clothes should have solid colors and not be too bright.

6. Compose your shot. Fill the frame. Get in close. The less wasted space around the subject, the more interesting the photo. Keep people in groups close together, and arrange them so height differences are minimized.

7. Don't move. If possible use a tripod to stabilize the camera, or shoot with your camera resting on a solid object. A shutter-release cable will prevent a heavy shutter-finger from blurring the photo.

8. Take lots of pictures. The professionals shoot many rolls of film to get that one good shot. If you shoot just a roll or two, you will have a good choice of photos for your card.

9. Now make one of the photo frames in this section for your card, referring to other sections for techniques where indicated. See the Machine-Printed Cards section if you want to have your photo printed on your card paper.

FINISHED CARDS

LIGHT BLUE CARD PAPER

USE A JAR LID AS CUTTING GUIDE

SCORE AND FOLD

FRONT PANEL

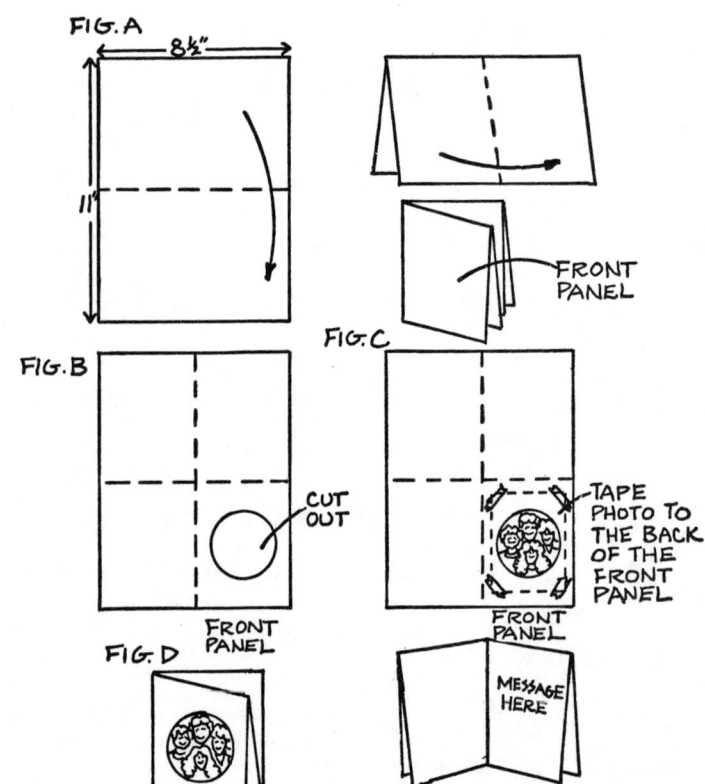

FIG. A

8½"

11"

FIG. B

FIG. C

FRONT PANEL

FIG. D

CUT OUT

FRONT PANEL

TAPE PHOTO TO THE BACK OF THE FRONT PANEL

FRONT PANEL

MESSAGE HERE

An All-Occasion Card

- **Additional materials:** duplicate photos (one for each card), X-acto knife
- Use 3" x 4" duplicate prints of your photo.
- Read the Pop-Up and Cutout Cards section for techniques and recommended paper.
- Cut, score, and fold your card paper (unfolded size 8½" x 11", fig. A). This is known as a French fold.
- Reopen your card and cut out the circle window on the front panel (cut one layer, fig. B). The size of the circle depends on the size of the image in your photo—choose the circle that "crops" your photo to its best advantage. Tape your photo to the back of the front panel (fig. C).
- Refold the card and write your message (fig. D).

Your finished card fits an A2 envelope.

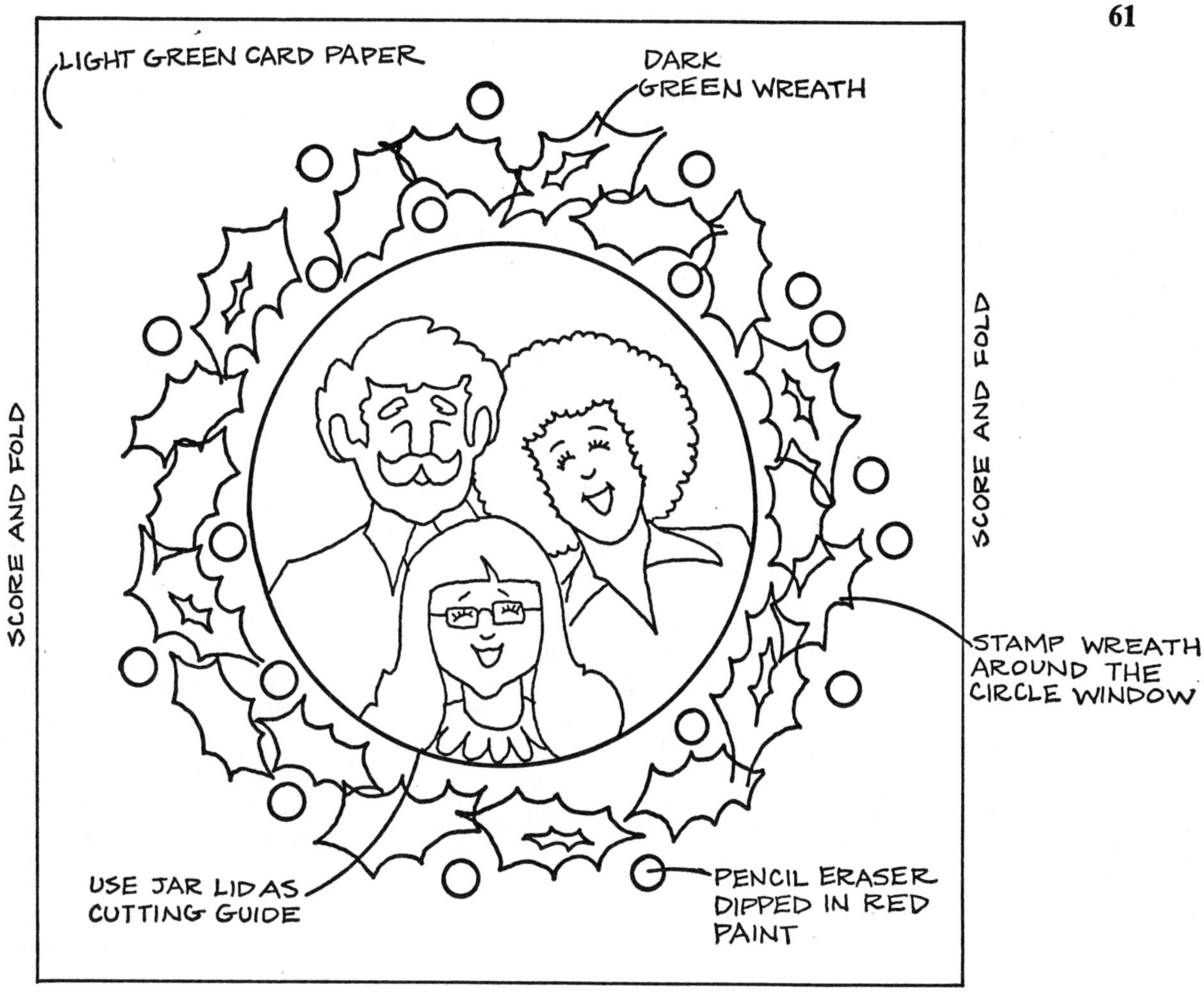

LIGHT GREEN CARD PAPER

DARK GREEN WREATH

SCORE AND FOLD

SCORE AND FOLD

STAMP WREATH AROUND THE CIRCLE WINDOW

USE JAR LID AS CUTTING GUIDE

PENCIL ERASER DIPPED IN RED PAINT

A Card for Christmas

- **Additional materials:** rubber-eraser stamp (for wreath), ink pad, scotch tape, duplicate photos (one for each card), gummed stickers, X-acto knife
- Use 3"x3" or 3"x4" duplicate prints of your photo.
- Read the Stamp-Out Cards section for techniques and recommended card paper.
- Cut, score, and fold your card paper (unfolded size 5"x15") into three panels, each 5"x5".
- Reopen the card and cut out a circle window on the right-hand panel (fig. A). Then fold the window panel over the center panel.
- Now make an eraser-stamp holly wreath around the outside of the window. See the Christmas Wreath card in the Stamp-Out Cards section.
- When the ink is dry, reopen the card and place your photo on the center panel. Fold the window panel over your photo. Center your photo (fig. B) within the window and then tape it to the center panel.
- Glue the window panel to the center panel (fig. C).

Your finished card is a self-mailer.

FIG. A

5" 5" 5"

CUT OUT

PHOTO TO GO HERE

5"

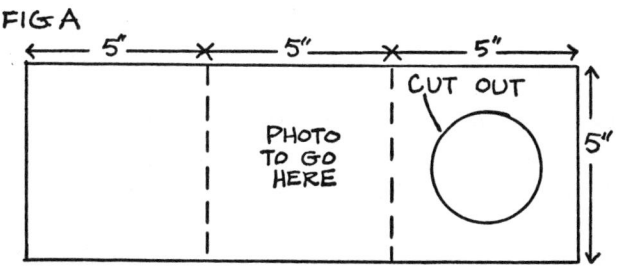

FIG. B

TAPE PHOTO

SIMPLE STAMP WREATH

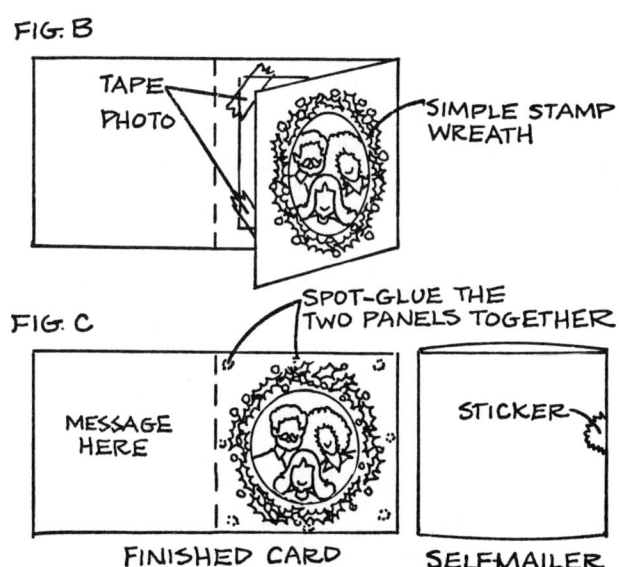

FIG. C

SPOT-GLUE THE TWO PANELS TOGETHER

MESSAGE HERE

STICKER

FINISHED CARD

SELFMAILER

Stencil Cards

Appearance: Simple designs, brushed with paints.
Skill required: Minimal.
Quantity/Time: Once you have your stencil, up to thirty cards can be made quite quickly.

MATERIALS	• Recommended paper: medium-weight, colored or white cover paper; coated card paper; or—in a pinch—construction paper (see All About Paper) • Easy Envelopes • Stencil paper (available at art supply stores, or use shirt cardboard, boxboard or railroad board, or old file folders) • Paper towels • Poster paints or any water-based paints • Backside of a breadboard, or heavy cardboard (to protect your table when cutting) • Tracing paper • Carbon paper
TOOLS	• X-acto knife • Stencil brush (available at art stores or use any <u>stiff</u> bristle brush, such as a glue or paste brush, but <u>not</u> a paint brush) • Paint reservoir: paper plate, aluminum foil pan, or a regular dinner plate lined with foil • Masking tape • Sharp pencil • See individual cards for additional materials and tools
HOW TO MAKE THE CARD	1. Cut a piece of stencil paper an inch or two larger than your card design. Then cover the card design with tracing paper and transfer the design onto the stencil paper with a pencil and carbon paper (see How to Transfer in Techniques section). 2. Carefully cut out of the stencil paper all the shaded areas of the design (this is where the color will appear). Use continuous, firm pressure to get a clean cut, turning the stencil paper so

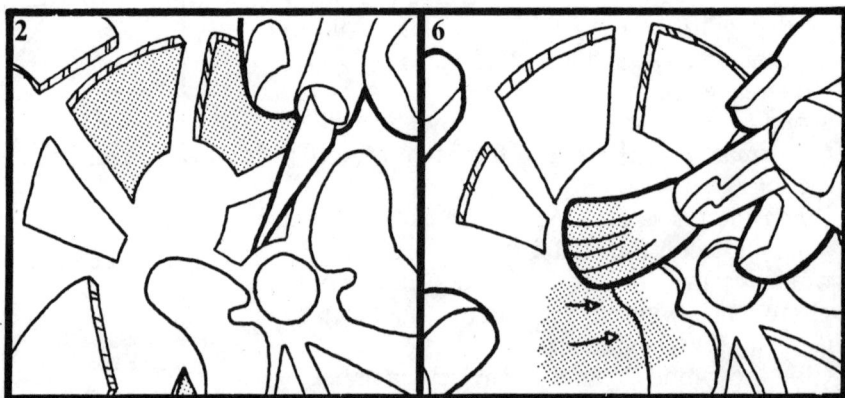

that you always cut along the outline toward you. Discard the cutouts.

3. Cut your card paper to the size indicated on the card design.
4. Put newspaper under your card paper to catch any stray paint. Place the stencil on your card paper so that the design is in the correct position according to the card design.
5. Pour your paint into the reservoir and dip the tip of the stencil brush into the color.
   Hint: The key to stenciling is to use a fairly dry brush, so dab the tip on a paper towel to remove excess paint.
6. Press the stencil down to prevent paint from seeping under the edges. Now brush with light, quick strokes from the outside edge of each hole in the stencil toward the center of the hole. Note that stenciling is not painting — you want a brushed look, not a solid coat of color.
7. Remove the stencil carefully. If the design is smeared, your brush wasn't dry enough. Try again.
8. When the paint is dry, score and fold your card, making sure the edges meet as shown in the card design.

---

1. After the paint is dry, glue materials such as ribbon, foil stars, or pictures cut from gift wrapping paper to your card.
2. Use a very dry brush to put on a first color, then go back and darken just the edges with an application of a second color, blending it into the first.
3. Repeat the same design several times with different colors by moving the stencil ⅛" or more every time you change colors. Be sure to let each color dry before stenciling another color over it.
4. Use a combination of spatter and stencil on each card (see Spatter Cards section).

VARIATIONS TO TRY AFTER MAKING YOUR FIRST CARD

FINISHED CARDS

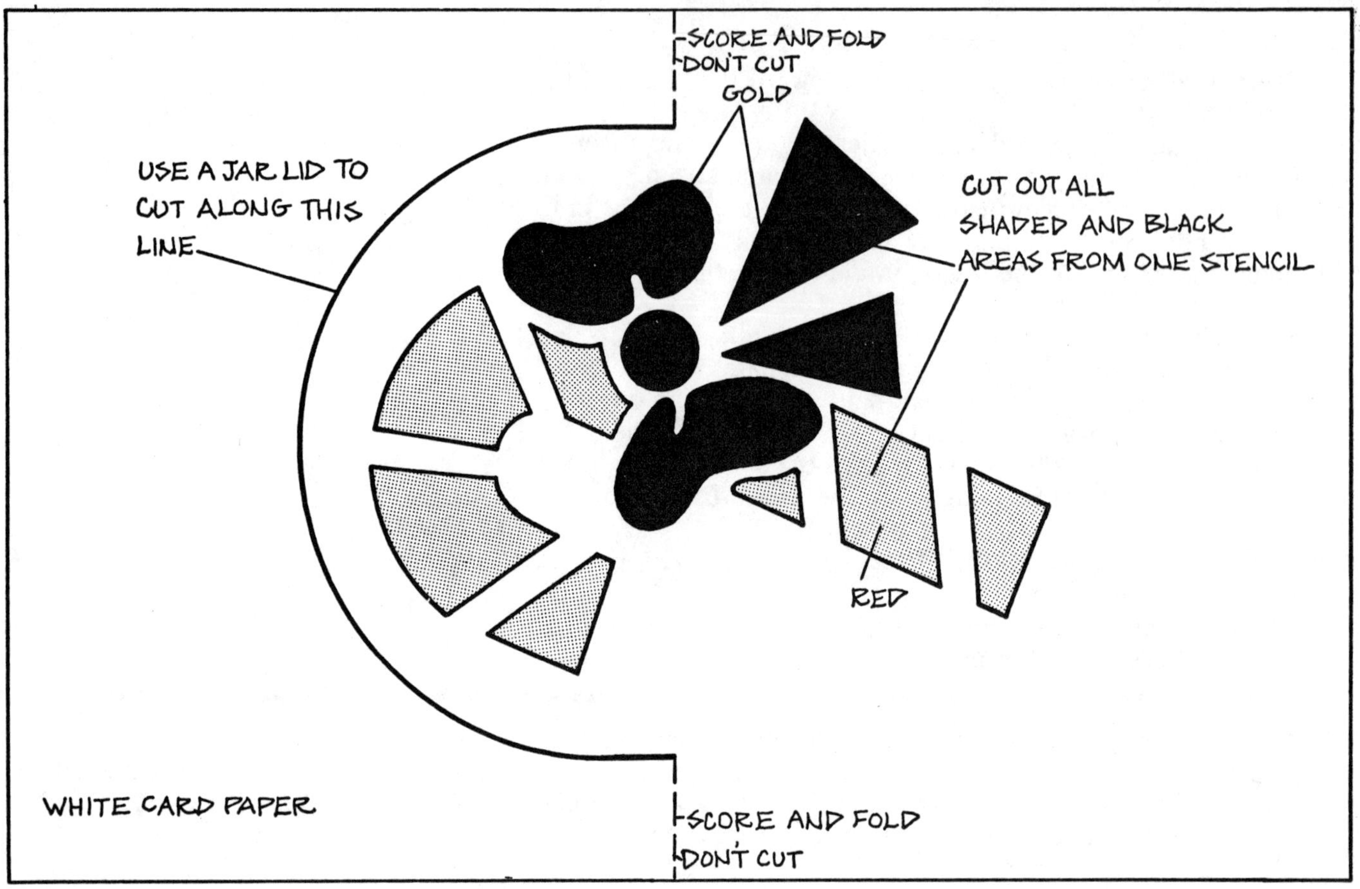

SCORE AND FOLD
DON'T CUT
GOLD

USE A JAR LID TO
CUT ALONG THIS
LINE

CUT OUT ALL
SHADED AND BLACK
AREAS FROM ONE STENCIL

RED

WHITE CARD PAPER

SCORE AND FOLD
DON'T CUT

CUT OUT ALL
SHADED AREAS FROM
YOUR STENCILS

SCORE AND FOLD

SCORE AND FOLD

A Candy Cane for Christmas

- After cutting your card paper (unfolded size 4½"x7¼"), score the short fold lines—don't score across the design area.
- Cut the semicircle only up to the score line on either side. You may find a jar lid and X-acto knife helpful in the cutting.
- Center the candy cane stencil in the semicircle as shown. Now stencil your card.

Your folded card measures 4½"x6" and fits into an A6 envelope.

MESSAGE HERE

A Christmas Song

- Cut, score, and fold your card paper (unfolded size 5" x 15") as illustrated in figures A to C—this is called a double gatefold.
- Prepare two stencils, one for the "Fa" and another for the "la."
- Unfold the card to stencil in your colors.

When dry and refolded, your card fits into a #6 Baronial envelope.

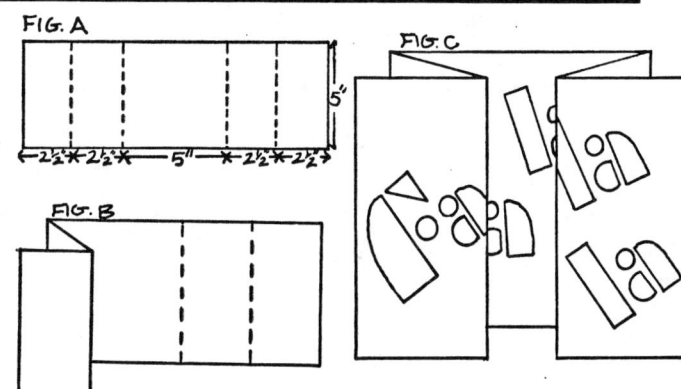

SCORE AND FOLD

SCORE AND FOLD

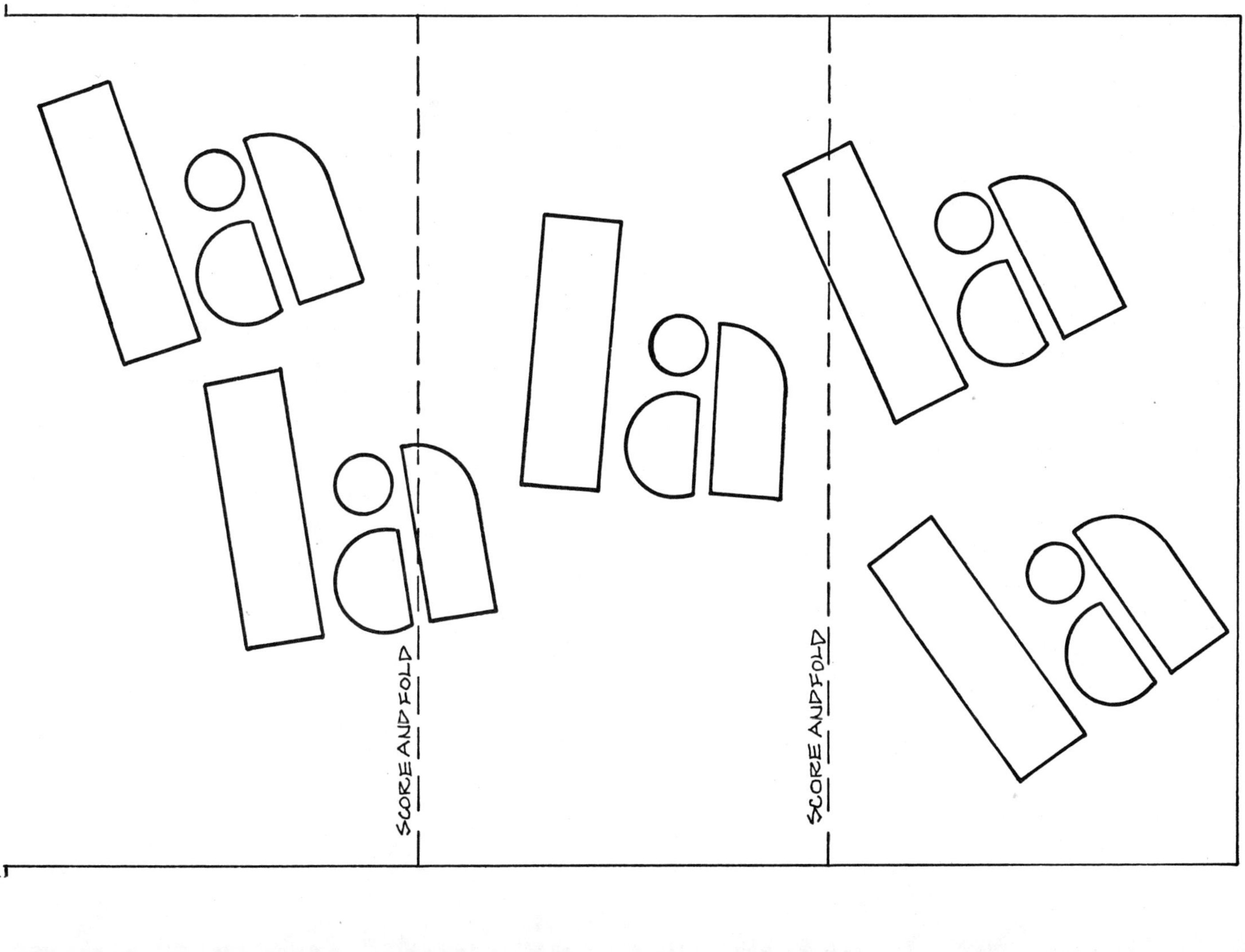

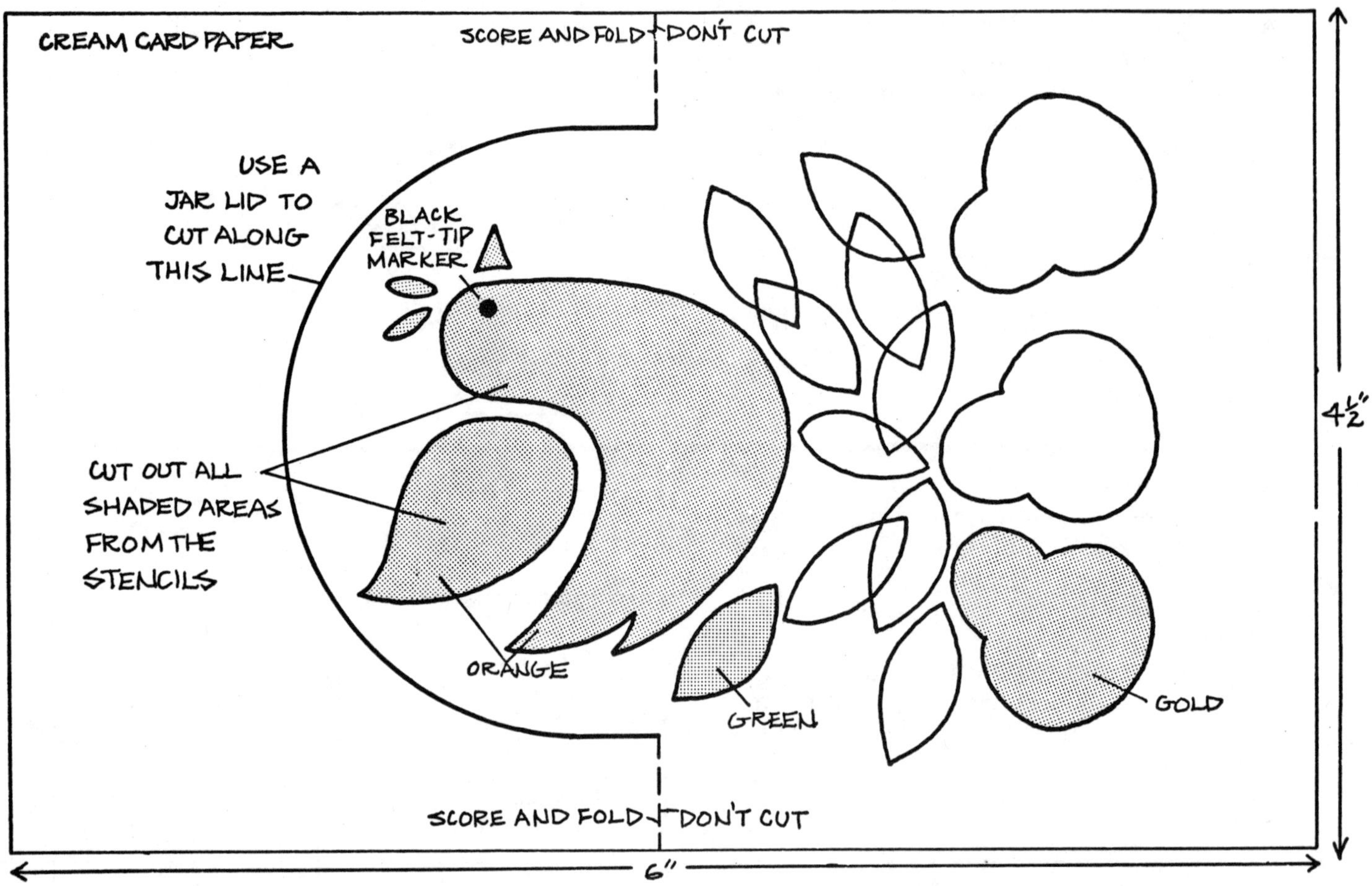

CREAM CARD PAPER   SCORE AND FOLD·DON'T CUT

USE A
JAR LID TO
CUT ALONG
THIS LINE

BLACK
FELT-TIP
MARKER

CUT OUT ALL
SHADED AREAS
FROM THE
STENCILS

ORANGE

GREEN

GOLD

4½"

SCORE AND FOLD·DON'T CUT

6"

FIG. A PARTRIDGE

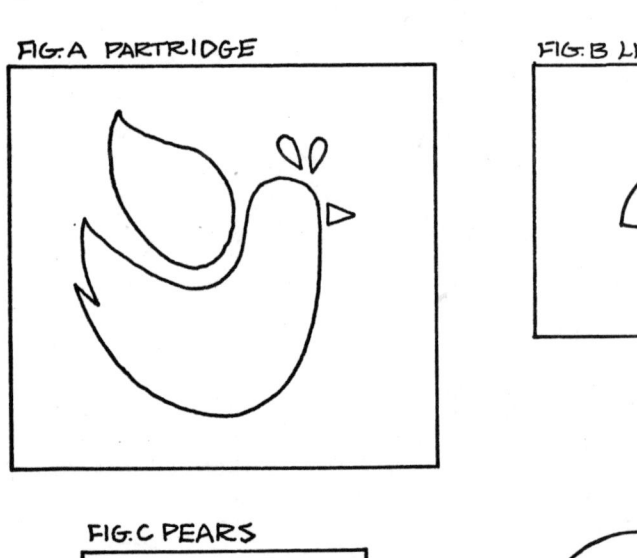

FIG. B LEAVES

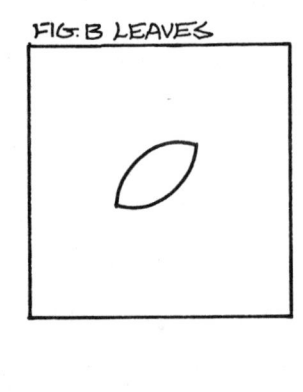

FIG. C PEARS

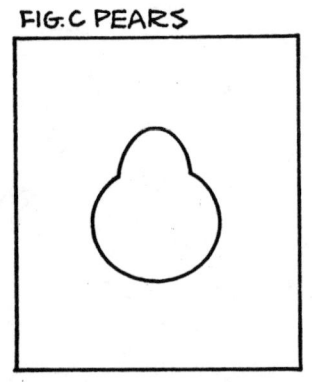

FINISHED CARD

Partridge in a Pear Tree

- **Additional material:** black felt-tip marker
- After cutting your card paper (unfolded size 4½" x 7¼"), score the short fold lines — *don't* score across the design area.
- Cut the semicircle only up to the score line on either side. You may find a jar lid and X-acto knife helpful in the cutting.
- Make a stencil for each design element (see figs. A to C).
- Stencil the bird first, centering it in the semicircle as shown; then stencil one leaf. Overlap the rest of the leaves, letting each dry before starting the next. Now stencil in the pears and draw the bird's eye with a black marker.

Your folded card measures 4½" x 6" and fits into an A6 envelope.

HAPPY
FOURTH

FINISHED CARD

A Fourth of July Card

- Follow the positioning of the design very carefully, so that when scored and folded the top half of the card meets the rim of Uncle Sam's hat.
- After the paint is dry, indicate where the folds are to go with light pencil lines (these should be erased later). Now score and fold the card.

The unfolded card size is 4"x10". Your folded card will fit into an A2 envelope.

Variation: Stencil Uncle Sam's hat or the firecrackers on place cards and name tags. Their size will be determined by which part of the design you use (see illustrations).

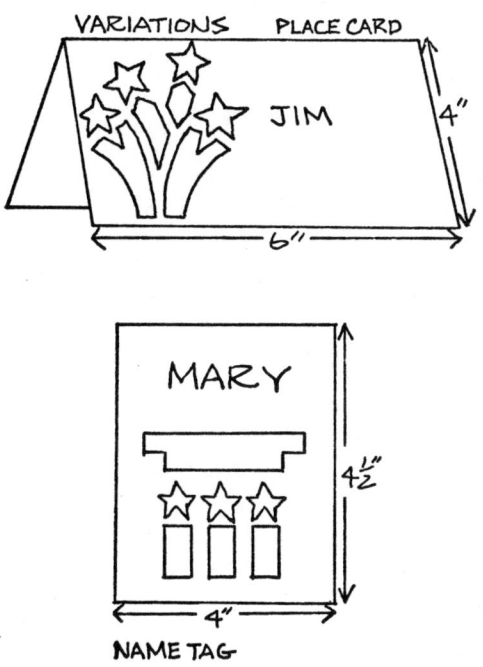

VARIATIONS   PLACE CARD

JIM

4"

6"

MARY

4½"

4"

NAME TAG

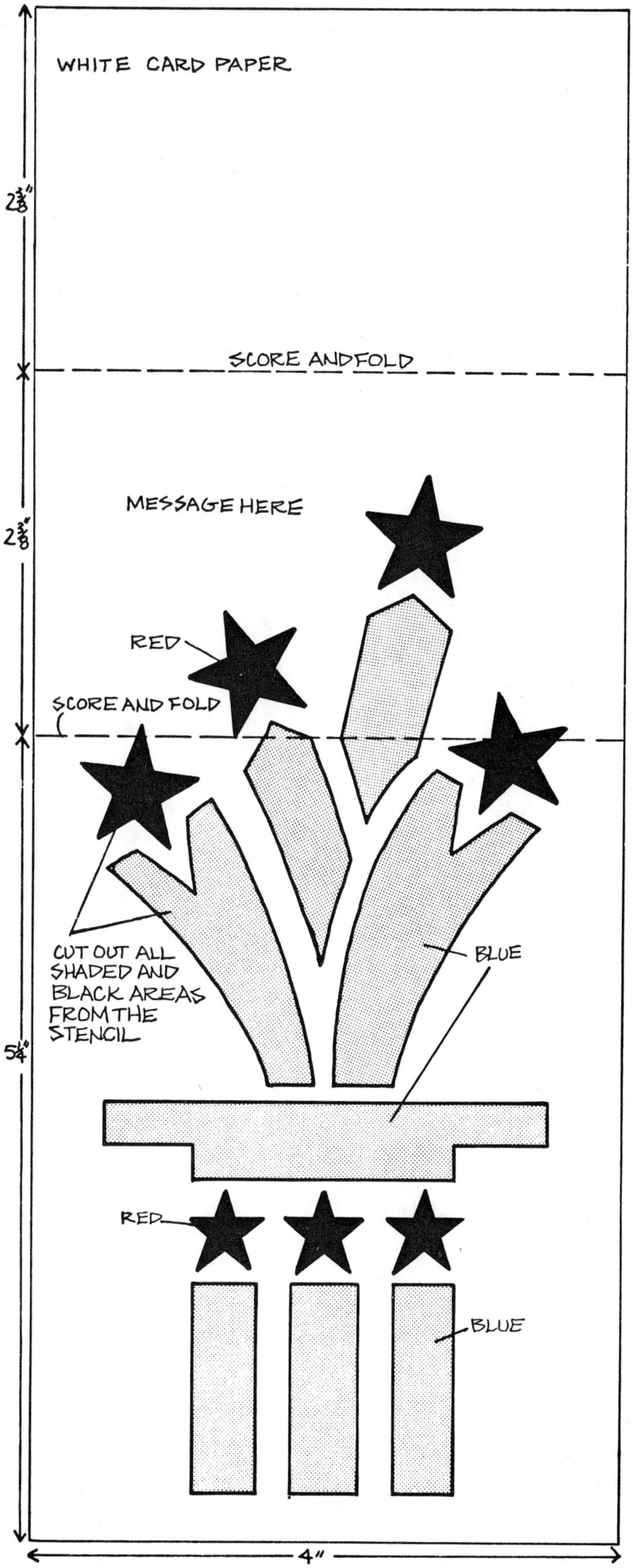

WHITE CARD PAPER

2⅜"

- - - SCORE AND FOLD - - -

MESSAGE HERE

2⅜"

RED

- - - SCORE AND FOLD - - -

CUT OUT ALL
SHADED AND
BLACK AREAS
FROM THE
STENCIL

BLUE

5¼"

RED

BLUE

4"

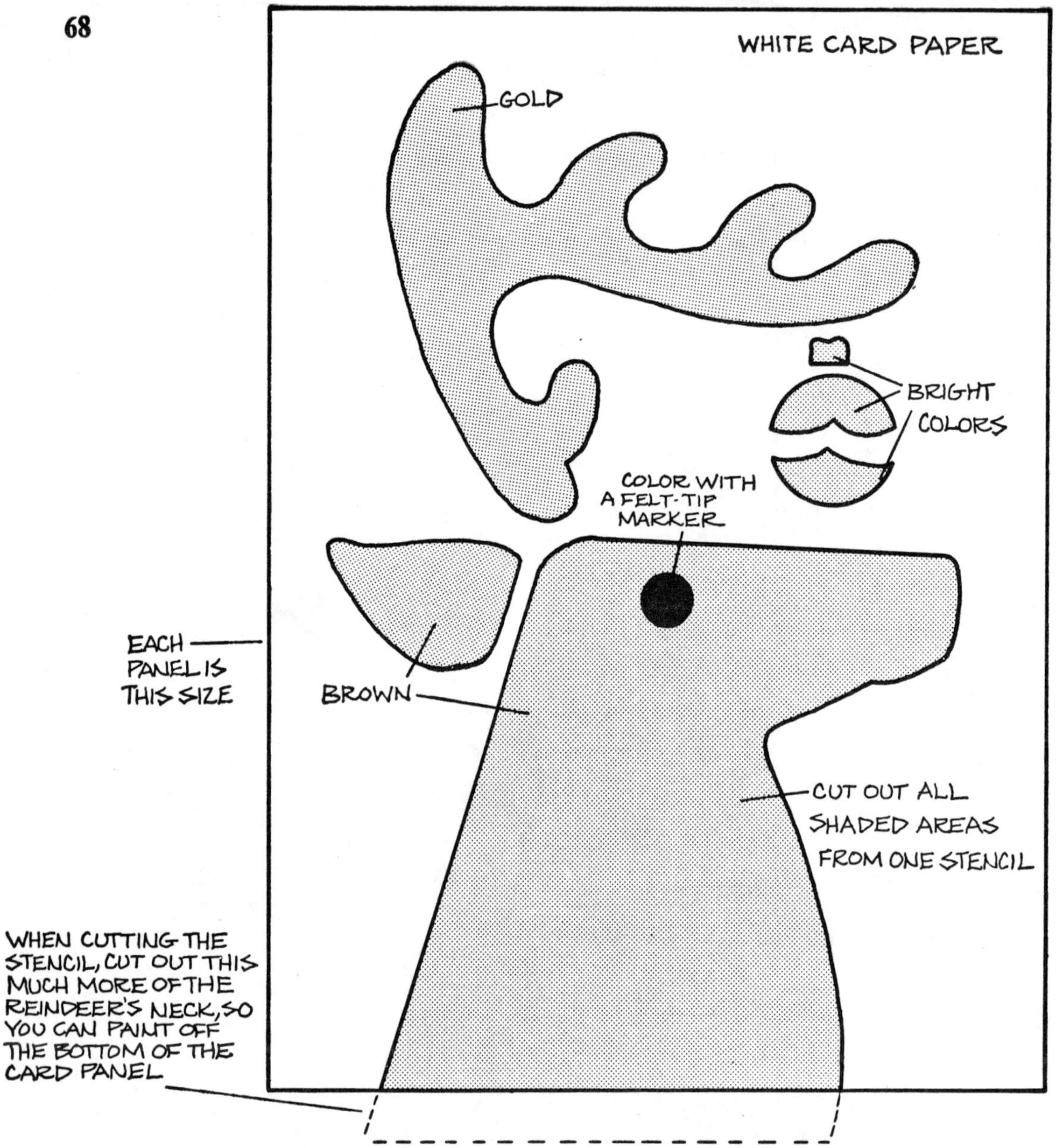

WHITE CARD PAPER

GOLD

BRIGHT COLORS

COLOR WITH A FELT-TIP MARKER

EACH PANEL IS THIS SIZE

BROWN

CUT OUT ALL SHADED AREAS FROM ONE STENCIL

WHEN CUTTING THE STENCIL, CUT OUT THIS MUCH MORE OF THE REINDEER'S NECK, SO YOU CAN PAINT OFF THE BOTTOM OF THE CARD PANEL

4½" 4½" 4½" 4½"

MESSAGE HERE

6"

FINISHED CARD

Santa's Reindeer Card

- **Additional material:** felt-tip markers
- Cut your card paper to 6" x 18". Score and fold your card before you begin stenciling to make certain each animal will be correctly positioned.
- Stencil the reindeer on the front, and on panels 1, 2, and 3. Center each reindeer on the panel, lining up the top and bottom of the stencil with the top and bottom of the card paper.
- Color in each reindeer eye with a felt-tip marker.

Your folded card fits into an A6 envelope.

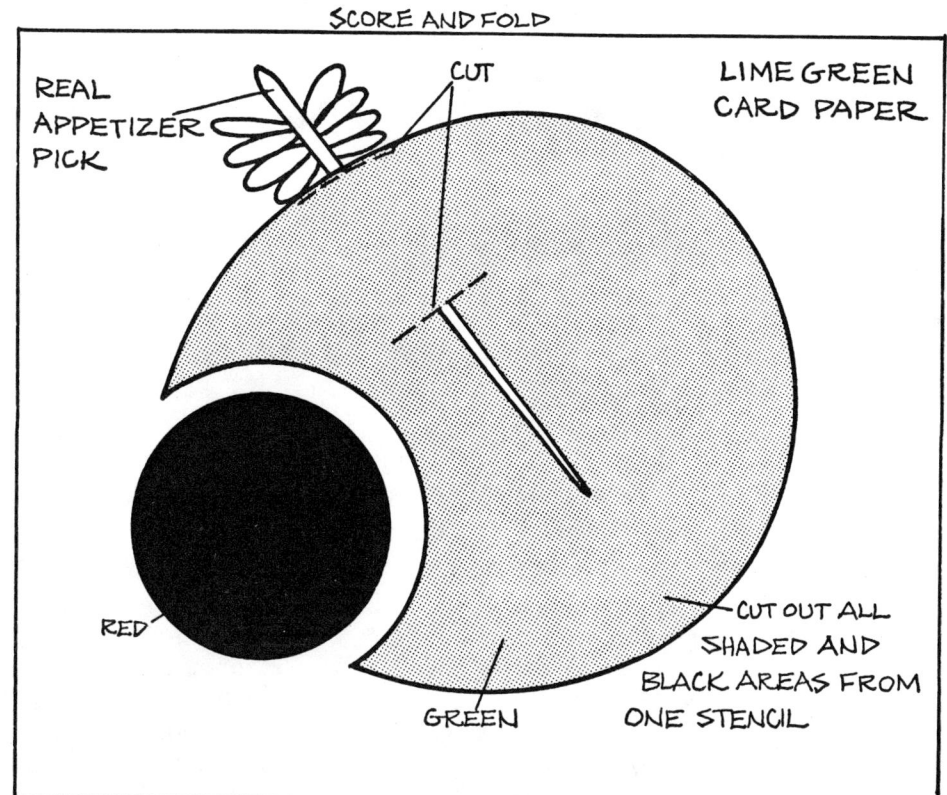

SCORE AND FOLD

REAL APPETIZER PICK

CUT

LIME GREEN CARD PAPER

RED

GREEN

CUT OUT ALL SHADED AND BLACK AREAS FROM ONE STENCIL

FRONT PANEL

Party Invitation Hors d'Oeuvre

- **Additional material:** appetizer picks (from party shop or drug store)
- To make it easier to position the design, cut, score, and fold your card before you begin stenciling.

The unfolded card measures 5"x8".

Your folded card fits into an A2 envelope.

Variation: Carry the motif to the envelopes, place cards, and napkins. Make a stencil of the small olive and paint it on. Or to simplify the printing, cut an olive stamp out of a potato or an eraser (see Stamp-Out Cards section).

FINISHED CARD

PLACE CARD

Lucy

3"

1¾"

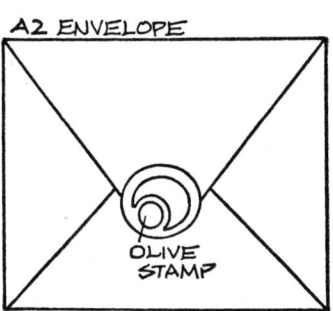

A2 ENVELOPE

OLIVE STAMP

HAPPY HALLOWEEN

Spatter Cards

Appearance: Dappled, airy, textured look.
Skill required: Quite simple, but potentially messy.
Quantity/Time: After mastering the spatter technique, many cards can be made quickly.

MATERIALS

- Recommended paper: medium-weight, colored or white cover paper; coated paper; or—in a pinch—construction paper (see All About Paper)
- Easy Envelopes
- Poster paints
- Carbon paper
- Masking tape
- Old clothes
- Stencil paper (available at art supply stores, or use light cardboard, shirt cardboard, boxboard or railroad board, or old file folders)
- Back side of a breadboard, or heavy cardboard (to protect your table when cutting)
- Newspaper to protect working area

TOOLS

- Old toothbrush
- Paint reservoir: paper plate, foil-lined dinner plate, or aluminum freezer-pan
- Scissors or X-acto knife
- Sharp pencil
- See individual cards for additional materials and tools

HOW TO MAKE THE CARD

1. Start with a piece of stencil paper an inch or two larger than your card paper (see card design). Then cover the card design with tracing paper and transfer it to the stencil paper with a pencil and carbon paper (see How to Transfer in Techniques section). You will need a separate stencil for each different-colored design part.
2. Cut out the design parts (all shaded areas) and save both cutouts and stencil.

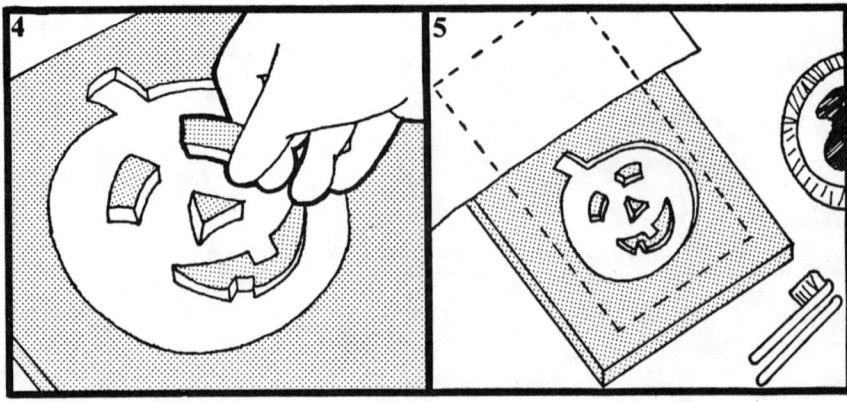

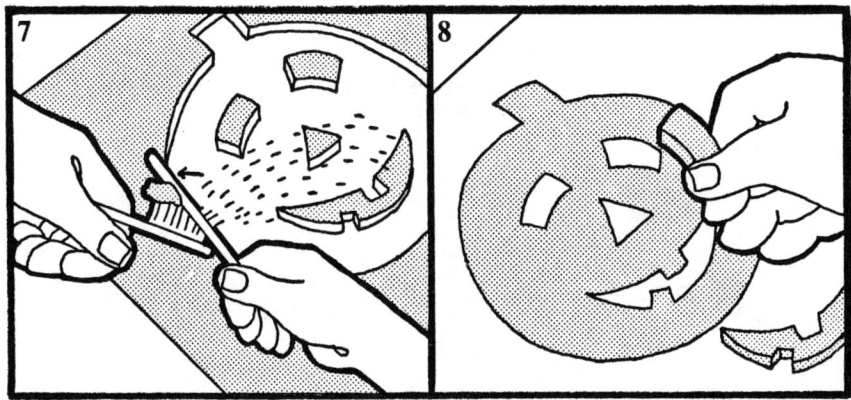

3. Cut your card paper to size. Spread newspapers over your working area and lay the card paper on top.

4. Place the cutouts or stencil (as required by design) on the card paper so that the design will be positioned properly when the card is folded.

5. Cover all areas where you do not wish color to appear using strips of scrap paper.

6. Pour a thin layer of paint into your paint reservoir.

7. Dip the toothbrush into the paint and then point the brush toward your card paper with the bristles up. Now run a pencil, or your finger, toward you over the bristles to create a spray. You must stroke toward you, or you will get a face full of paint. Keep the brush angled toward the paper as you brush the bristles until the paper is evenly spattered. Don't overspatter. **Hint:** Be sure everything within reach of the spray is well protected, including you and your clothes. The key to successful spattering is controlling your spray. Practice on a piece of scrap paper before you begin making your card.

8. Remove the stencil and scrap paper, being careful of the wet paint.

9. Let the paint dry. Then score and fold your card as shown.

VARIATIONS TO TRY AFTER MAKING YOUR FIRST CARD

1. Brush the toothbrush over a piece of window screen or through a kitchen strainer, rather than spattering directly onto the card.

2. Spatter one color over another color. Let the first color dry thoroughly before applying the second.

3. Reverse the areas that receive color—if you used cutouts to make your card, use the stencil this time.

4. Use spray paint. Spray paints are available in small 3.2-ounce sizes.

5. Use a paper doily as your spattering stencil.

6. Spatter over pine needles, leaves, bottle caps, or any found items to create other interesting patterns.

7. Spatter a design and let it dry. Then move the stencil pattern slightly (⅛" to the side) and spatter again.

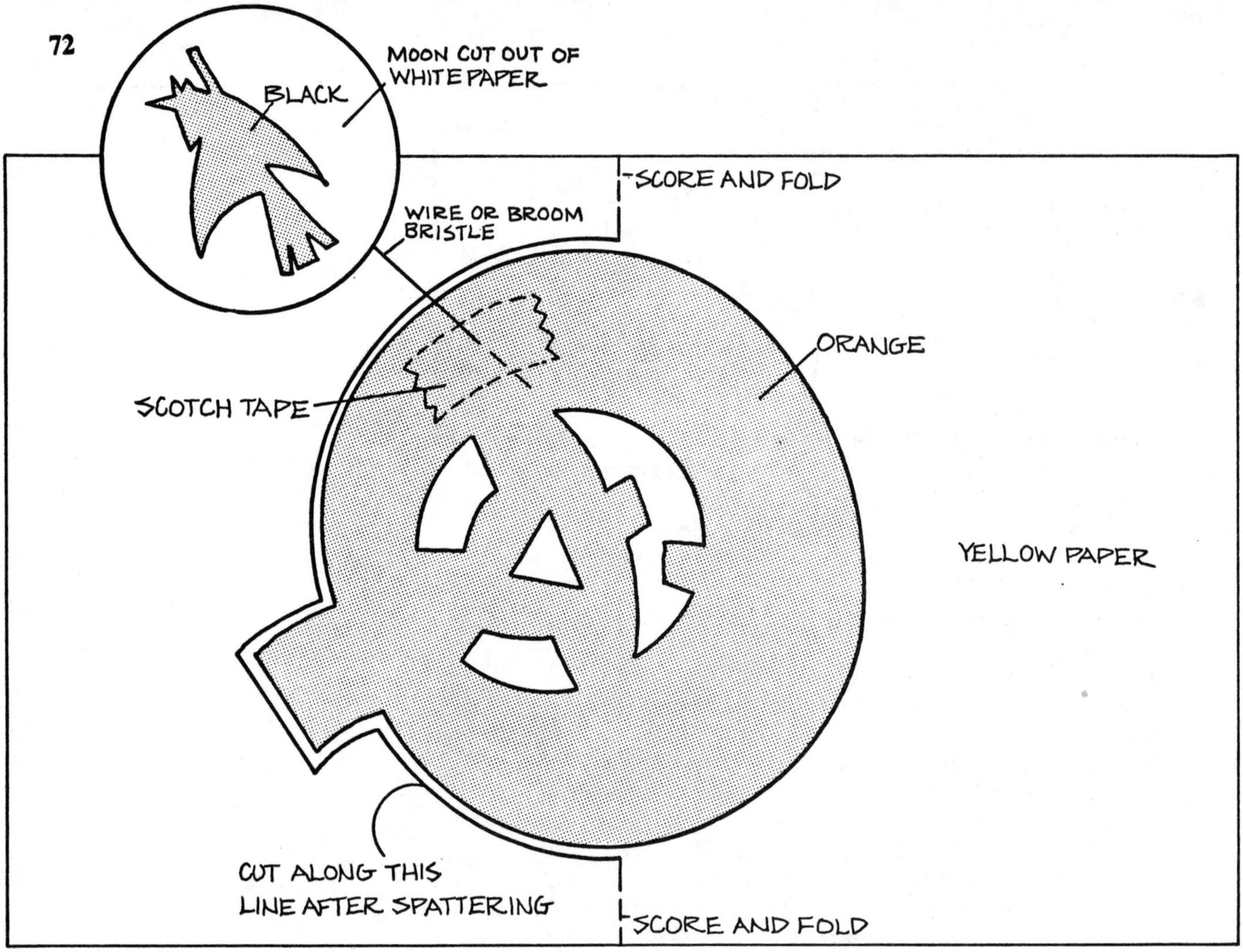

BLACK

MOON CUT OUT OF WHITE PAPER

WIRE OR BROOM BRISTLE

SCORE AND FOLD

ORANGE

SCOTCH TAPE

YELLOW PAPER

CUT ALONG THIS LINE AFTER SPATTERING

SCORE AND FOLD

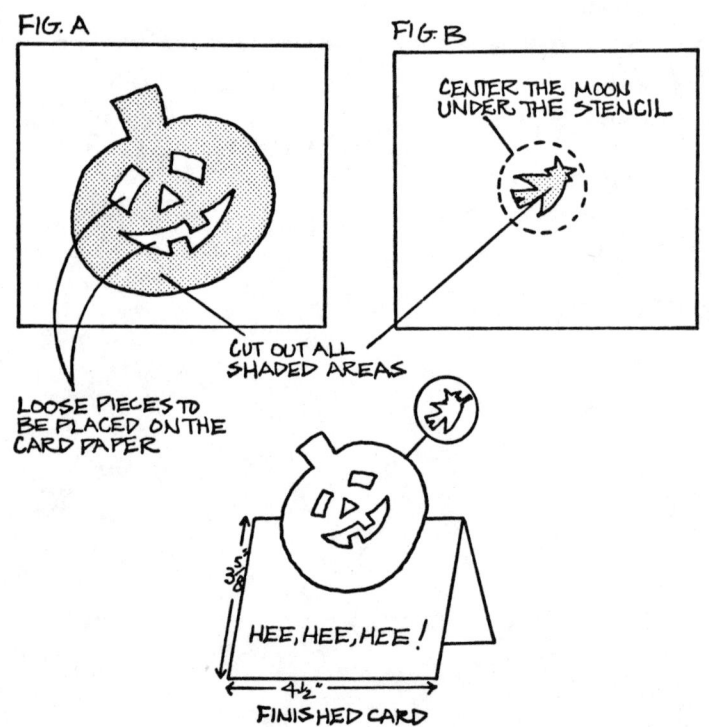

FIG. A

LOOSE PIECES TO BE PLACED ON THE CARD PAPER

CUT OUT ALL SHADED AREAS

FIG. B

CENTER THE MOON UNDER THE STENCIL

HEE, HEE, HEE!

4½"

FINISHED CARD

A Halloween Pumpkin

- **Additional materials:** broom bristle or springy wire
- After you cut your card paper, mark the fold lines lightly with pencil (these should be erased later) and score them.
- Make two stencils and then spatter each on a different paper, as shown in figures A and B.
- Before you put the witch in place, cut around the top of the pumpkin, but only up to the score line on either side. A jar lid and an X-acto knife will guide you to a perfect cut.
- Take a bristle from your witch's broom or use a piece of springy wire to keep her soaring. Tape one end of the bristle or wire to the back of the pumpkin, the other end to the back of the moon.

Mail this card unfolded so that the wire doesn't bend, or the bristle break. Your unfolded card measures 4½" x 7¼" and fits into a 5½" x 7½" open-end envelope

A Christmas Stocking

- **Additional materials:** hole punch, Christmas stickers
- You need patience and a steady hand here.
- Use a hole punch to cut the small circles.

The unfolded card measures 5½" x 8½". Folded, your card is a self-mailer, requiring only a Christmas sticker to seal.

4¼" 4¼"

5½"

MERRY CHRISTMAS

FINISHED CARD

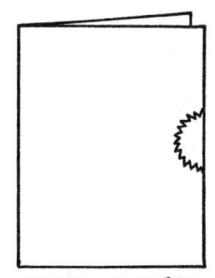

SELF-MAILER

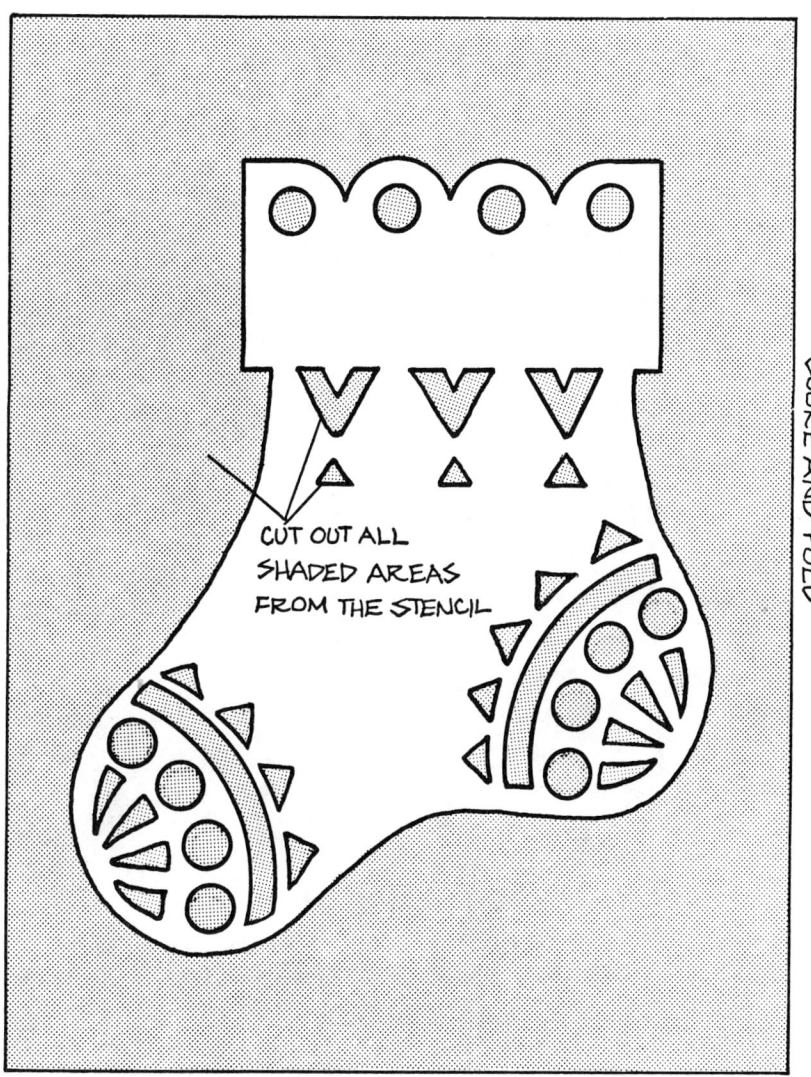

SCORE AND FOLD

CUT OUT ALL SHADED AREAS FROM THE STENCIL

Need place cards for a Halloween party?

- Cut out your card paper and then lightly pencil in fold marks (these should be erased later).
- Put the stencil over your card paper.
- Spatter and let dry.
- Now use a jar lid to guide you in cutting the semicircle, but stop at the fold marks.

Score the short fold marks and fold as shown.

CONNIE

1½"

3½"

FINISHED PLACE CARD

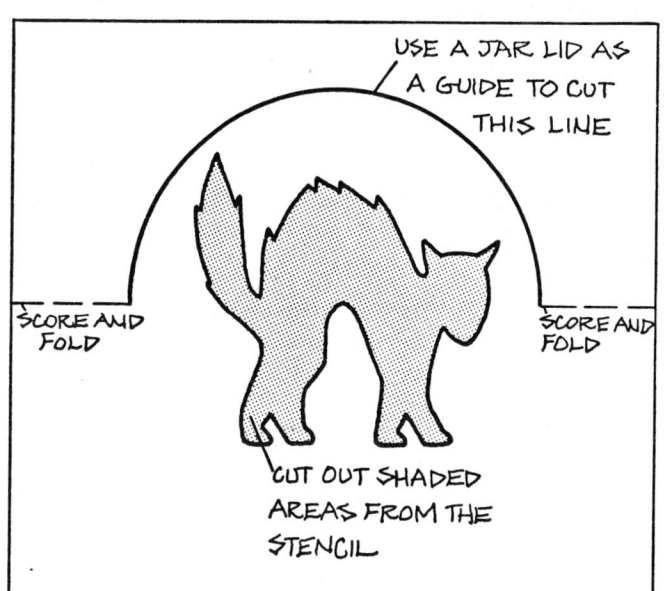

USE A JAR LID AS A GUIDE TO CUT THIS LINE

SCORE AND FOLD

SCORE AND FOLD

CUT OUT SHADED AREAS FROM THE STENCIL

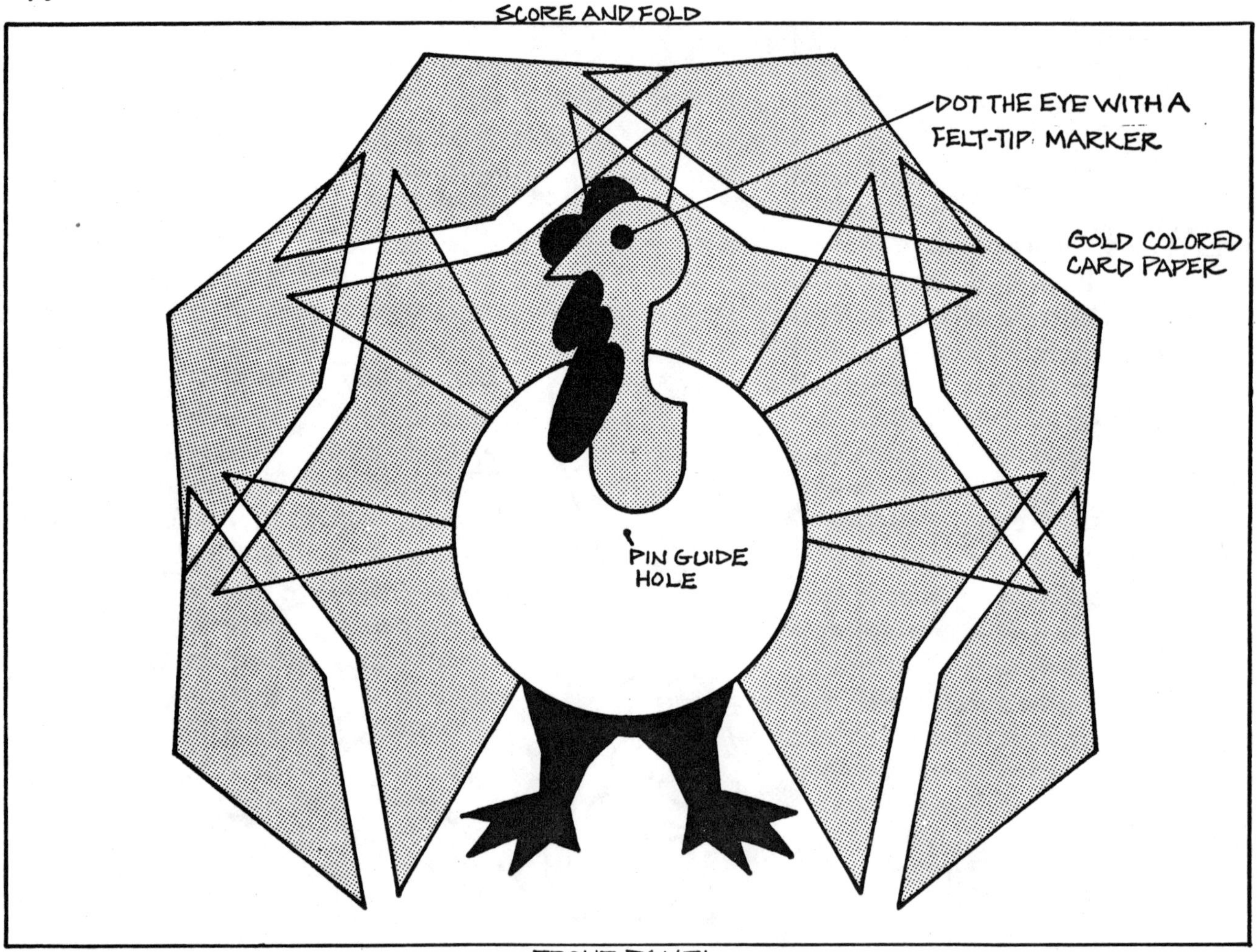

SCORE AND FOLD

DOT THE EYE WITH A
FELT-TIP MARKER

GOLD COLORED
CARD PAPER

PIN GUIDE
HOLE

FRONT PANEL

A Thanksgiving Day Turkey

- **Additional materials:** straight pin, felt-tip marker
- Make the three stencils shown in figures A to C.
- Registration is important here. Be sure to push the straight pin through both stencil and card firmly into your board (corrugated cardboard is excellent for this).
- Cut, score, and fold your card paper (unfolded size 7" x 10").

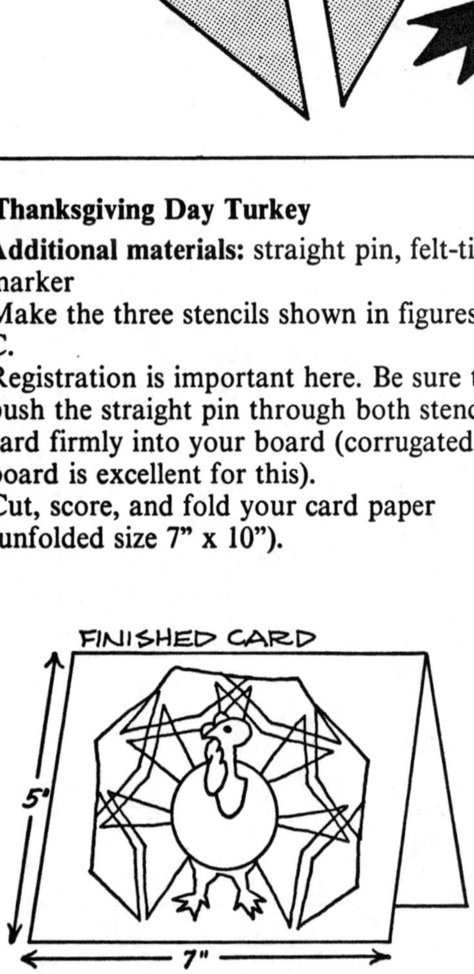

FINISHED CARD

5"

7"

- Stencil A: Hold stencil to card with a straight pin, positioned as shown in the card design. Now spatter the feathers. Let dry a moment and then rotate the stencil until you can spatter in between the feathers you just spattered. Now spatter again and let paint dry completely.
  Hint: If you use a combination of colors, wait a moment or two for each spatter to dry before applying the next color.
- Stencil B: Remove stencil A when paint is dry and now hold stencil B to the card with a straight pin. Position as shown in the card design and then spatter the turkey head. Let dry completely.
- Stencil C: Put your turkey on his feet with stencil C. Change stencils and align on the turkey's head. Now spatter. The body of the turkey will remain the color of your card paper. Let dry completely before stuffing.

The finished card will fit into an A7 envelope.

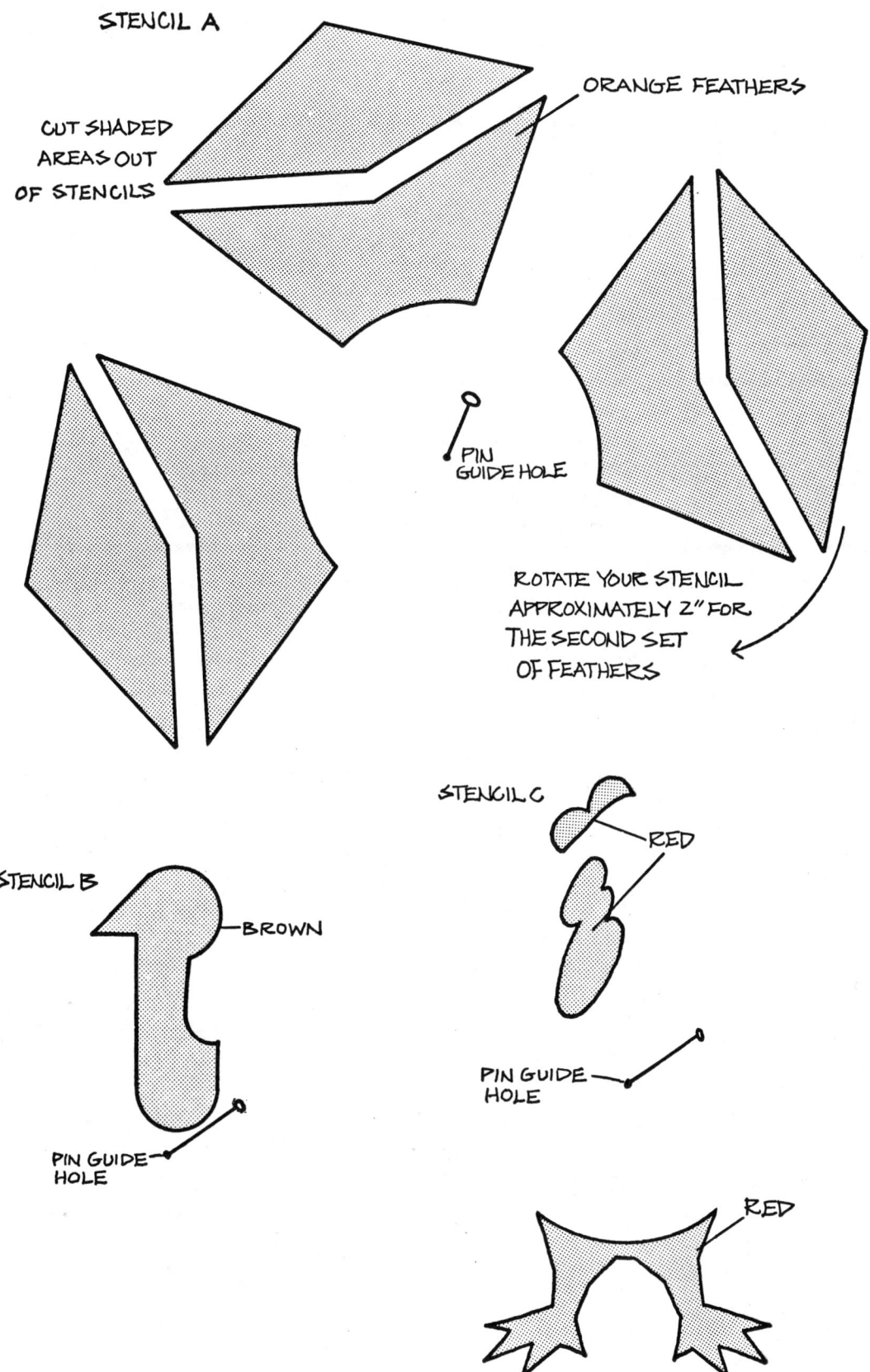

STENCIL A

CUT SHADED
AREAS OUT
OF STENCILS

ORANGE FEATHERS

PIN
GUIDE HOLE

ROTATE YOUR STENCIL
APPROXIMATELY 2" FOR
THE SECOND SET
OF FEATHERS

STENCIL C

RED

PIN GUIDE
HOLE

STENCIL B

BROWN

PIN GUIDE
HOLE

RED

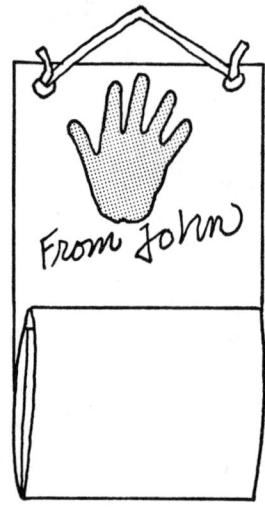

Hand Stamp Cards

Appearance: Bold, primitive design.
Skill required: None.
Quantity/Time: As many as you want, very quickly.

MATERIALS

- Recommended paper: medium-weight, colored or white cover paper; coated paper; or—in a pinch—construction paper (see All About Paper)
- Easy Envelopes
- Newspaper
- Poster paints
- Hands and feet

TOOLS

- Paint reservoir: paper plate or aluminum foil pan
- Ruler
- Scissors or an X-acto knife
- Felt-tip marker or ball-point pen
- Sharp pencil
- See individual cards for additional materials and tools

HOW TO MAKE THE CARD

1. Cut, score, and fold your card paper, as shown.
2. Draw light pencil guidelines on your card as indicated in the card design. These are to keep your hands where they belong.
3. Spread a thin layer of poster paint on the bottom of your paint reservoir.
4. Now, have each family member press a hand into the paint to cover the surface of the hand, then onto newspaper to blot off the excess paint. Don't worry—poster paint washes off easily with water.
   Hint: You'll know you have just the right amount of paint if the impression you make on the newspaper shows up the lines and swirls of your hand. Practice a few times until you achieve this effect.
5. Press your paint-coated hand firmly onto the card paper in the

proper position—the hand stamp. You can get about two imprints from each inking. Continue stamping until your card is complete and then lay it aside to dry.

6. If you are using more than one color, let the first one dry before pressing a different color handprint over it.

7. When all the prints are dry, have each family member sign his or her print with a colorful felt-tip marker or ball-point pen.

---

1. Alternate two colors: red hand, green hand, red hand, etc.
2. Instead of a hand stamp, trace around each family member's hand with a colorful felt-tip marker.

VARIATIONS TO TRY AFTER MAKING YOUR FIRST CARD

Birth Announcement

- **Additional materials:** stamp pad, heavy-weight paper
- A heavy-weight paper is best to use since the card (4" x 5") does not fold.
- Ink the baby's feet. This can be simple if you use a regular stamp pad (you may use a brayer and tempera paint if you wish — see Glossary).
- Then press the card paper against the feet, *not* the feet against the card.

When dry, the card goes into an A2 envelope.

BABY ANNOUNCEMENT

IT'S A GIRL
RED
PINK CARD PAPER
4"
5"
FINISHED CARD

The Original Family Hand Stamp

- **Additional materials:** ribbon or yarn, hole punch, gummed stickers, roll paper (butcher paper, shelf paper)
- No measurements here. Your card size depends on the number of people in your family.
- Just remember two things: Make the paper wide enough for the largest hand, and long enough so there is a panel for each artist. If you have a big family, make your card from a roll of paper.
- A handy hanger is made by punching a hole at the top and looping through ribbon or yarn.

Your card becomes a self-mailer with the fold-after-fold method (fig. A) and a gummed sticker.

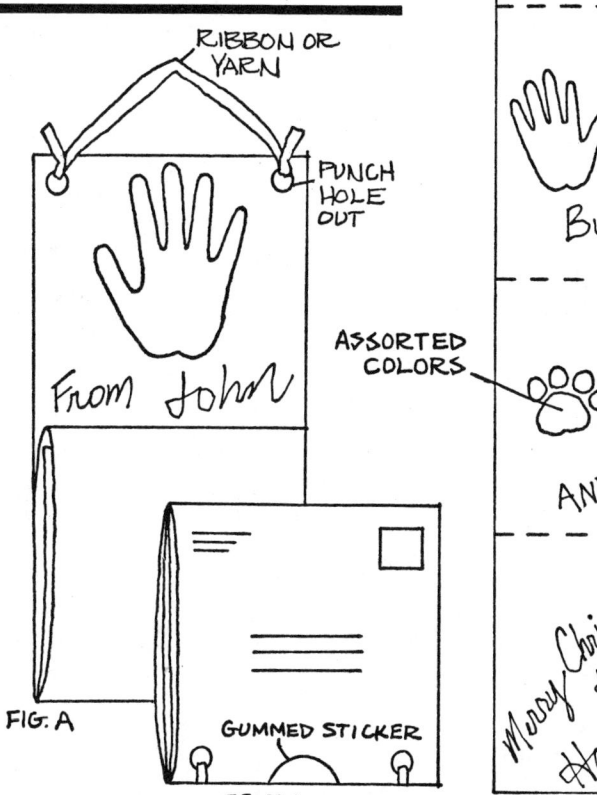

RIBBON OR YARN
PUNCH HOLE OUT
From John
FIG. A
GUMMED STICKER
SELF-MAILER

FAMILY HAND STAMP
From John
SCORE & FOLD
Mary
WRITE YOUR NAME BELOW YOUR HANDSTAMP
Buddy
ASSORTED COLORS
AND FIDO
Merry Christmas & Happy New Year
FINISHED CARD

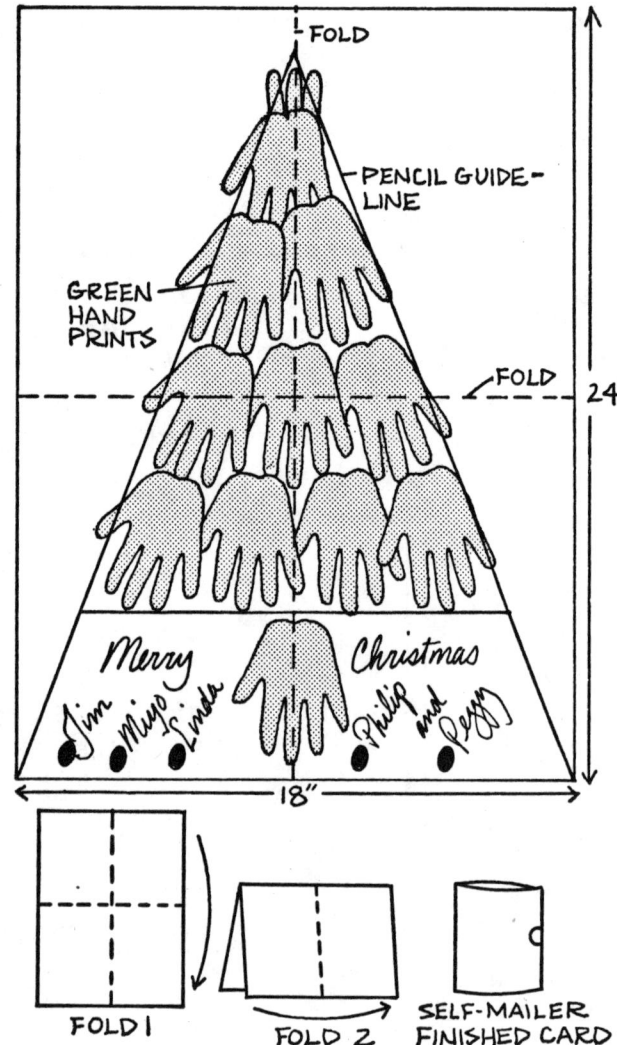

FOLD

PENCIL GUIDE-
LINE

GREEN
HAND
PRINTS

FOLD 24"

Merry Christmas
Jim Miyo Linda Philip and Peggy

18"

FOLD I

FOLD 2

SELF-MAILER
FINISHED CARD

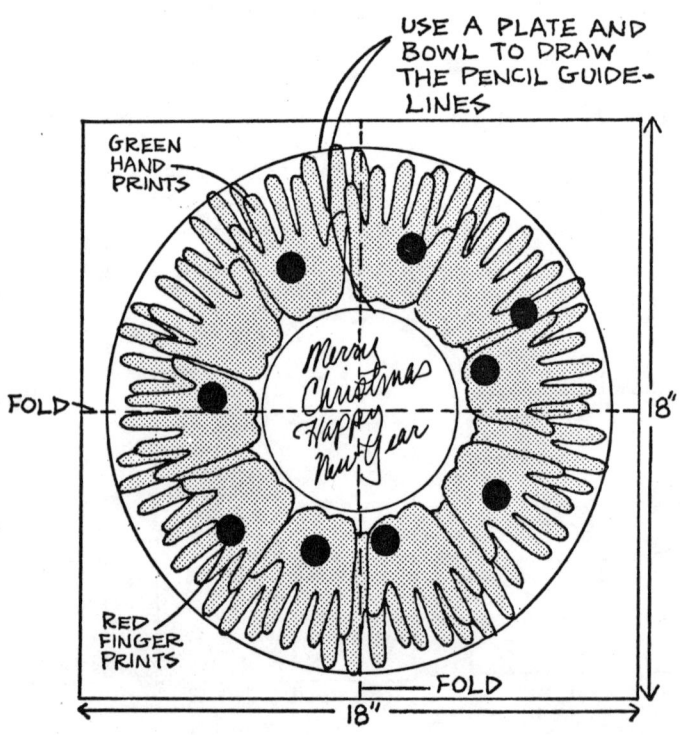

USE A PLATE AND
BOWL TO DRAW
THE PENCIL GUIDE-
LINES

GREEN
HAND
PRINTS

FOLD

Merry
Christmas
Happy
New Year

18"

RED
FINGER
PRINTS

FOLD

18"

A Handy Christmas Tree

- **Additional material:** gummed stickers
- Make yours any size you want, but we suggest a card of 18" x 24" to give you a well-shaped tree.
- Draw your guidelines. Lightly pencil one from the top center of the card to each of the two bottom corners; another horizontally, where you want the base of your tree to be (leave enough room beneath for the trunk and family thumbprints). Keep all handprints within these pencil lines to maintain the Christmas tree shape.
- To hand stamp begin at the top. Imprint just your three middle fingers. Then reverse your palm (or the paper) so that the handprints are upside down, and make the rest of the ever-widening handprint branches. Use a moderate amount of overlapping, as shown. One handprint makes the trunk; a thumb dipped in a variety of bright colors provides the tree ornaments.
- Each member of the family signs at the bottom with a thumbprint and their name.

Fold your card as shown, and seal with a gummed sticker.

A Handy Christmas Wreath

- **Additional materials:** string, straight pin, gummed stickers
- Make yours any size you want. We suggest an almost life-size one on 18"x 18" paper.
- Draw your circle guidelines in the center of your card paper using one large round platter (or a round wastebasket) and a small salad bowl as drawing guides. If you don't have the right sizes, cut a piece of string a bit longer (for tying knots) than the larger radius and tie one end to a pencil, the other to a pin. Stick the pin in the center of your paper, tighten the string, and lightly draw the circle you need. Shorten the string for the inner circle.
- To hand stamp, just go to it. Point your handprints away from the center of the card, with the heel of your palm resting on the edge of the inner circle. Keep within the circle to assure a round wreath. This wreath can take quite a bit of overlapping, but keep the application of paint light so the card paper color will show through.
- A scatter of holly berries adds sparkle and is easily done with a fingertip dipped in red paint.

Write your message in the center of your wreath. Fold your card as shown, and seal with a gummed sticker.

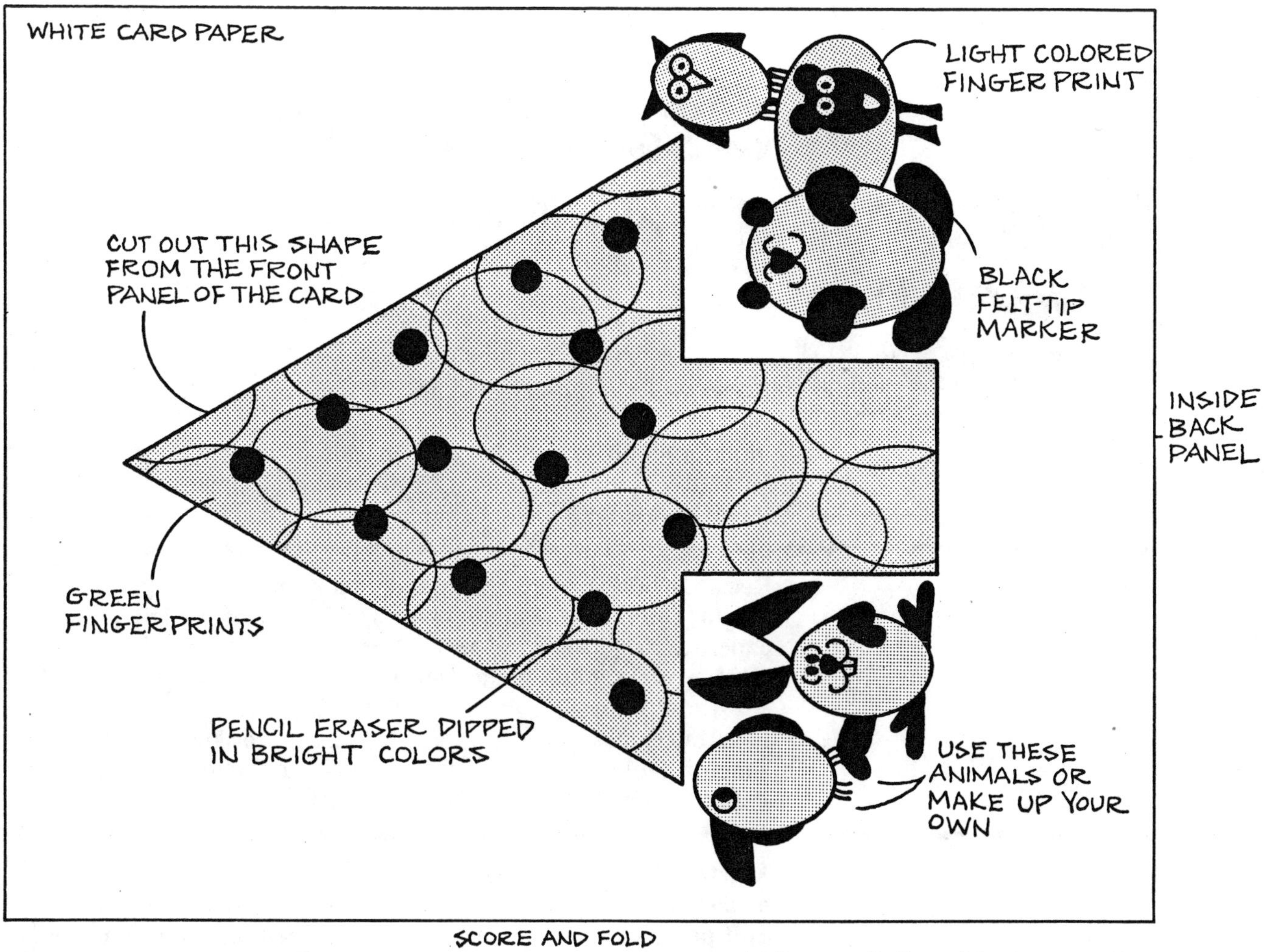

WHITE CARD PAPER

CUT OUT THIS SHAPE
FROM THE FRONT
PANEL OF THE CARD

LIGHT COLORED
FINGER PRINT

BLACK
FELT-TIP
MARKER

INSIDE
BACK
PANEL

GREEN
FINGER PRINTS

PENCIL ERASER DIPPED
IN BRIGHT COLORS

USE THESE
ANIMALS OR
MAKE UP YOUR
OWN

SCORE AND FOLD

A Thumbprint Christmas Tree

- **Additional materials:** tracing paper, carbon paper, light cardboard, fine-point black felt-tip marker.
- First cut and score your card paper (fig. A, unfolded size 6½" x 10").
- Make a cardboard cutting guide of the Christmas tree (see How to Transfer in Techniques section). Place the cardboard tree on the face of your card in the proper position and cut around the guide to form a tree-shaped window. Fold the card as indicated (fig. B).
- Now use the window cutout as a stencil for your fingerprints. Put branches on your tree by dipping your family's fingers into green poster paint (or onto a stamp pad) and then pressing them onto the inside card paper through the window. Don't be afraid to paint on the edges of the window—this gives a desirable effect to the face of your card (fig. C).
- Cover the entire tree with fingerprints, but go easy on the paint (or ink)—you want the impressions to be recognized as fingerprints. Let the card dry.
- Open the card and decorate your tree. Use the

eraser end of a pencil dipped into assorted bright colors to stamp out ornaments.
- For the finishing touch, each animal body is made with one fingerprint. Use light colors (such as oranges and pinks) so that when the body dries you can draw in the ears, face, feet, and paws with a fine-point black felt-tip marker. Then each artist signs his own animal (fig. D).

After your family card is dry, write your message, refold, and put the finished card into an A7 envelope.

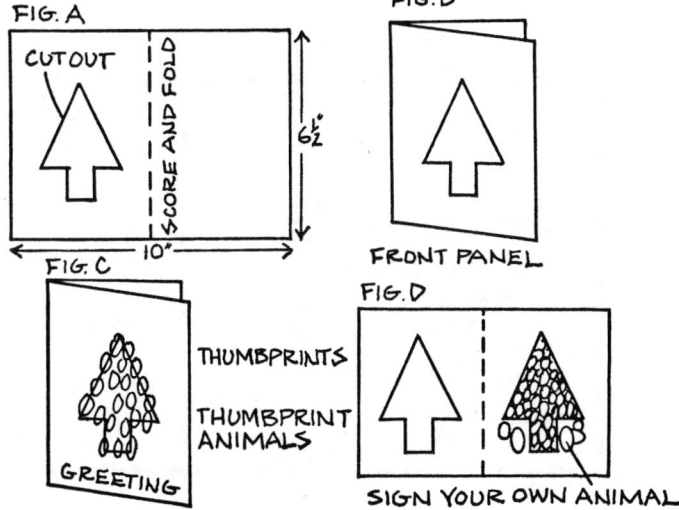

FIG. A

CUTOUT

SCORE AND FOLD

6½"

10"

FIG. B

FRONT PANEL

FIG. C

GREETING

THUMBPRINTS

THUMBPRINT
ANIMALS

FIG. D

SIGN YOUR OWN ANIMAL

Stamp-Out Cards

Appearance: A variety of simple designs put together any way you want.

Skill required: Very little. You only need to make a single stamp.

Quantity/Time: Once you have the stamp, a great many cards can be made quickly.

MATERIALS

- Recommended paper: medium-weight, colored or white cover paper; coated paper; or—in a pinch—construction paper (see All About Paper)
- Easy Envelopes
- Tracing paper
- Paper towels
- Stamp pad, poster paints, ink, food coloring, or any paints you might have on hand
- Cotton rag or strip of an old T-shirt
- Material for stamp: a raw potato or rubber eraser (a Pink Pearl brand is best)

TOOLS

- X-acto knife or small pocket or paring knife
- Soft pencil (HB or 2B, see Glossary)
- Saucer or plate
- See individual cards for additional materials and tools

HOW TO MAKE THE CARD

1. Choose the material to make your stamp. Eraser stamps last longest and make the best impressions; potato stamps make the largest prints and are easiest to cut. Be careful when working with a potato—the juice can leave starch stains on your clothes.
2. Lay a sheet of tracing paper over your card design and trace it with a soft, sharp pencil. Make a heavy impression. Go over it twice if necessary.
3. Check that your stamp is large enough to accommodate the design. If you are using a potato, cut it in half to provide a flat surface (cut across length or width). If it is moist, blot it on a paper towel.

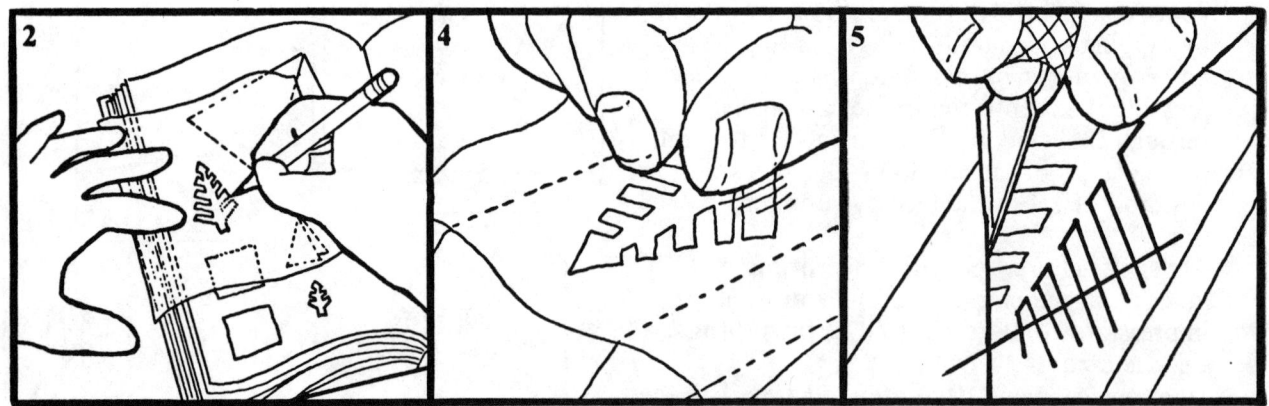

4. Place your tracing paper, pencil-side down, on top of the eraser or cut potato. Hold it firmly in place and transfer the design to the stamp by rubbing over the tracing paper with your thumbnail.

5. Now cut your stamp. First, cut into the stamp material all around the design outline to about ⅛" deep (see illustration). Keep the knife blade slanted *away* from the design (to give the stamping area a strong base).

6. Next, starting at the outer edges of the stamp, pare *toward* the design at a depth of about ⅛". Trim away excess areas of stamp material until the design stands out (see illustration). Be sure not to cut underneath the design—stop each paring cut when you reach your outline cut—or the stamp will weaken and break down after only a few prints. Also be sure to keep your fingers away from the blade.

7. After the stamp is cut, cut your card paper.

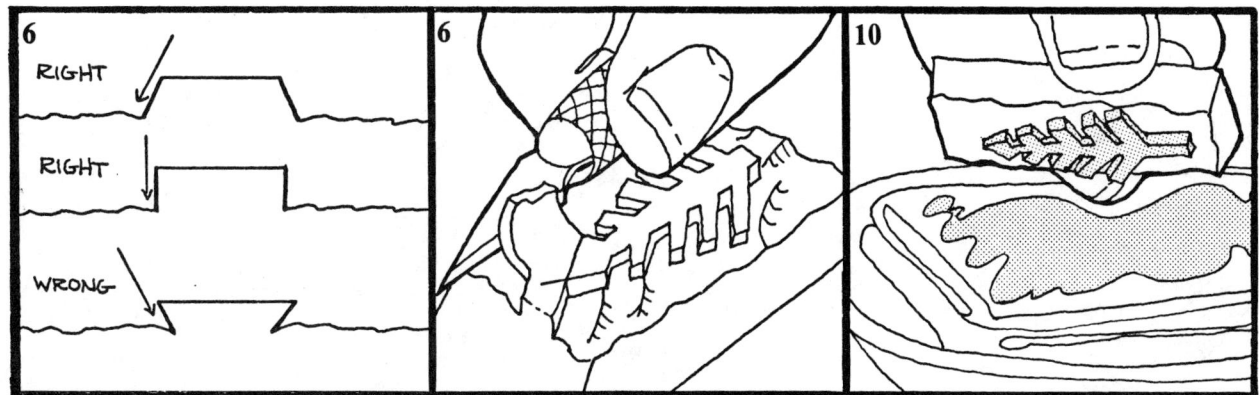

8. Before printing your card, stamp a few times on a practice sheet to be sure you are using the right amount of ink and to see that the design is cut properly. Try holding the stamp in different ways and printing with different pressures to see what effects you can get. You can get four or five imprints with each application of ink.

9. If you are using a stamp pad to make your prints, simply press the stamp onto the inked pad and then firmly onto your card paper in the proper position. Press the stamp down on all sides so the entire design will print.

10. If you are using poster paint, ink, or food coloring, make your own stamp pad by folding a piece of cotton cloth into a square. Put it on a plate and pour your color over the cloth until it is saturated. Then proceed as in step 9. If you want a heavier coat of paint, dip the stamp right into paint poured into a saucer or plate, blot off the excess, and stamp.

11. When your print is dry, score and fold your card as shown in the card design.

VARIATIONS TO TRY AFTER MAKING YOUR FIRST CARD

1. For a multicolored print, press the top of your stamp into one color and the bottom into another.

2. Stamp your design or message on your envelope to carry through the theme of your card.

3. Use your stamp to decorate gift-wrapping paper (use white or colored tissue paper, shelf paper, butcher paper, or colored wrapping paper), a tablecloth, or place mats.

82

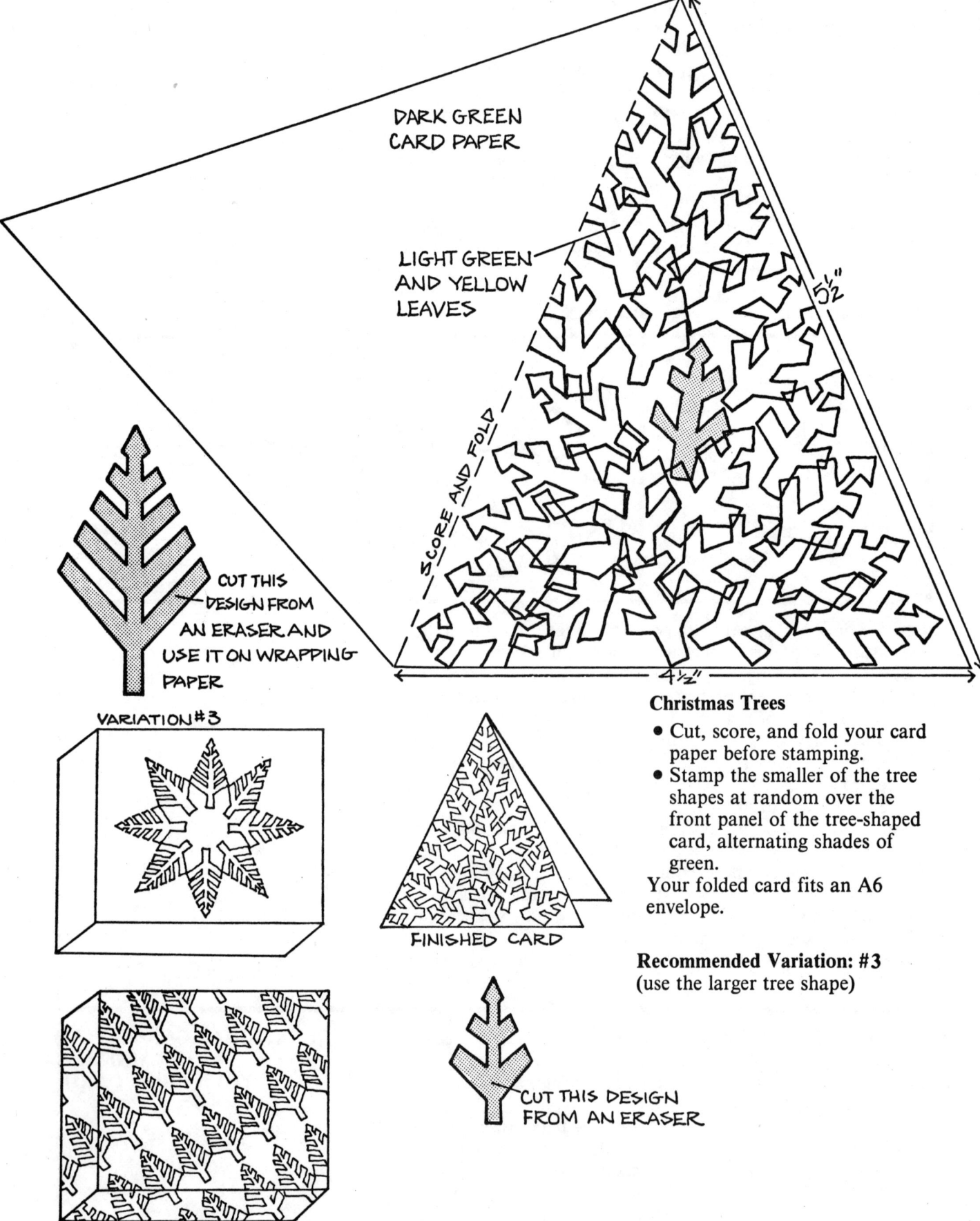

DARK GREEN
CARD PAPER

LIGHT GREEN
AND YELLOW
LEAVES

SCORE AND FOLD

5½"

4½"

CUT THIS
DESIGN FROM
AN ERASER AND
USE IT ON WRAPPING
PAPER

VARIATION #3

FINISHED CARD

Christmas Trees

- Cut, score, and fold your card paper before stamping.
- Stamp the smaller of the tree shapes at random over the front panel of the tree-shaped card, alternating shades of green.

Your folded card fits an A6 envelope.

Recommended Variation: #3
(use the larger tree shape)

CUT THIS DESIGN
FROM AN ERASER

A Thanksgiving Cornucopia

- **Additional materials:** fruits and vegetables that are in season, carbon paper, light cardboard, paper towels
- Cut, score, and fold your card paper (unfolded size 4½" x 11"). Unfold to print.
- Cut the cornucopia design out of a large potato (fig. A).
- Stamp it on the face of your card (fig. B).
- Cover the card design with tracing paper and transfer the oval shape to light cardboard with a pencil and carbon paper (see How to Transfer in Techniques section).
- Cut the oval out of the cardboard. This is your drawing and cutting guide to make the window in the front of your card. With the guide in position on the card, trace lightly around the cardboard oval, then cut around it to remove the window.
- Now choose firm (not juicy) fruits or vegetables with interesting shapes and textures: apple, cauliflower, lime, bell pepper, broccoli, or mushroom. Cut them in half with a sharp knife to get a flat, even stamping surface. If they are at all moist, dry the wet section with a paper towel before inking.
- Print them on the inside of the card, so that the most interesting shapes show through the front window when folded. Save space inside for your message.
- This card has the added appeal of scent, so don't overdo the onions.

Your refolded card fits into an A6 envelope.

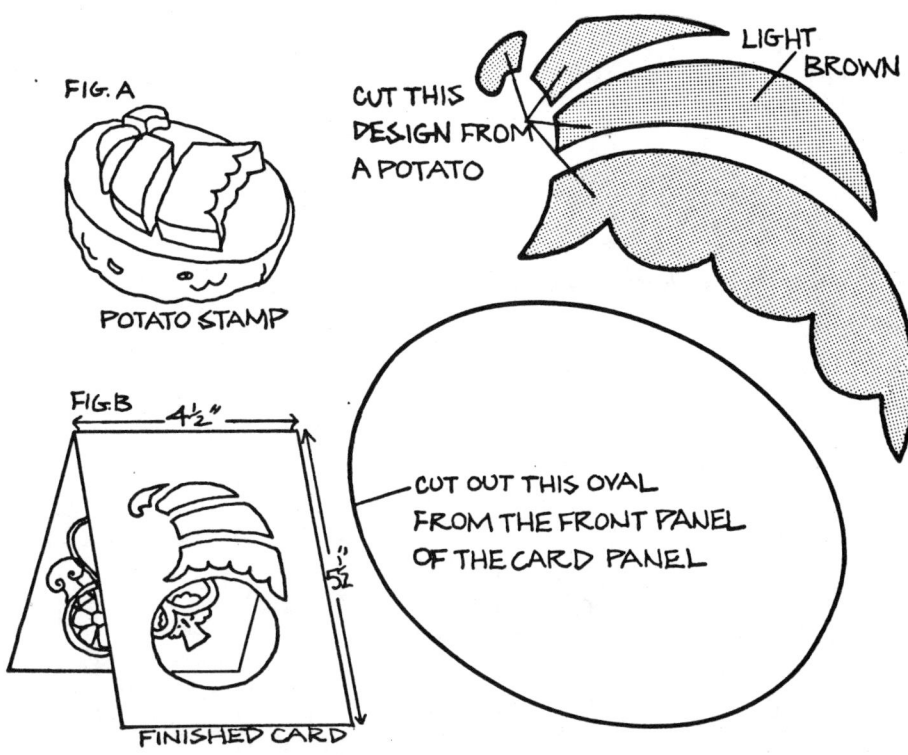

FIG. A

POTATO STAMP

CUT THIS DESIGN FROM A POTATO

LIGHT BROWN

FIG B   4½"

5½"

FINISHED CARD

CUT OUT THIS OVAL FROM THE FRONT PANEL OF THE CARD PANEL

LIGHT ORANGE CARD PAPER

MESSAGE HERE

BRIGHT COLORS— RED, PINK, YELLOW

INSIDE PANEL

FIG. A
CUT LETTERS FROM
POTATOES

A New Year Invitation
- **Additional material:**
  gummed stickers
- Make each of the three words
  out of a large potato (fig. A).
- Cut, score, and fold your
  card paper (figs. B and C,
  unfolded size 5" x 15") into
  four panels. Unfold to stamp.
- Stamp each of the first three
  panels with its own word and
  put your invitation on the
  fourth panel.

Your refolded card is a self-
mailer (fig. D). Seal with a
gummed sticker.

FIG. B

3¾"   3¾"   3¾"

5"

HO   HA   HO
HO   HA   H
HO   HA

3¾"

FINISHED CARD

FIG. C

HO
HO
HO

FIG. D

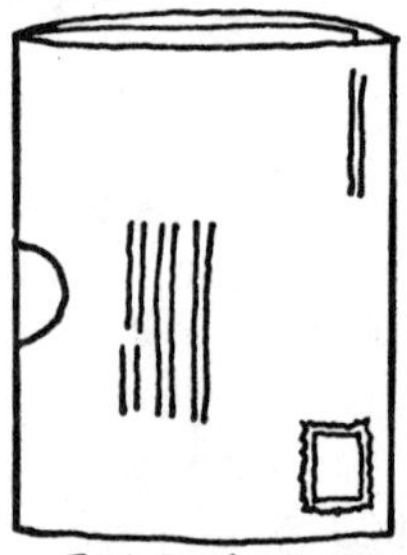

SELF-MAILER

HO — red

HA — ORANGE

HO

HO

HA

HA

HO

HA

SCORE AND FOLD

SCORE AND FOLD

A Thank You Card

- Cut a stamp for each word.
- Cut, score, and fold your card (unfolded size 5" x 8") and unfold for printing. Your refolded card fits into an A2 envelope.

Recommended Variations: #2 and #3. Use thin rows of red, yellow, and blue side by side for a rainbow effect.

THANK YOU
THANK YOU
THANK YOU

4"

5"
FINISHED CARD

PALE BLUE CARD PAPER

GREEN

DARK BLUE

THANK YOU
THANK YOU
THANK YOU

WHITE CARD PAPER

LIME GREEN

MESSAGE
HERE

HEE
HEE
HEE

SCORE
AND FOLD

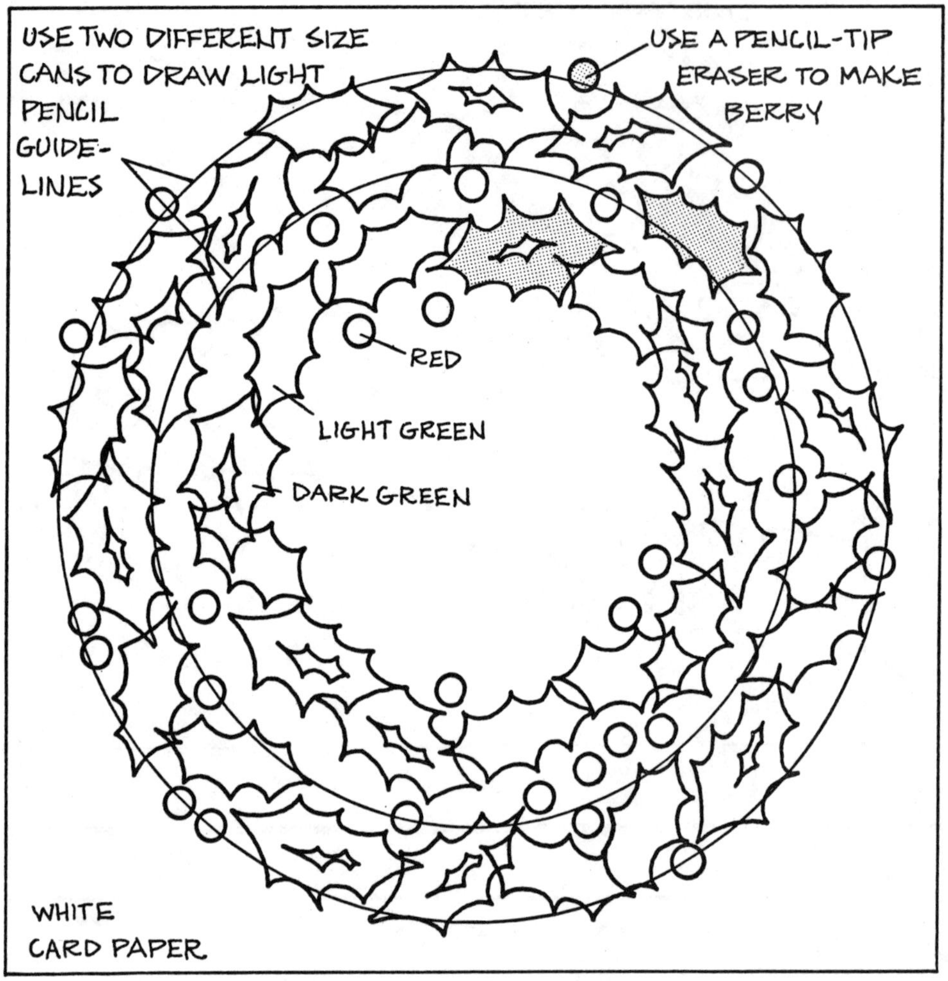

USE TWO DIFFERENT SIZE
CANS TO DRAW LIGHT
PENCIL
GUIDE-
LINES

USE A PENCIL-TIP
ERASER TO MAKE
BERRY

RED

LIGHT GREEN

DARK GREEN

WHITE
CARD PAPER

INSIDE BACK PANEL

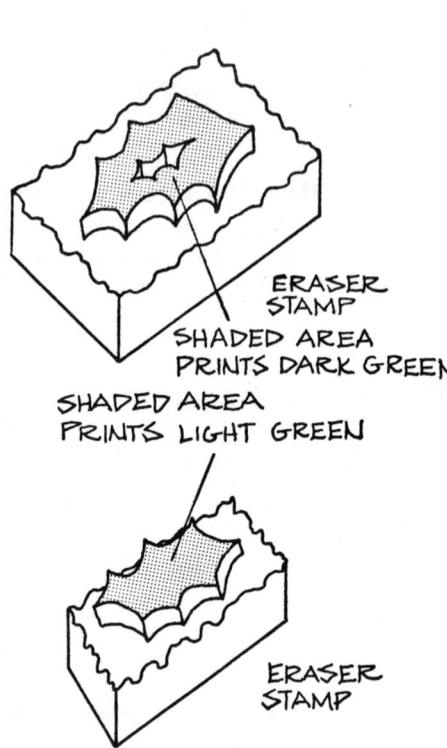

ERASER
STAMP

SHADED AREA
PRINTS DARK GREEN

SHADED AREA
PRINTS LIGHT GREEN

ERASER
STAMP

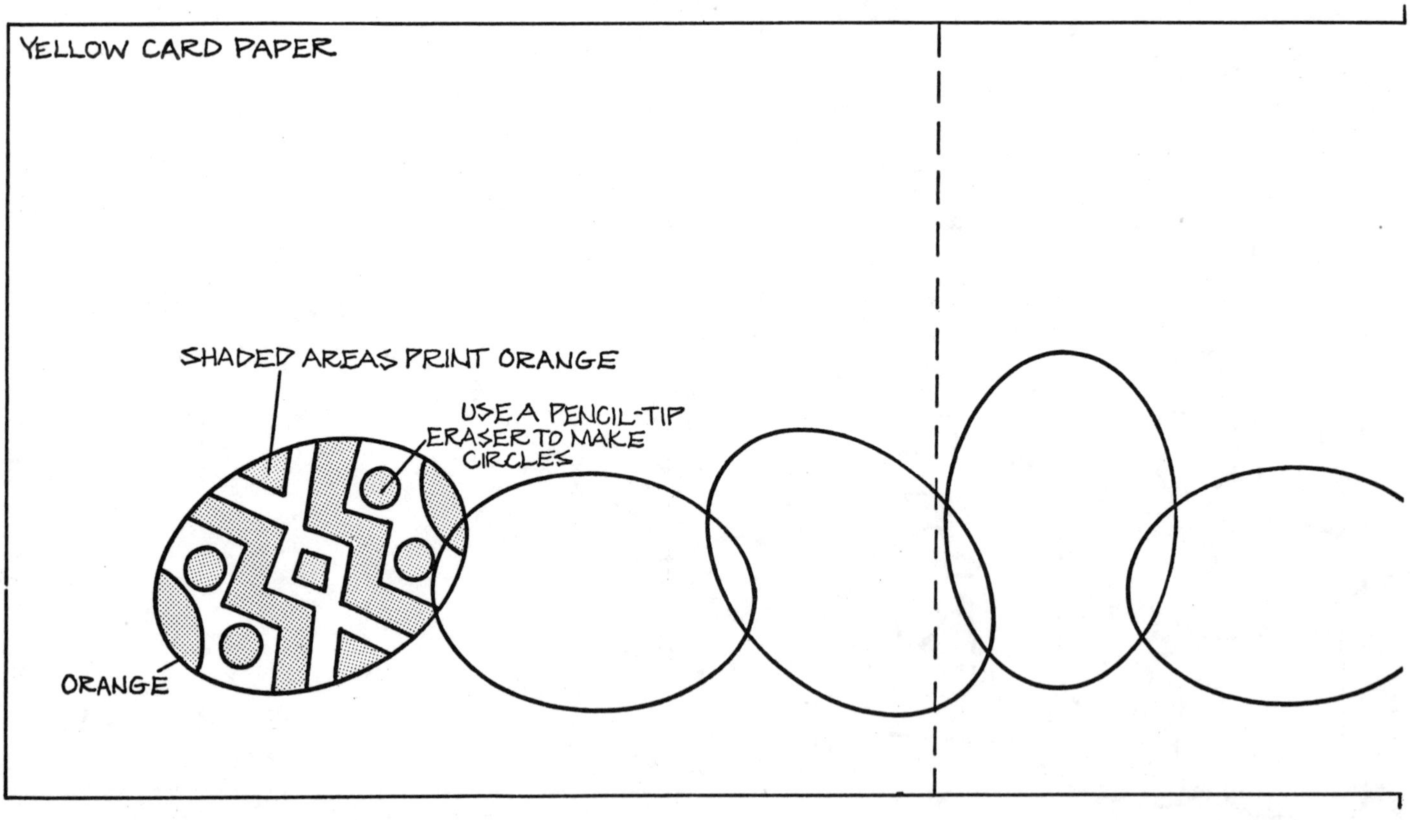

YELLOW CARD PAPER

SHADED AREAS PRINT ORANGE

USE A PENCIL-TIP
ERASER TO MAKE
CIRCLES

ORANGE

A Christmas Wreath

- **Additional materials:** new pencil-tip eraser, gummed stickers
- Cut the two kinds of holly leaves out of an eraser—you'll want to use this stamp over and over.
- Cut, score, and fold your card paper (unfolded size 5" x 10"). Unfold for printing.
- Lightly pencil a circle within a circle on your card paper by using two different-sized cans as drawing guides. These circles will assure that your wreath stays round.
- Now stamp on the two kinds of holly, alternating shades of green, and then let dry.
- Dip the eraser end of a pencil into bright red paint to add holly berries to your wreath.

Your folded card is a self-mailer. Seal with a gummed sticker.

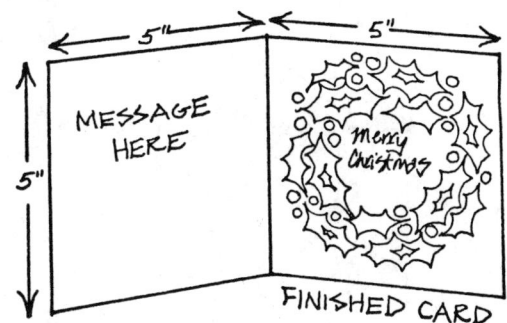

An Easter Egg Card

- **Additional material:** new pencil-tip eraser
- When tracing your design don't copy the small circles—they are added later.
- Cut, score, and fold your card paper (unfolded size 4" x 15"). Use an accordion fold (fig. A) or the self-mailer fold (fig. B), but unfold for printing.
- Stamp the eggs as shown.

Your refolded card fits an A2 envelope. If a self-mailer, send with a gummed sticker or Easter seal.

Stained-Glass-Look Cards

Appearance: Translucent, bright colors, surrounded by dark frames in a stained-glass motif.
Skill required: A steady hand with cutting tools.
Quantity/Time: Involves tracing, cutting, and coloring cards on an individual basis. Moderately fast.

MATERIALS	• Recommended paper: heavy- to medium-weight cover paper (see **All About Paper**) • Easy Envelopes • Tracing paper • Carbon paper • Light cardboard • White ink and crow quill pen (see Glossary) to write your message • Scotch and masking tapes • White glue or glue stick
TOOLS	• Black permanent felt-tip marker (<u>not</u> water soluble) • Colored watercolor felt-tip markers (<u>must be</u> water soluble) **Note: If the marking pen specifications are not followed, the black will run into the other colors.** • X-acto knife or scissors • Sharp pencil • Back side of a breadboard, or heavy cardboard (to protect your table when cutting) • See individual cards for additional materials and tools
HOW TO MAKE THE CARD	1. Lightly tape a piece of tracing paper over your card design. 2. Trace the thick lines of your design with the permanent black felt-tip marker. Be sure your lines are the same thickness as the design lines, so the card will look like stained glass. 3. Remove your tracing from the book. Now color in the different traced areas with your water-soluble color markers. Make each part of the design one solid color to create the stained-glass effect. Trim the colored tracing to the size indicated in the card design, and set aside for the moment.

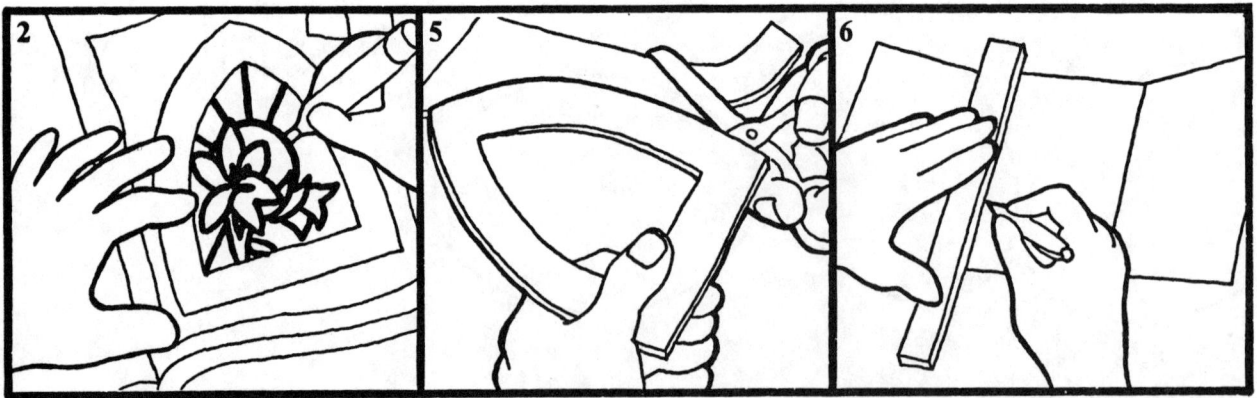

4. Cover the card design with tracing paper again and transfer the frame of the window (arch or circle) to light cardboard with a pencil and carbon paper (see How to Transfer in Techniques section).

5. Cut the window frame out of the light cardboard. This is your drawing guide.
   Hint: A dinner plate makes a good guide for cutting the arch, a 1-lb. coffee can for the circle.

6. Cut, score, and fold your card paper.

7. Now use the drawing guide to help you cut the window frame out of your card paper, according to the instructions for the card design.

8. Center the stained glass between your two window frame panels, as shown, and tape in place with scotch tape.

9. Glue the inside edges of the window panels. Then press the two panels together with the stained glass in between. Place under a book until dry.

10. Write your message in white ink with a crow quill pen (see Glossary) or any other type of pen that can be dipped in ink.

FINISHED CARDS

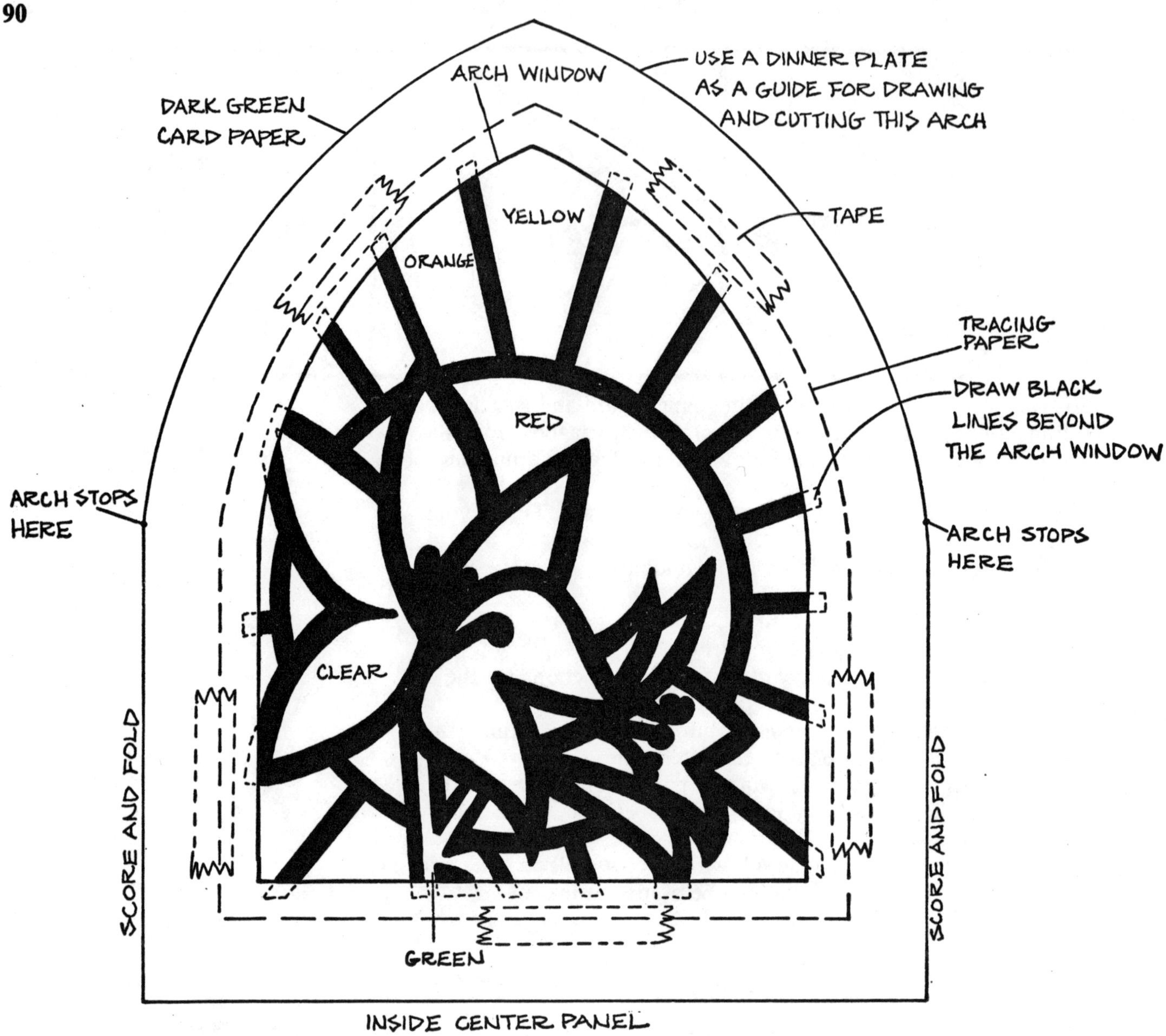

DARK GREEN
CARD PAPER

ARCH WINDOW

USE A DINNER PLATE
AS A GUIDE FOR DRAWING
AND CUTTING THIS ARCH

YELLOW

ORANGE

TAPE

RED

TRACING
PAPER

DRAW BLACK
LINES BEYOND
THE ARCH WINDOW

ARCH STOPS
HERE

ARCH STOPS
HERE

SCORE AND FOLD

CLEAR

SCORE AND FOLD

GREEN

INSIDE CENTER PANEL

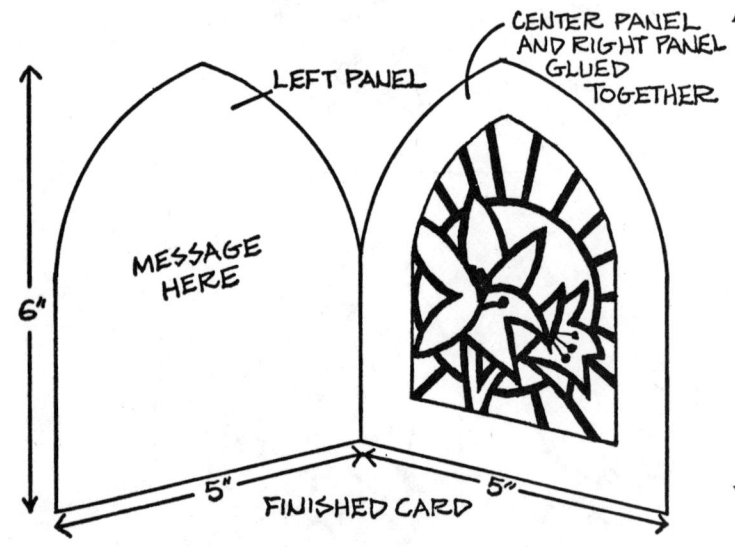

LEFT PANEL

CENTER PANEL
AND RIGHT PANEL
GLUED
TOGETHER

MESSAGE
HERE

6"

5"   5"

FINISHED CARD

An Easter Lily

- Cut, score, and fold your paper in thirds (unfolded size 6" x 15").
- To make the arch: lay your cardboard drawing guide over the folded card and lightly pencil around the *outside* of the guide (the part of the arch to be cut). Then cut along this line through all three layers of paper.
- To make the window frame: Open the front panel of your card, leaving the last two panels folded together. Lay your drawing guide over the two panels and lightly pencil entirely around the *inside* of the guide. Now cut along this line through both layers of paper and you have your frame.

When folded, your card fits into an A7 envelope.

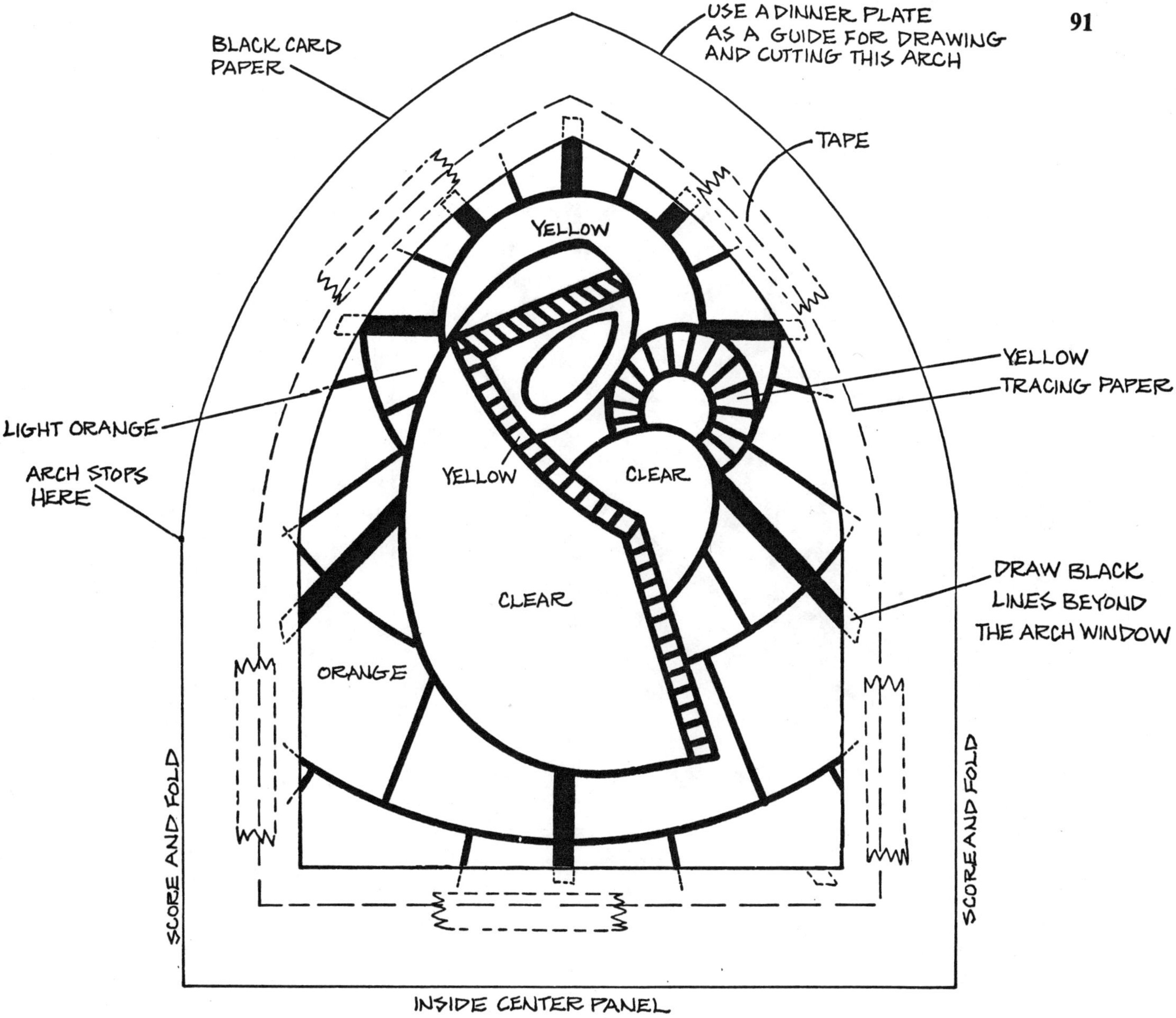

USE A DINNER PLATE
AS A GUIDE FOR DRAWING
AND CUTTING THIS ARCH

BLACK CARD
PAPER

TAPE

YELLOW

YELLOW
TRACING PAPER

LIGHT ORANGE

YELLOW

CLEAR

ARCH STOPS
HERE

CLEAR

DRAW BLACK
LINES BEYOND
THE ARCH WINDOW

ORANGE

SCORE AND FOLD

SCORE AND FOLD

INSIDE CENTER PANEL

A Christmas Madonna

- Cut, score, and fold your card paper in thirds (unfolded size 6" x 15").
- To make the arch: lay your cardboard drawing guide over the folded card and lightly pencil around the *outside* of the guide (the part of the arch to be cut). Then cut along this line through all three layers of paper.
- To make the window frame: Open the front panel of your card, leaving the last two panels together. Lay your drawing guide over the two panels and lightly pencil entirely around the *inside* of the guide. Now cut along this line through both layers of paper and you have your frame.

When folded, your card fits into an A7 envelope.

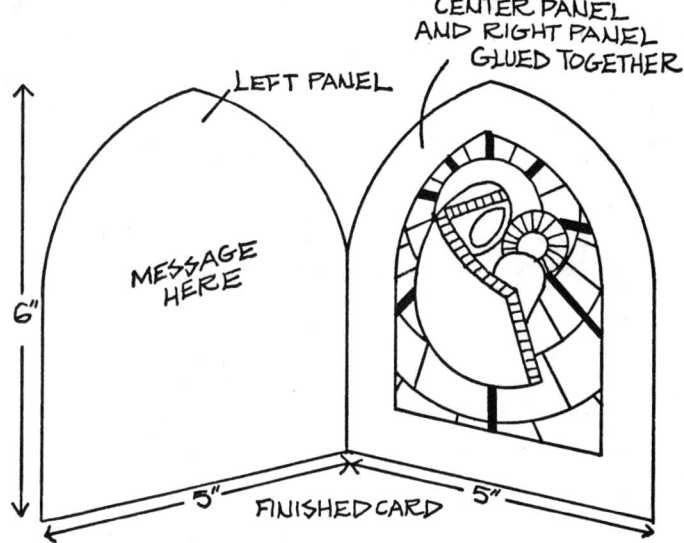

CENTER PANEL
AND RIGHT PANEL
GLUED TOGETHER

LEFT PANEL

MESSAGE
HERE

6"

5"   5"

FINISHED CARD

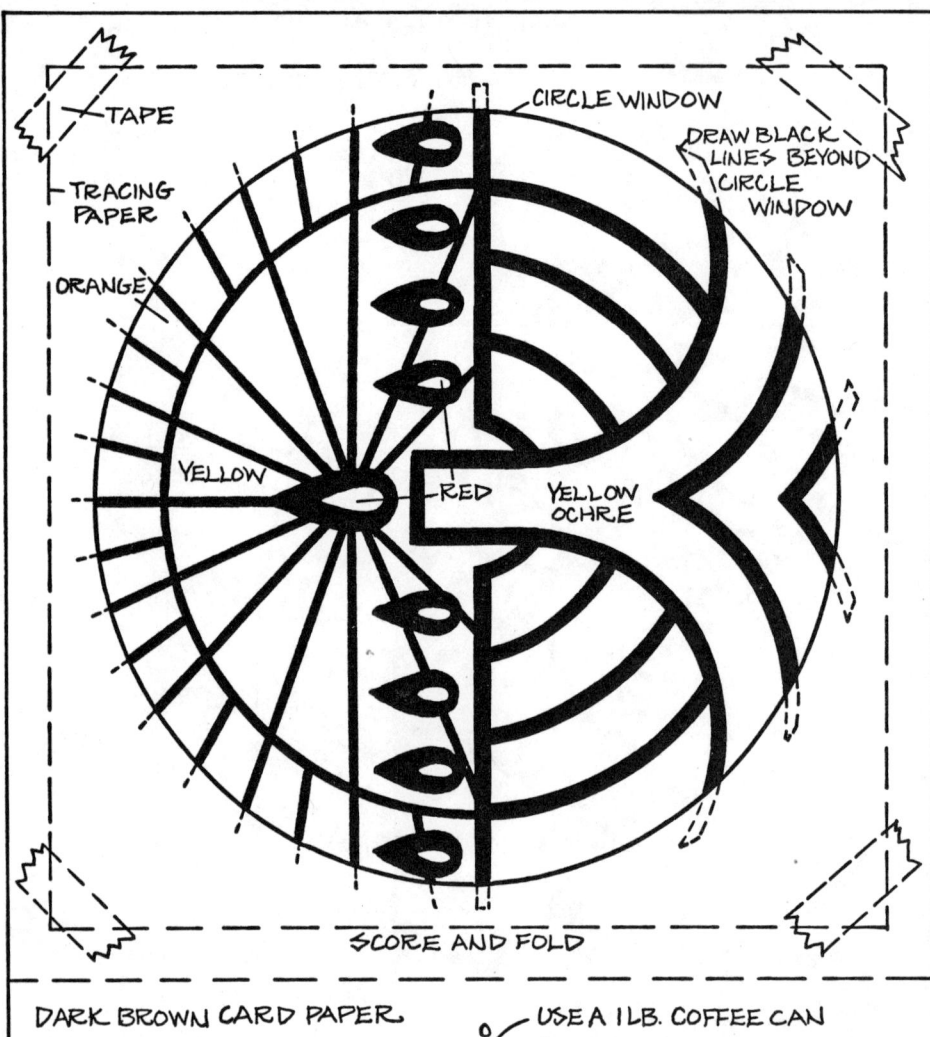

TAPE

TRACING PAPER

ORANGE

YELLOW

RED

YELLOW OCHRE

CIRCLE WINDOW

DRAW BLACK LINES BEYOND CIRCLE WINDOW

SCORE AND FOLD

A Hanukkah Greeting

- Cut, score, and fold your card paper in half (unfolded size 5" x 10").
- Lay your cardboard drawing guide over the folded card and pencil around the circle. Then cut along the line through both layers to make your window frame.
- For a more accurate drawing or cutting guide, use a 1 lb. coffee can.
- Write your message in white ink on the face of the card.

Your folded card measures 5" x 5". Send it in the unique Pinwheel Envelope (see Easy Envelopes).

TRACING PAPER

CUT

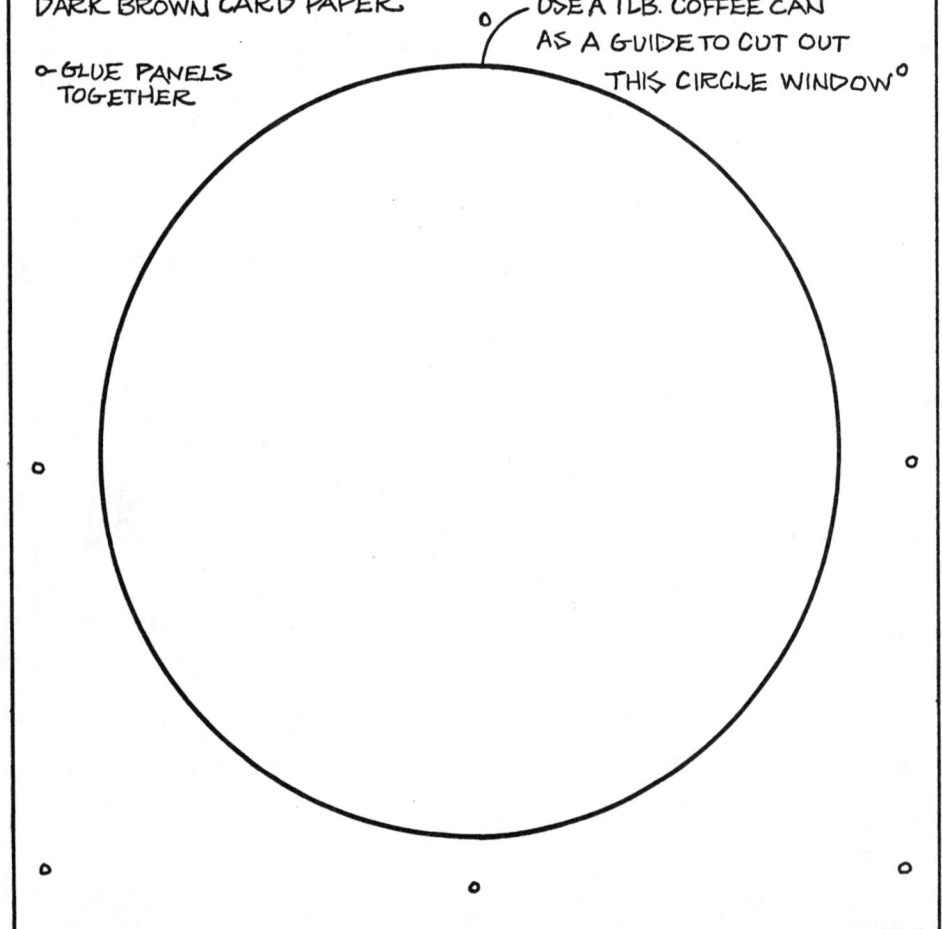

DARK BROWN CARD PAPER.

GLUE PANELS TOGETHER

USE A 1LB. COFFEE CAN AS A GUIDE TO CUT OUT THIS CIRCLE WINDOW

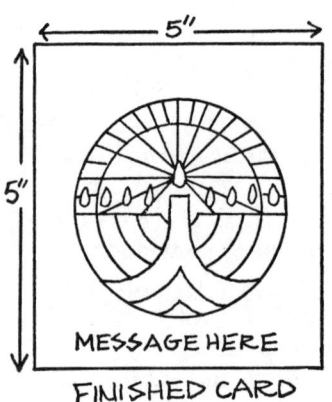

5"

5"

MESSAGE HERE

FINISHED CARD

A Stained-Glass Snowflake

● To make this card, follow the instructions given for the Hanukkah card.
Your folded card measures 5" x 5". Send it in the unique Pinwheel Envelope (see Easy Envelopes).

MESSAGE HERE

FINISHED CARD

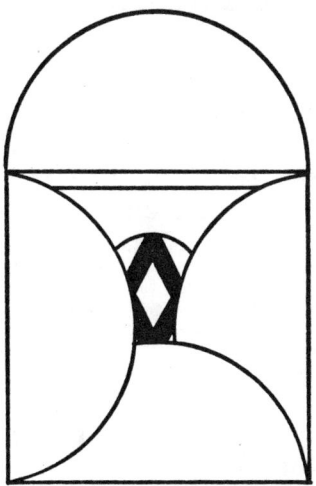

PINWHEEL ENVELOPE
SEE EASY ENVELOPES

TAPE

TISSUE

CLEAR

LIGHT GREEN

CIRCLE WINDOW

LIGHT BLUE

TURQUOISE

EXTEND BLACK LINES BEYOND THE CIRCLE WINDOW

SCORE AND FOLD

DARK BLUE CARD PAPER

○ GLUE PANELS TOGETHER

USE A 1 LB. COFFEE CAN AS A GUIDE TO CUT OUT THIS CIRCLE WINDOW

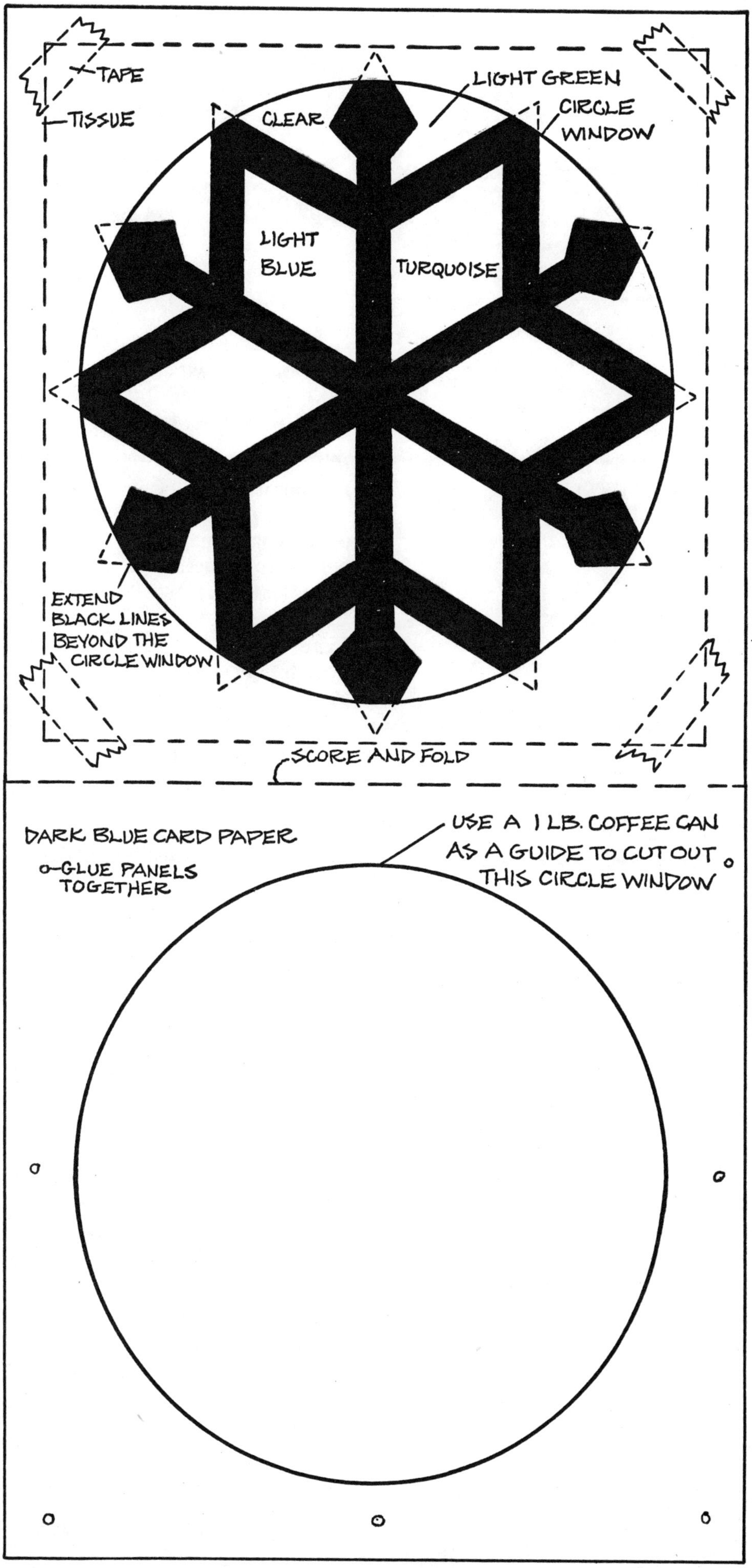

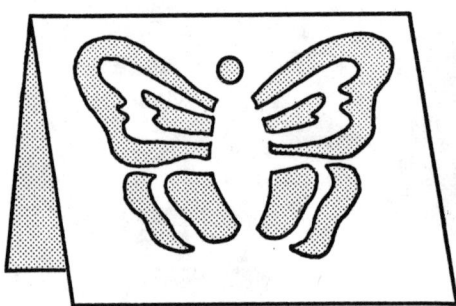

Crayon Melt Cards

Appearance: Swirls of blended color from melted crayons.
Skill required: Very little. You cut only one simple stencil.
Quantity/Time: Moderate. Each card must be made individually.

MATERIALS	
• Recommended paper: medium-weight, colored or white cover paper; coated paper; or—in a pinch—construction paper (see All About Paper) • Easy Envelopes • Paper towels • Scotch tape • White glue or glue stick	• Carbon paper • Light cardboard • Aluminum foil • Old crayons • Cloth rag or sponge • Erasable bond or typing paper • Back side of a breadboard, or heavy cardboard (to protect your table when cutting)

TOOLS	
• Electric food-warming tray (or foil-covered cookie sheet over low burner heat) • Scissors or X-acto knife	• Sharp pencil • See individual cards for additional materials and tools

---

HOW TO MAKE THE CARD

1. Select one of the designs and cut, score, and fold your card paper.
2. Cover the warming tray with aluminum foil, taping the edges down. Don't begin coloring until the tray is warm.
3. Choose two or three colors of crayons and peel off the paper. Now rub them over the foil as if you were coloring, letting the crayons melt and swirl together. Don't touch the melted wax.
   Hint: Any more than three colors tends to muddy the melt.
4. When the crayons have melted, lay a sheet of bond paper over the wax and lightly rub the paper with a cloth or dry sponge. You want a thin coating of crayon to stick to the paper and cover an area slightly larger than the size of your folded card.

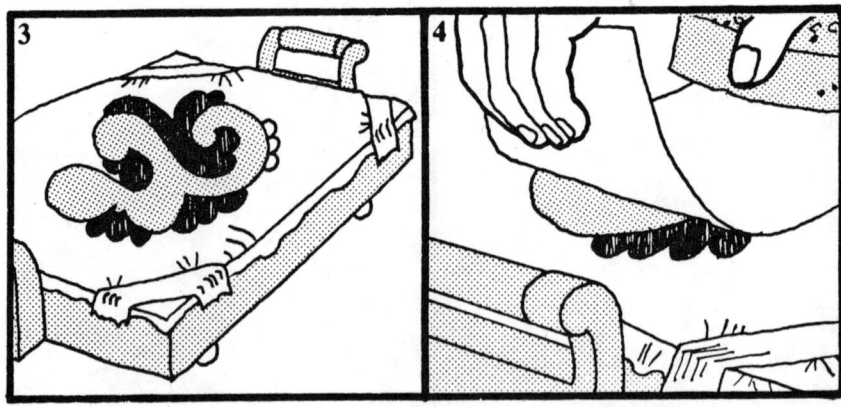

5. Lift the paper off carefully, taking care not to let the wax drip to the other side of the paper or onto your clothes or skin. Set aside to harden on a piece of paper towel.

6. While your melt is hardening, cover your card design with tracing paper and transfer it to light cardboard with a pencil and carbon paper (see How to Transfer in Techniques section).

7. Cut out the shaded areas on the cardboard. The resulting stencil is your drawing guide to transfer your design to the card paper.

8. Place the stencil over the card paper so the design is in its proper place. Then trace around the inside of the stencil with a sharp pencil.

9. Now cut out the penciled design on the card paper. You will have a window on the front of your card.

10. To finish your card, cut your crayon melt about ¼" smaller than the folded card size and slip it behind the window so the color shows through. Fix it neatly in place with scotch tape.

---

1. For a swirled effect, twist the paper slightly as you lift it off the melted crayons.

2. Use designs from other parts of this book. The simple designs used in the sections on Spatter, Stencil, and Embossed cards work best.

3. For note cards, cut your crayon melt into a rectangle slightly smaller than the card size and glue it on the front panel of your card.

**VARIATIONS TO TRY
AFTER MAKING
YOUR FIRST CARD**

FINISHED CARDS

A Christmas Card Ornament

- **Additional materials:** hole punch, yarn or ribbon
- As a card, use one design for the front, one for both front and back, or a different design for front and back. Tape a crayon melt in back of each cutout design.
- As an ornament, put designs on front and back. String yarn or ribbon through a hole punched out at the top so the card can hang on a Christmas tree.

The unfolded card measures 4¾"x10". Your folded card fits into a # 6 Baronial envelope.

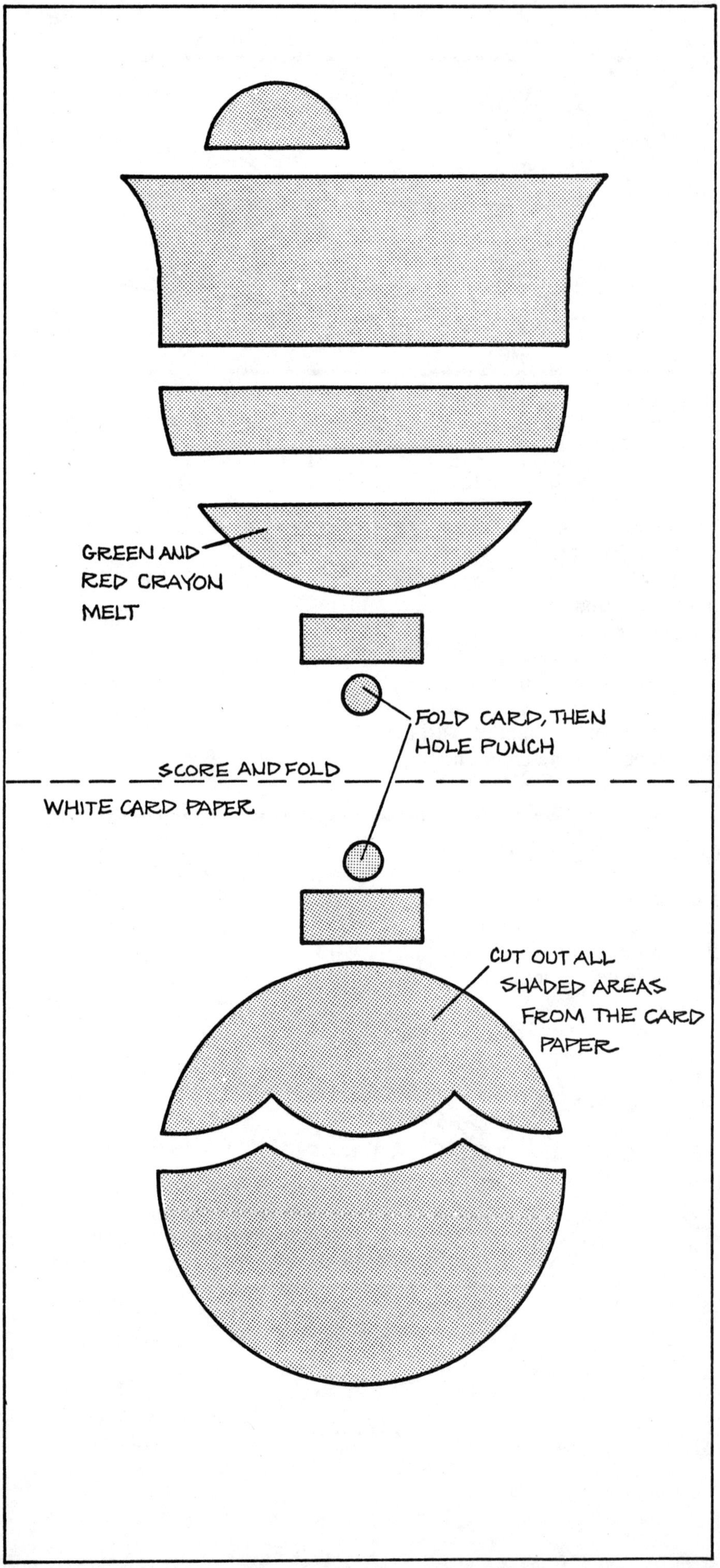

GREEN AND RED CRAYON MELT

FOLD CARD, THEN HOLE PUNCH

SCORE AND FOLD

WHITE CARD PAPER

CUT OUT ALL SHADED AREAS FROM THE CARD PAPER

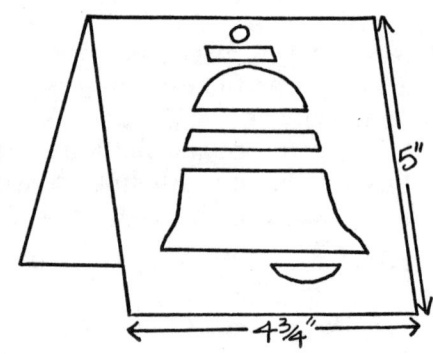

USE YARN OR RIBBON TO HANG AS AN ORNAMENT

FINISHED CARD

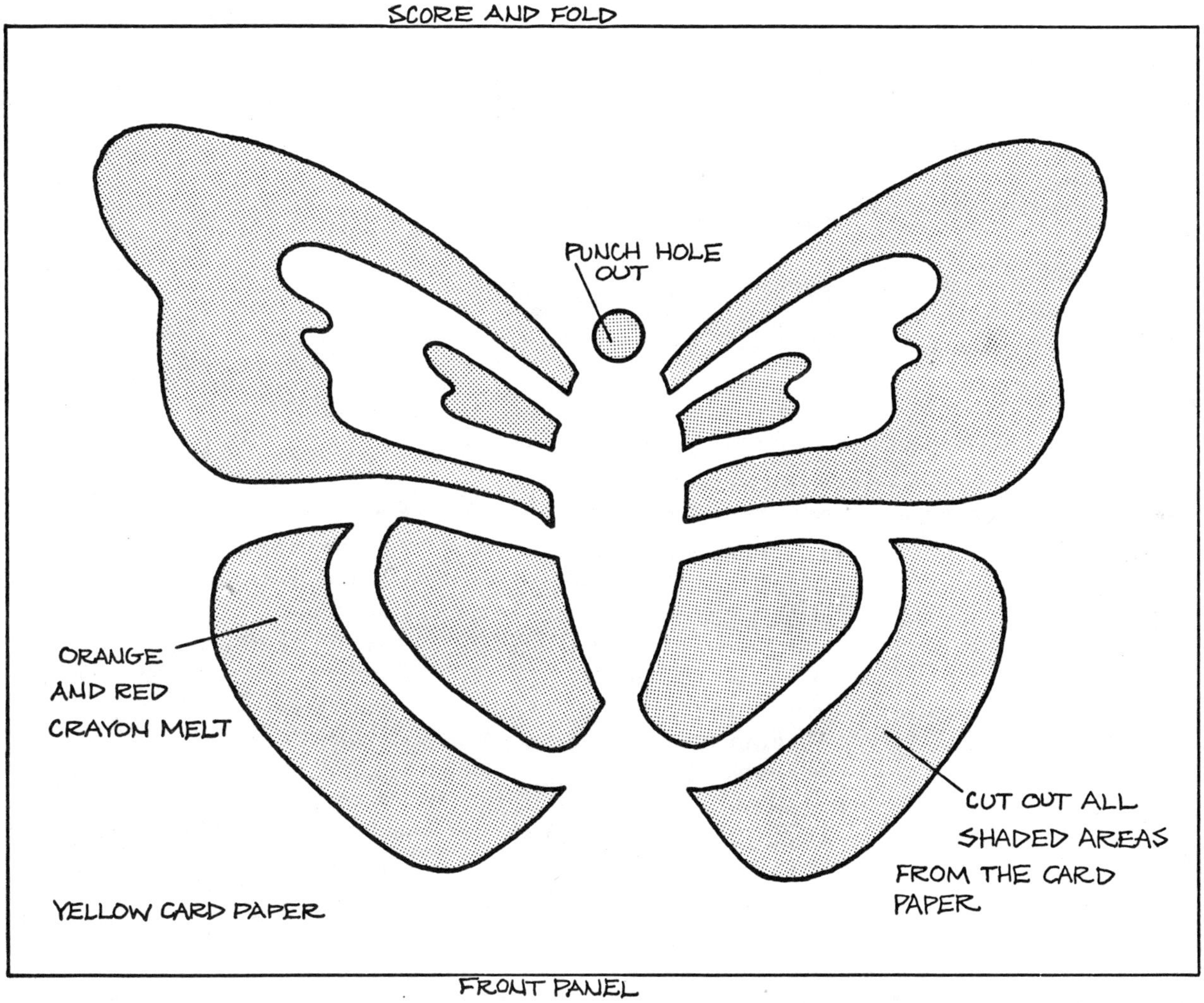

SCORE AND FOLD

PUNCH HOLE
OUT

ORANGE
AND RED
CRAYON MELT

CUT OUT ALL
SHADED AREAS
FROM THE CARD
PAPER

YELLOW CARD PAPER

FRONT PANEL

A Butterfly Greeting Card

- **Additional material:** hole-punch
- Make a stencil for the head
  and only half the design (fig.
  A). By turning the stencil over
  after drawing one half of the
  design, you can draw the
  other half—both sides match
  perfectly.
- Use the butterfly's head to
  line up the two halves
  correctly, when you flop the
  stencil.

The unfolded card measures
6½" x 10". Your folded card fits
into an A7 envelope.

FIG. A

5"

6½"

FINISHED CARD

Paraffin Print Cards

Appearance: An antique, weathered look—definitely handmade.
Skill required: Many processes, but all of them easy.
Quantity/Time: Once you have your paraffin block, up to fifty cards can be made fairly quickly.

MATERIALS

- Recommended paper: medium-weight, colored or white cover paper; coated paper; or—in a pinch—construction paper (see *All About Paper*)
- Easy Envelopes
- Paraffin wax (1-lb. box from a grocery store)
- Water-base block printing ink (from an art supply store)
- Tracing paper
- Wax paper
- Carbon paper
- Light cardboard (light poster-board from an art store, or shirt cardboard)
- Heavy cardboard (hot-press illustration board from an art store)
- Paper towels
- Coffee or shortening can (1-lb. size)
- Pan of water big enough to hold can (about 1½ qt.)
- Roll of masking tape (1" width)
- Inking surface: dinner plate (or aluminum foil)

TOOLS

- Felt-tip marker (permanent, <u>not</u> water-base)
- Sharp pencil
- Scissors or X-acto knife
- Linoleum-block cutter (from an art store)
- Stove (or hot plate)
- Potholders
- See individual cards for additional materials and tools.

HOW TO MAKE THE CARD

1. Place a sheet of wax paper over the card design. The paper should be larger than the design by an inch on all sides.
2. With the felt-tip marker, trace the design (including the surrounding rectangle) onto the wax paper. Do not smear the tracing—the ink

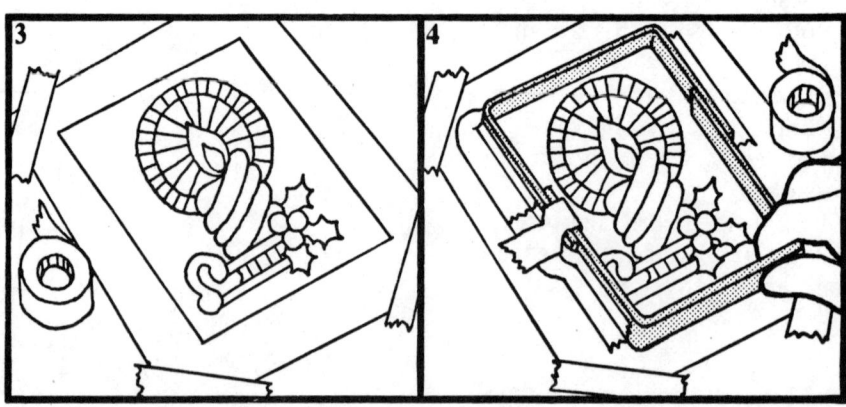

will only rest lightly on the surface of the paper and it should be handled carefully.

3. Center the wax paper, tracing-side up, on the smooth side of a piece of illustration board, leaving at least an inch of board outside the paper. Tape down the corners of the paper, stretching it so that it is absolutely flat against the board.

4. Now make a border by cutting long, 1"-wide strips of the light cardboard. The cut edges should be very straight and even (use an X-acto knife and a ruler) so the cardboard will make a tight seal with the wax paper. Place these strips on edge—like a fence—along the outside rectangle you traced around the design, and then bend the strips at the corners and join the ends (overlapping) with masking tape on the straight sides.

5. Press masking tape all around the outside of the cardboard fence where it meets the paper, so that half the tape is on the fence and half is on the cardboard. The tape will be a seal against the wax leaking through. Reinforce every joint and corner with extra pieces of tape.

6. Put 1 lb. of paraffin in the coffee can and place the can in a large pan of water on top of the stove. Bring the water to a slow boil until the paraffin is melted.

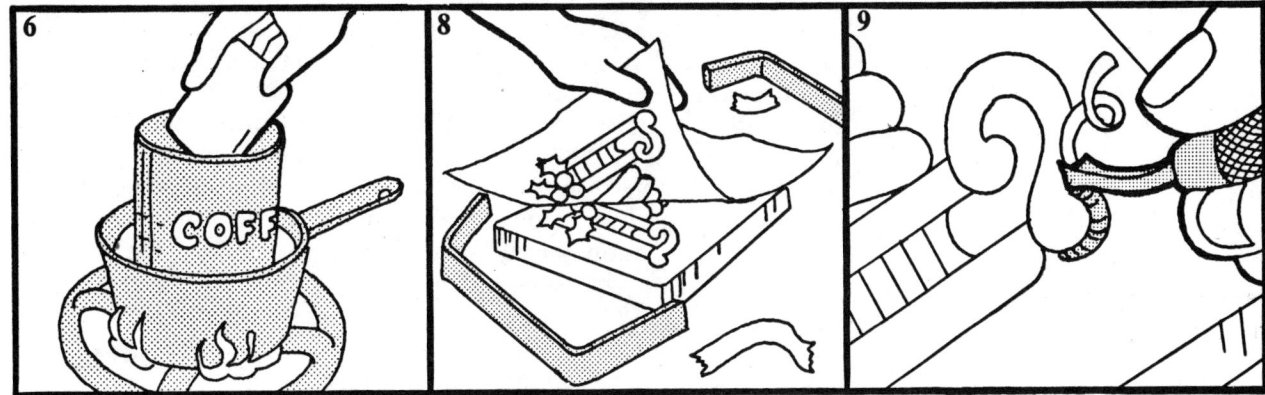

7. Before you pour the wax, set the hot can on some paper towels to dry the bottom so no stray drops of water will fall into the mold. Then pour the melted paraffin into the mold until it is at least ¼" deep. When you pour, try not to make any air pockets in the wax. Leave the mold on a level surface until it hardens, which takes about two hours—less if placed in the refrigerator. Don't freeze.
Hint: Try to pour the wax where it is to be left to harden. The less you move the mold when it is still liquid, the better your block will be. A small amount of leakage is okay—it will stop.

8. When the wax is hard, carefully peel off the cardboard mold and the wax paper. Be careful not to crack the wax block. The felt-tip marker design is now transferred to the paraffin block. The design will be backward on the paraffin, but it will print correctly.

9. Now cut the block with the linoleum-block cutter, carving grooves in the paraffin along the lines shown on the design. The smallest V-shaped blade (Speedball #1) is best for this. Then the shaded areas of the card design should be completely scooped out, using one of the U-shaped cutters.
Hints: When cutting the paraffin block with the smallest V-shaped tool, make clean and definite cuts. The care you give to cutting will be rewarded in the printed design.

If you do make a mistake in cutting the block, simply melt it down again and make a new mold. One lb. of wax makes about three to four molds.

10. When you have finished carving the design, rinse off any loose pieces of wax from the printing surface (the raised portion) and from within the grooves. Dry carefully before applying ink.

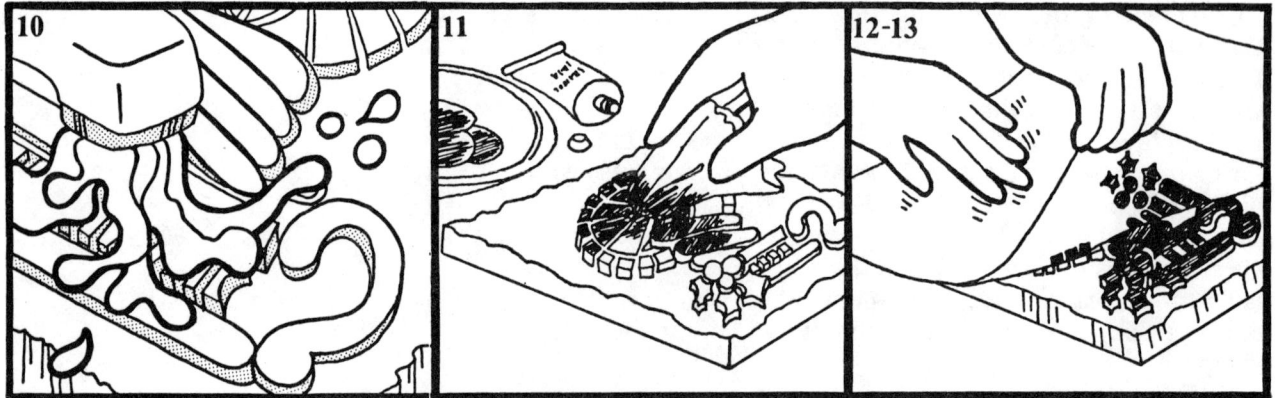

11. Squirt some printing ink onto an old plate or some aluminum foil and spread it around a bit. Dab a paper towel or a rag into the ink, and then onto the face of the paraffin block to cover the design evenly and completely. Not too much ink, or the grooves will fill.

12. Put a piece of blank card paper (an inch larger than the finished size) over the inked design and—taking care that the paper does not shift—rub your fingers over the paper so you can feel the raised surface of the block. Cover the whole design, pressing firmly. Take care that no ink gets on the back of the card from your fingers.

13. Now carefully peel the paper off the paraffin. This is your test print, and it will show you if there are any problems: if the cutting is correct, if the inking is complete, if you have pressed down too lightly (or too heavily), which parts of the design may need extra pressure to print clearly, and if you have positioned the paper correctly. Make the necessary adjustments.

14. Print the rest of your cards, re-inking the paraffin block as needed, and set them aside to dry. If the grooves fill with ink, wash the block, dry, and re-ink.

15. When your prints are completely dry, cut to size, score, and fold.

VARIATIONS TO TRY AFTER MAKING YOUR FIRST CARD

1. Instead of dabbing the ink, wipe it across the face of the design, either randomly or spreading it in one direction. The streaks will add drama to the design.

2. Dab several colors, one at a time, onto various parts of the paraffin design. Or highlight certain design elements with bright colors, or streak them across the design like a rainbow.

3. Cut out the printed designs and mount them on paper of another color and texture. This technique works especially well with children's prints—it allows them to be less careful when printing.

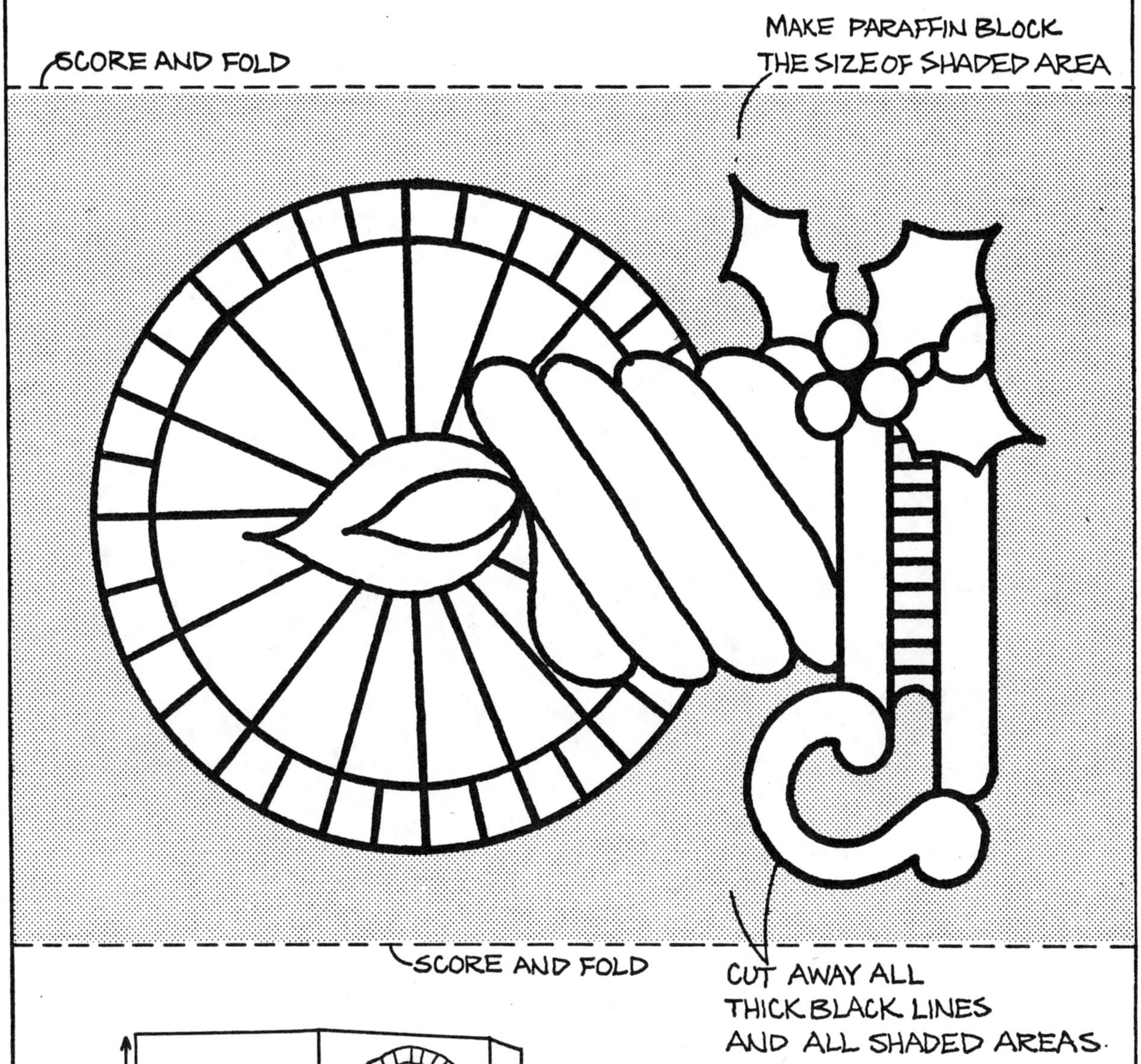

SCORE AND FOLD

MAKE PARAFFIN BLOCK
THE SIZE OF SHADED AREA

SCORE AND FOLD

CUT AWAY ALL
THICK BLACK LINES
AND ALL SHADED AREAS.

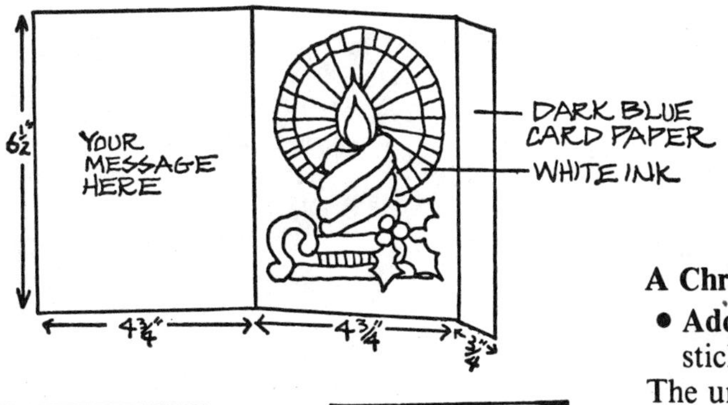

YOUR
MESSAGE
HERE

6½"

4¾"

4¾"

¾"

DARK BLUE
CARD PAPER

WHITE INK

GUMMED
STICKER

FINISHED CARDS

A Christmas Candle

• **Additional material:** gummed stickers

The unfolded card measures 6½"x10¼". Folded, your card is a self-mailer. Use a Christmas seal to keep the card closed.

Recommended Variation: #3

THE TWO PANELS MEET

SCORE AND FOLD

SCORE AND FOLD

CUT AWAY ALL THICK BLACK LINES
AND ALL SHADED AREAS.

MAKE PARAFFIN BLOCK
THE SIZE OF SHADED AREA

FIG. A

FOLD

YOUR MESSAGE
HERE

FOLD

4½"

3" 6" 3"

FIG. B

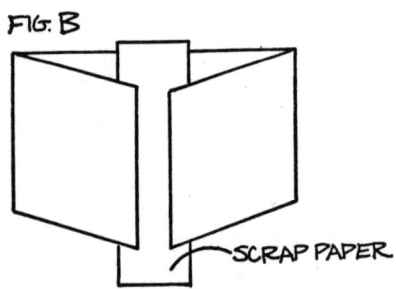

SCRAP PAPER

FINISHED CARD

YELLOW
CARD PAPER

GREEN INK

A Garden Note Card

- Cut, score, and fold your card
  before printing (fig. A, unfolded size 4½"x12").
- To print, place the front of the
  folded card (where the two
  panels meet) centered face
  down on the inked linoleum
  block. Put a piece of scrap
  paper behind the crack (fig. B)
  to prevent ink from squeezing
  through to the inside. Be especially careful not to let the
  paper shift while printing.
- Peel your card off carefully
  and let it dry.

When it has dried, your card will
fit into an A6 envelope.

5"

3"

YOUR MESSAGE
HERE

7"

Christmastime

The unfolded card measures
5" x 10". Folded, your card fits
an A7 envelope.

Recommended Variation: #2

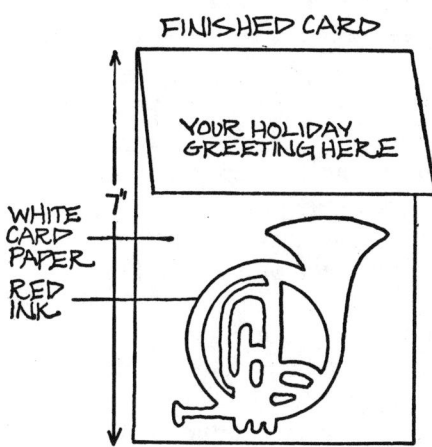

FINISHED CARD

YOUR HOLIDAY
GREETING HERE

7"

WHITE
CARD
PAPER

RED
INK

CUT AWAY ALL
THICK BLACK LINES
AND ALL SHADED AREAS

MAKE PARAFFIN BLOCK
THE SIZE OF SHADED AREA   SCORE AND FOLD

Linoleum Print Cards

Appearance: Dramatic, high contrasts. An artistic look.
Skill required: Carving the linoleum block demands some skill and practice. Making the print from the block is a snap.
Quantity/Time: Once you have your linoleum block, up to fifty cards can be made fairly quickly.

MATERIALS	<ul><li>Recommended paper: medium-weight, colored or white cover paper; coated paper; or—in a pinch—construction paper (see All About Paper)</li><li>Easy Envelopes</li><li>White glue or glue stick</li><li>Aluminum foil</li></ul> <ul><li>Linoleum block (from an art supply store)</li><li>Water-soluble ink for block printing (from an art store)</li><li>Carbon paper</li><li>Masking tape</li></ul>

TOOLS	<ul><li>Linoleum cutter with U- and V-shaped tips (from an art store; other tips are optional and can give you more variety of cuts)</li><li>Rubber roller or brayer (from an art store)</li><li>Rolling pin or large jar with straight, smooth sides</li><li>Nails and hammer</li></ul> <ul><li>Inking surface: cookie sheet, glass plate, or old dinner plate</li><li>Sharp pencil</li><li>Work surface of smooth wood able to take nails, either scrap or from lumberyard</li><li>Bench hook (optional from an art store)</li><li>See individual cards for additional materials and tools</li></ul>

HOW TO MAKE THE CARD

1. Cover your card design with tracing paper and transfer it centered onto your linoleum block with a pencil and carbon paper (see How to Transfer in Techniques section). Any words or designs you want to print must be backwards on the face of the block in order to print correctly. The designs in this section are already reversed.
   Hint: A good way to check your design is to look at it on the block in a mirror. What you see in the mirror is what you will get on the print.
2. Anchor the linoleum block. This can be done by pounding nails around the block edges into a larger piece of wood (see illustration) or by getting an inexpensive bench hook (see Glossary) from an art supply store. (The bench hook uses the side of your table to brace the block, and doubles as an inking plate.) If you use nails, be sure that your wood work surface is also braced, either against a wall or by nails driven through the wood to catch against the edge of the table.
   Hint: Make sure nail heads are well below the printing surface of the block.

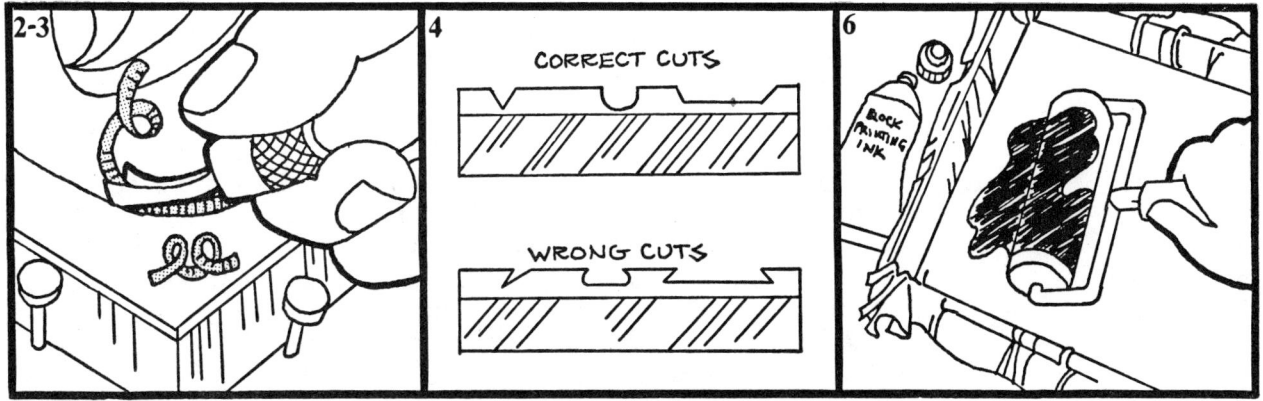

3. Begin cutting the outline of the design with the smallest V-shaped blade (Speedball #1). Hold the tool firmly: it can slip unexpectedly. *Always push the tool away from you:* change your position or the position of the block in order to cut away from your body. Make sure all hands and arms are safely out of the way of the direction of the blade. Slowly carve along the design lines about $\frac{1}{16}$" deep, watching each cut, and use a deliberate, steady pressure.
   Hint: Linoleum cuts easier when it is warm. Wash it in warm water before you transfer the design, or hold it between your hands just before cutting. If you mess up while cutting, don't be discouraged—the linoleum block effect is an uneven one and you can touch up small mistakes during inking. Your skill will improve with each block you cut.

4. When the outline is cut, the large shaded areas can be gouged away with the U-shaped blade (Speedball #3 or #5). Be careful not to undercut the linoleum for it will break down and print poorly (see illustration). Don't worry if the lines on the block are wavy—these give a desirable effect.

5. When the block cutting has been completed, brush the face of the block clean and lift it out of its brace. Wash it with soap and water to remove any oils from your hands that may interfere with the inking.

6. Squirt some ink onto a cookie sheet covered with foil (or other flat surface large enough to roll out ink). Spread the ink evenly with a rubber roller or brayer until the roller is completely covered with ink. Then roll off the excess on a clean part of the cookie sheet.

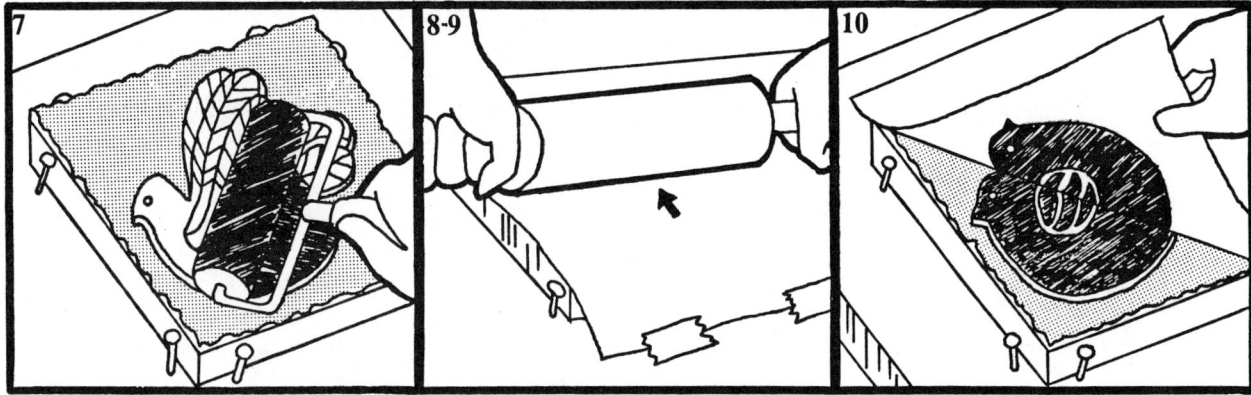

7. Anchor the linoleum block on your wood surface with nails. Roll the inked brayer across the carved design until all raised areas have a uniform coating of ink. Don't use too much ink or the grooves may fill and you will have to wash the block and re-ink.

Hint: Particularly difficult spots may be touched up with a Q-tip dipped in the ink, but remember the linoleum block effect is not a uniform one.

8. Lightly and carefully lay your card paper on top of the inked linoleum block. The paper should be at least four inches longer than the finished card size for you will need some extra paper to stick out beyond the block. Tape one end of the paper to the wood surface to hold it in place while printing (see illustration).

9. Now, press the paper evenly down on the linoleum block with a rolling pin, rolling the pin away from the taped end of the paper several times. Be careful not to let the paper shift on the block, or the print will smear.

10. When you're finished printing carefully peel up one edge of the paper and with a quick steady lift pull the rest of the paper clear of the block. The linoleum block effect is textured. The design should be clear, but irregularities of inking on the colored part of the card are desirable.

11. Use this first print as a guide. Comparing the print with the block will tell you if there is more cutting to do, if the inking was complete, or if you pressed hard enough while printing. Wash the block in warm water and recut any portion that needs correction, or apply more ink where needed. Cut your first card to finished size, score and fold: if your design placement is off, adjust your paper accordingly.

12. After you have made any corrections, print your cards, adding more ink as needed, and lay the finished prints on a flat surface to dry. If the grooves fill with ink after several printings, simply wash and re-ink.

13. When the ink is completely dry, cut, score, and fold your cards as shown.

**VARIATIONS TO TRY
AFTER MAKING
YOUR FIRST CARD**

1. Use other designs in this book, but remember they must be reversed. To reverse a design, trace the design onto a piece of tracing paper, flop it traced-side down on your block, and trace over the design again. This second tracing transfers the pencil lines to the linoleum.

2. Use two or three colors side by side on the cookie sheet. Roll the inks out with the brayer, trying not to mix them. They should all print at the same time and give a rainbow effect.

3. Instead of rolling the ink, lightly dab different parts of the block with different colors for a full-color or stained-glass effect.

4. Cut out your print and mount it on card paper of a contrasting color.

5. If the design permits, double print. Print the first color—preferably the lighter one—and let it dry. Clean the block, re-ink with another color, place the printed card on the block in a different position, and print the second color.

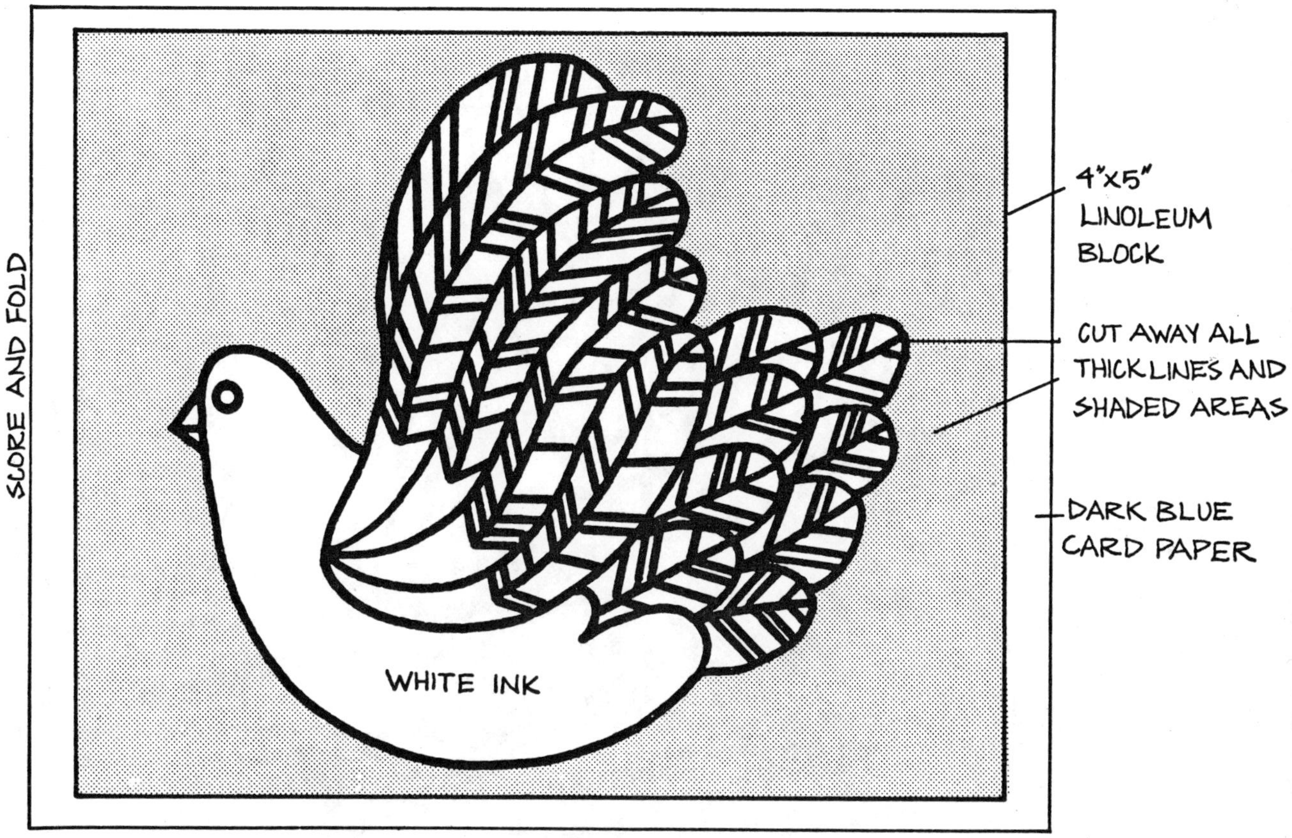

SCORE AND FOLD

4"x5"
LINOLEUM
BLOCK

CUT AWAY ALL
THICK LINES AND
SHADED AREAS

DARK BLUE
CARD PAPER

WHITE INK

FRONT PANEL

A Christmas Dove

- Use a 4" x 5" linoleum block.
- Pastel colors will give you the most pleasing cards.
- Your card paper for the single dove measures 4½" x 11" unfolded.

Your folded card fits into an A2 envelope.

Recommended Variation: #5.

Remember to print the lightest color first. Your card paper for the three-dove card measures 6¾"x10" unfolded. Your folded card fits into an A7 envelope.

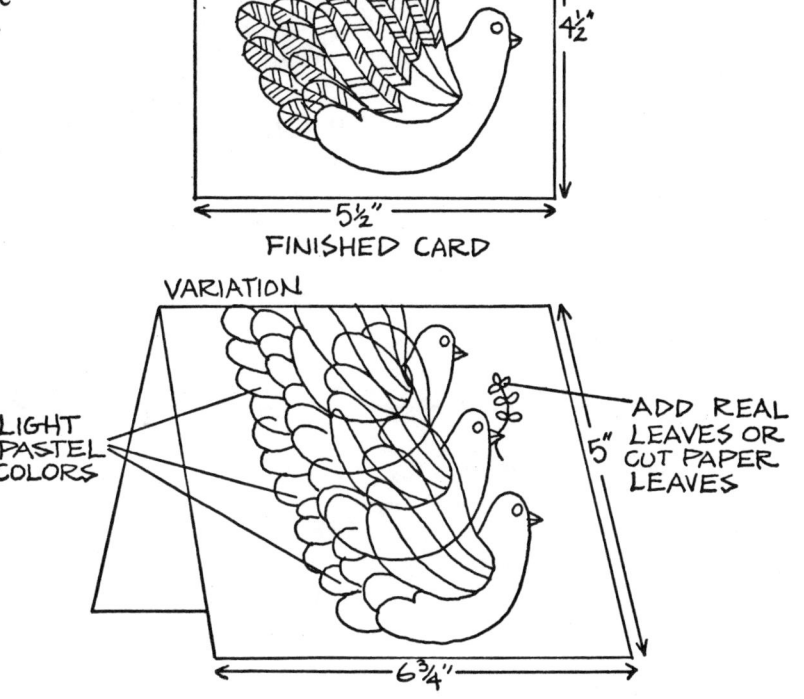

4½"

5½"

FINISHED CARD

VARIATION

LIGHT
PASTEL
COLORS

ADD REAL
LEAVES OR
CUT PAPER
LEAVES

5"

6¾"

108

SCORE AND FOLD

5"x7"
LINOLEUM
BLOCK

BROWN
INK

CUT AWAY
ALL BLACK
LINES

WHITE OR CREAM
CARD PAPER

FRONT PANEL

An Open-House Card

- Use a 4" x 5" linoleum block.
- Cut, score, and fold your card paper before printing (fig. A, unfolded size 5" x 8").
- To print, place the front of your folded card (where the two panels meet) centered face down on the inked linoleum block—the card and block are the same size. Put a piece of scrap paper behind the crack (fig. B) to prevent ink from squeezing through to the inside of the card.
- Peel your card off carefully and let it dry.

When it has dried, your card will fit into an A2 envelope.

Recommended Variation: #2

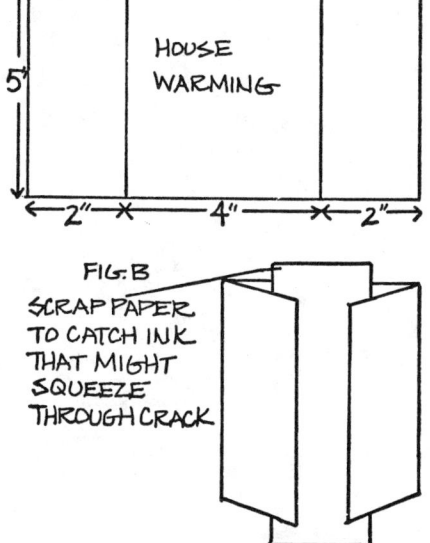

FIG. A

HOUSE WARMING

5"

2" — 4" — 2"

FIG. B

SCRAP PAPER TO CATCH INK THAT MIGHT SQUEEZE THROUGH CRACK

THE TWO PANELS MEET

SCORE AND FOLD

SCORE AND FOLD

FRONT PANEL

CUT AWAY ALL BLACK AND SHADED AREAS

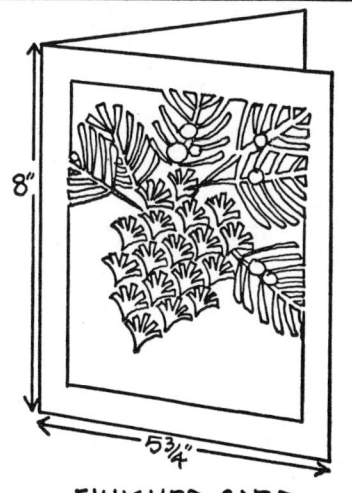

LIGHT BROWN CARD PAPER

BEIGE INK

FINISHED CARD

Holiday Season Pine Cone

- This design is shown larger than the recommended 5" x 7" linoleum block size: you have the option of making a larger card (8" x 10" linoleum block size). For the smaller card use the part of the design within the 5" x 7" rectangle.
- For a natural effect, try to make each pine needle with one cut, pressing lightly at the narrow end and harder at the wider end.

The unfolded card measures 8" x 11½". Your folded card fits into an A10 envelope.

Recommended Variation: #4

8"

5¾"

FINISHED CARD

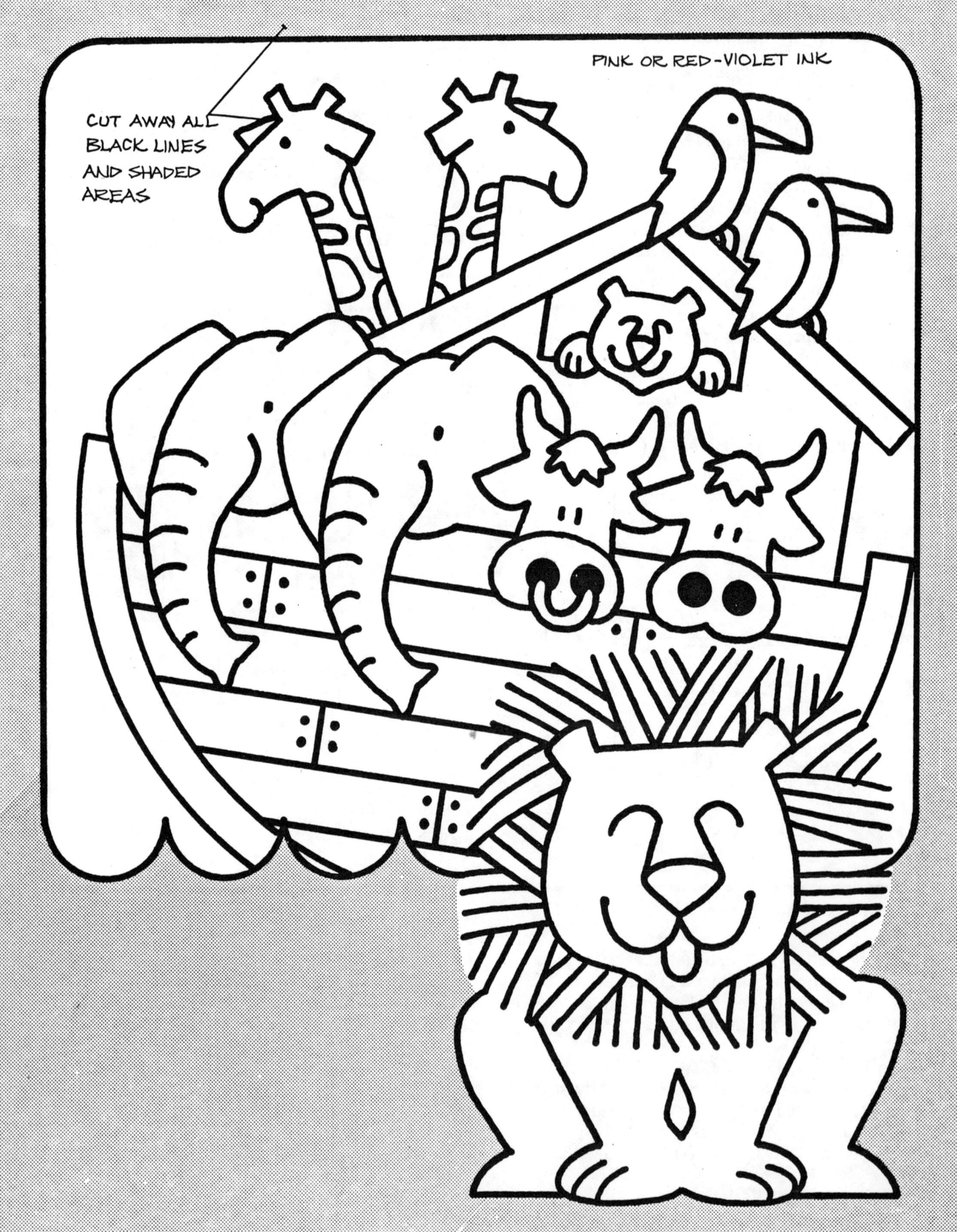

Noah's Ark Party Invitation

- **Additional material:** gummed stickers
- Center the design on a 8" x 10" linoleum block.
- Print the card centered on a 8½" x 11" piece of medium-weight cover paper.

Your folded card measures 5½" x 8½" and is a self-mailer. Seal with a gummed sticker.

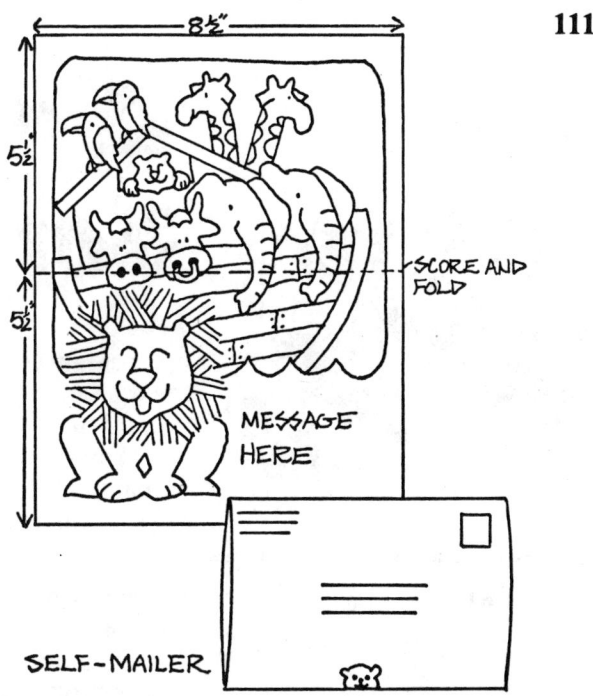

SELF-MAILER

A Santa Postcard

- **Additional material:** postcard-weight paper
- Center the design on a 3" x 5" linoleum block.
- Use heavy paper (postcard weight) for your card. White ink on a red card paper will give this card a snow-like effect.
- Trim your card to its finished size of 4" x 6".

On the back: Write your greeting on the left-hand side; the stamp and address go on the right.

FINISHED CARD

Simple Silk Screen Cards

Appearance: Very professional look. Designs have a sharp outline and an even ink distribution.

Skill required: Multiple simple techniques, needing only careful workmanship.

Quantity/Time: After preparation of the screen, up to thirty cards can be made fairly quickly.

MATERIALS		
	• Recommended paper: medium-weight cover paper (see *All About Paper*) • Easy Envelopes • Tracing paper • Wax paper • Masking tape (1" wide)	• Water-soluble silk screen ink (from an art supply store) • Household cleanser (like Ajax or Comet) • Cardboard • Newspapers • Paper towels

TOOLS		
	• Silk screen frame kit, 10" x 14", with hinged baseboard (from an art store) • Silk screen squeegee (from an art store) • Spoon	• X-acto knife (with extra blades) or scissors • Sharp pencil • Small scrub brush • Screwdriver • See individual cards for additional materials and tools

HOW TO MAKE THE CARD

1. Assemble your silk screen kit. (If the kit does not include directions, see instructions following this section.)
2. Clean the screen to remove the fabric sizing with a bristle or nylon brush and household cleanser and water. The brush should be stiff enough to clean, but not so hard that it might tear the fabric. Look through the screen at a bright window: you should be able to see through the fabric more clearly after you have scrubbed the screen.
3. After the screen is thoroughly dry, put masking tape around the edges where screen and frame meet. Put tape on the inside—half on

the screen and half on the frame—and on the back, over the groove. To get maximum adhesion, rub the tape with the back of a spoon. This tape will prevent the ink from leaking under the screen frame during printing and will keep the edges of your prints clean.

4. Cover one of the designs with tracing paper and transfer it to a 12" x 14" piece of wax paper by centering the wax paper beneath the design page and tracing over the lines with a sharp pencil (see How to Transfer in Techniques section). Use just enough pressure so that the design will show as a white line on the wax paper. Also be sure to transfer the rectangular border of the card.

5. Cut out and discard all shaded and black areas on the card design. Make your cut edges smooth and even—these will show in the printing. After cutting, your stencil should be one piece with one or two smaller cutout pieces.

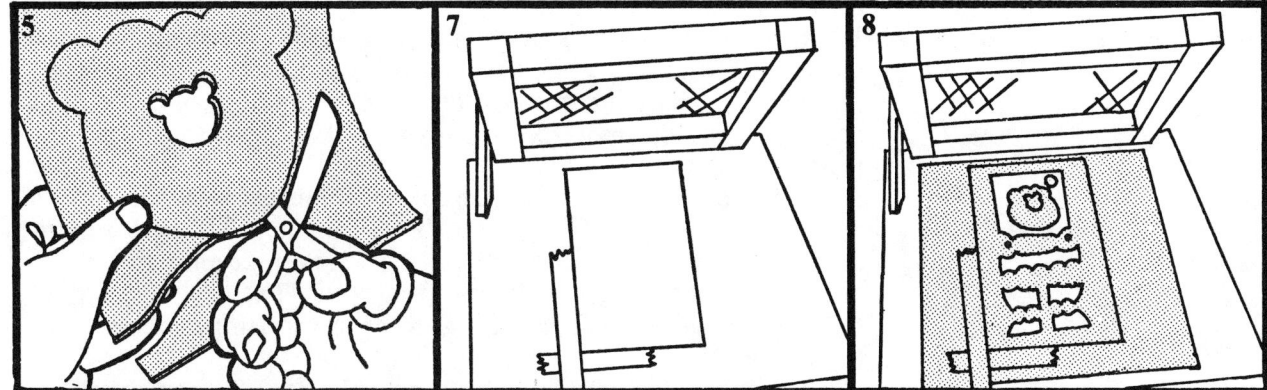

6. Cut your card paper larger than the finished card size (see card design for sizes). Be sure that each piece of card paper is exactly the same size—you will be making several cards from one stencil and alignment, or registration (see Glossary), is important. This is especially critical when you are printing two colors, because the colors must align with each other.

   Hint: Most art supply stores have paper cutters. When you buy your card paper, ask the salesperson to cut all your cards for a particular design at once. They will then be exactly the same size for registration and should align perfectly for printing. You can trim them yourself to the final size.

7. Spread newspapers over your work area and have a supply of paper towels ready for quick clean-ups. Now place a piece of card paper on the baseboard under the screen frame and in the center of the silk screen. Put masking tape on the baseboard along two sides of a corner of the paper to use as a guide for the rest of the cards. This guide is especially important in two-color cards, and you should construct it so each card will be positioned in exactly the same place and at the same angle.

   Hint: An extra thickness or two of tape will make it easier to align the paper, but too much will interfere with the printing.

8. Lay the wax paper stencil and any required cutout pieces on the card paper in the correct position and lower the screen. Be sure the wax paper extends beyond the taped edges of the screen.

9. Spoon out a strip of ink along the hinge edge of the screen. The ink should be very thoroughly stirred and mixed before using: its texture should be even and creamy.

10. Place the squeegee behind the ink strip (near frame edge) and angle it so that a sharp edge of the rubber rests on the screen. With a

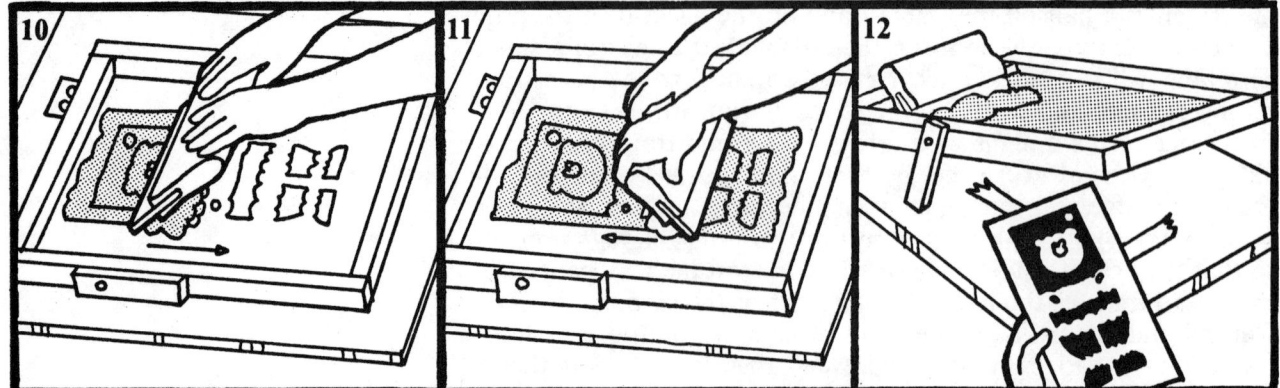

steady and firm downward pressure, pull the squeegee towards you across the screen until you have passed the design.

11. Lift the squeegee over the ridge of ink and make a return stroke towards the hinged end. Use more pressure this time, but keep the movement smooth and even (if the squeegee chatters, make another stroke till smooth). This stroke will clean excess ink from the screen.
Hint: You may need to brace the silk screen assembly while you are making the printing strokes with the squeegee. The best way to do this is to have a friend hold the screen down, keeping it steady and in contact with the card paper beneath it. The next best way is to brace the baseboard against a wall, or use a clamp to secure it to your work table.

12. When you have completed the return stroke, the squeegee will be back at the hinge end of the screen. Let it rest against the frame and raise the screen to remove the print. The wax paper stencil and pieces will stick to the screen for your next print (if there are any loose flaps of wax paper, tape them to the frame). If the print has stuck to the screen, peel it off carefully. Put the card aside on some newspapers to dry.
Hint: If the ink doesn't print, you may not be pressing hard enough, the screen may not be clean (don't let ink dry on it), or you may simply need more ink. The angle at which you hold the squeegee is also important. Experiment in order to find the angle that gives a desirable effect. Silk screen should give a solid, even color. The printed surface has a raised texture and crisp edges—it is a very professional look.

13. Place a new piece of card paper on the baseboard between the tape guidelines, lower the screen, and proceed as in step 10. Add more ink as necessary.

14. When your cards are dry, cut them to finished size, score, and fold as shown in the card design.

VARIATION TO TRY AFTER MAKING YOUR FIRST CARD

Try a two-color card. Simply print the stencil for one color, usually the lighter color first, and let all the cards dry. Peel off the stencil, clean the screen thoroughly with the brush and cleanser, and let dry. Then place one of the printed cards in the tape guidelines, align the stencil for the second color on top of the card, and print again. The placement of the second color stencil should be done carefully so the colors will be in register. See the two-color card in this section.

These instructions apply to the silk screen kit made by Speedball, which you can find in most art supply stores. (If your store doesn't carry the kit, write to Speedball, Hunt Manufacturing Co., 1405 Locust St., Philadelphia, PA 19102.) The kit contains: a baseboard, the silk screen stretched on its frame, two hinge sets with screws, and a kickleg. There are pilot holes in the base and frame to help you position these pieces and start the screws. Line up the screen frame and the baseboard so the pilot holes face up and are matched to each other. The silk should touch the baseboard. Put together the hinges with their hinge pins and place them correctly over the pilot holes: the two-bearing hinge should go on the base. Screw the hinges in place, keeping the whole assembly aligned while you work. The kickleg goes on the side of the frame. If there is no pilot hole, put the screw in the center of the frame depth (so the frame will still lie flat to the baseboard) and at least five inches from the end. The kickleg drops down when you lift the screen and holds it up while you replace the card papers on the baseboard. The hinge pins allow you to detach the screen frame for cleaning. Make sure that the frame contacts the baseboard evenly, or you will have to hold down the frame while printing to make sure all parts of the card are printed evenly.

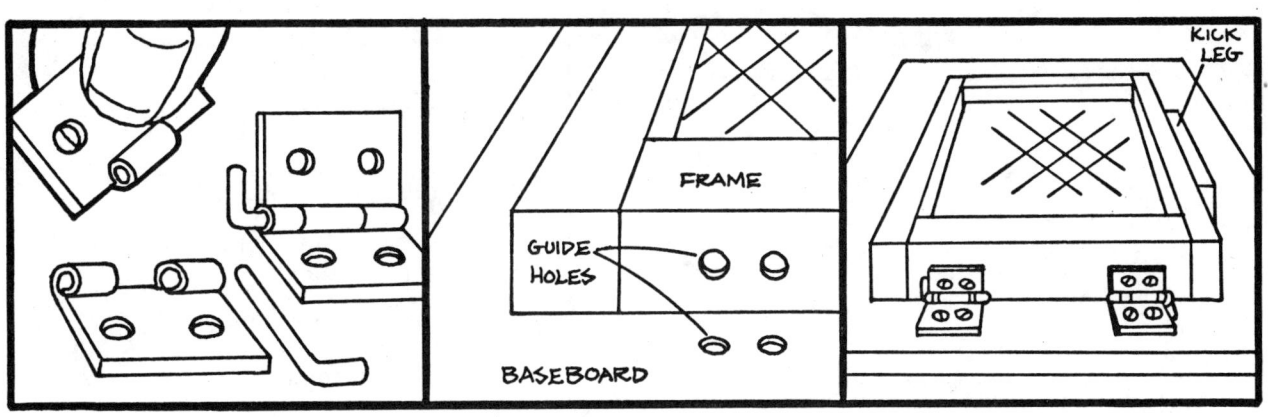

FINISHED CARDS

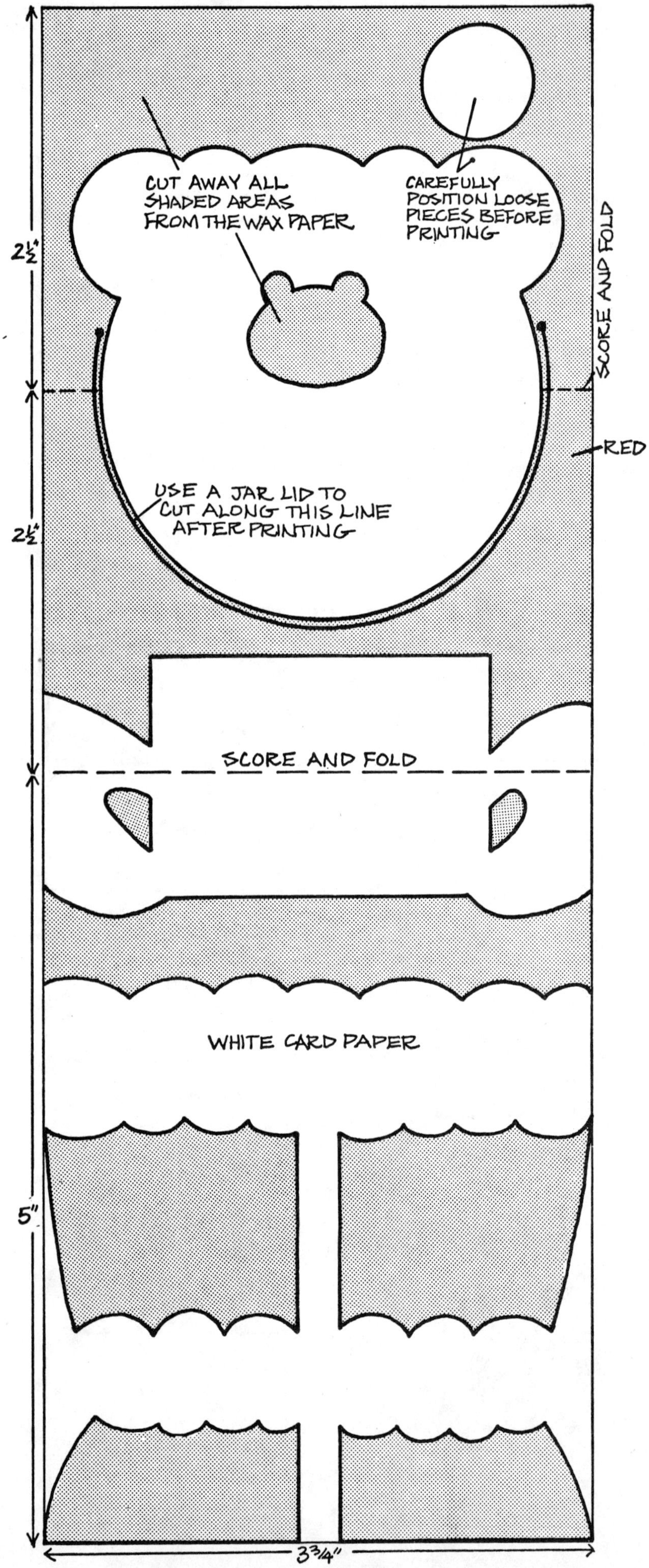

CUT AWAY ALL
SHADED AREAS
FROM THE WAX PAPER

CAREFULLY
POSITION LOOSE
PIECES BEFORE
PRINTING

SCORE AND FOLD

RED

USE A JAR LID TO
CUT ALONG THIS LINE
AFTER PRINTING

2½"

2½"

SCORE AND FOLD

WHITE CARD PAPER

5"

3¾"

WAX PAPER

CARD PAPER BEFORE
PRINTING

TRIMMED CARD
SIZE

A Santa for Christmas

- Cut your card paper to 5½" x
  12". This will be trimmed
  after printing.
- When card is dry, cut along
  the printed edges to trim your
  card to its final size (3¾" x 10")
  and also cut around Santa's
  beard where indicated.
- Score and fold.

Your folded card fits into an A2
envelope.

FINISHED CARD

WHITE CARD PAPER

CUT ALONG
THIS LINE
AFTER PRINTING

RED

ORANGE

SCORE AND FOLD

FRONT PANEL

Christmas Presents

- This is a two-color card. See the Variation in the general instructions for the procedure.
- Cut your card paper to 5" x 12". This will be trimmed after printing.
- Make two stencils: refer to the small illustrations of design elements (figs. A and B) and transfer the appropriate elements by tracing the card design.
- Print the lighter color first, and let it dry before printing the second color.

When your card is completely dry, trim to its final size (4" x 10½"), score, fold, and cut away excess paper as shown. Your finished card fits into an A6 envelope.

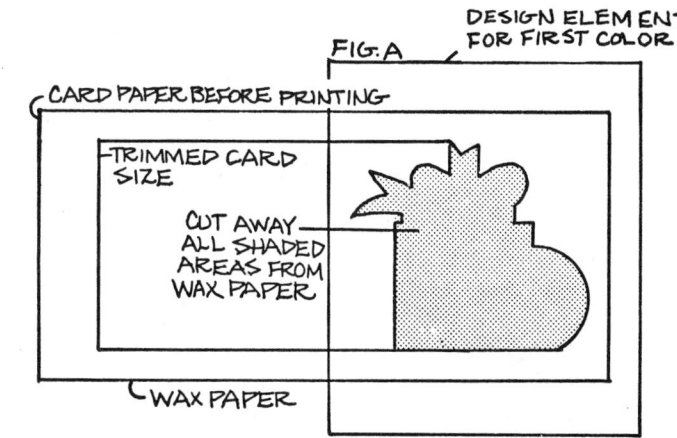

DESIGN ELEMENTS FOR FIRST COLOR

FIG. A

CARD PAPER BEFORE PRINTING

TRIMMED CARD SIZE

CUT AWAY ALL SHADED AREAS FROM WAX PAPER

WAX PAPER

FINISHED CARD

4"

5¼"

DESIGN ELEMENTS FOR 2ND COLOR

FIG. B

WAX PAPER AROUND NOSE

CUT AWAY ALL BLACK AREAS FROM WAX PAPER

MED. BLUE PAPER

CUT OUT ALL
SHADED AREAS FROM
THE WAX PAPER

BE CAREFUL IN
POSITIONING LOOSE
PIECES FOR PRINTING

SCORE AND FOLD

WHITE
REINDEER

INSIDE FRONT PANEL

WAX PAPER

CARD PAPER BEFORE PRINTING

TRIMMED CARD SIZE

MESSAGE
HERE

4½"

5"   5"   1"

FINISHED CARD

A Christmas Reindeer

- **Additional material:** gummed stickers
- Cut your card paper to 5½" x 12". Note as you position your paper that the card will be trimmed at the reindeer's neck. This is done to keep ink from squeezing around the edge of the card paper during printing.
- When the ink has dried, trim your card to its final size (4½" x 11"), score, and fold. Your folded card is a self-mailer. Seal with a gummed sticker.

WHITE CARD PAPER (OR SCHOOL COLOR)

1⅝"

SCORE & FOLD

1⅝"

SCORE AND FOLD

GLUE ON A STORE-BOUGHT TASSLE, OR MAKE YOUR OWN

YOUR SCHOOL COLOR

DRAW IN THE SMILING MOUTH AFTER PRINTING

6¼"

4½"

For Graduation

- **Additional material:** tassel (from a fabric store)
- For a very personal touch, use school colors for the card paper and ink, and glue on a real tassle.
- Cut your card paper to 5½ x 11". Note as you position your paper, that the card will be trimmed at the bottom of the gown.
- When the ink has dried, trim your card to final size (4½" x 9½"), score, and fold.

Your folded card fits into an A6 envelope.

WAX PAPER
CARD PAPER BEFORE PRINTING
TRIMMED CARD SIZE
YOUR MESSAGE GOES HERE

FINISHED CARD

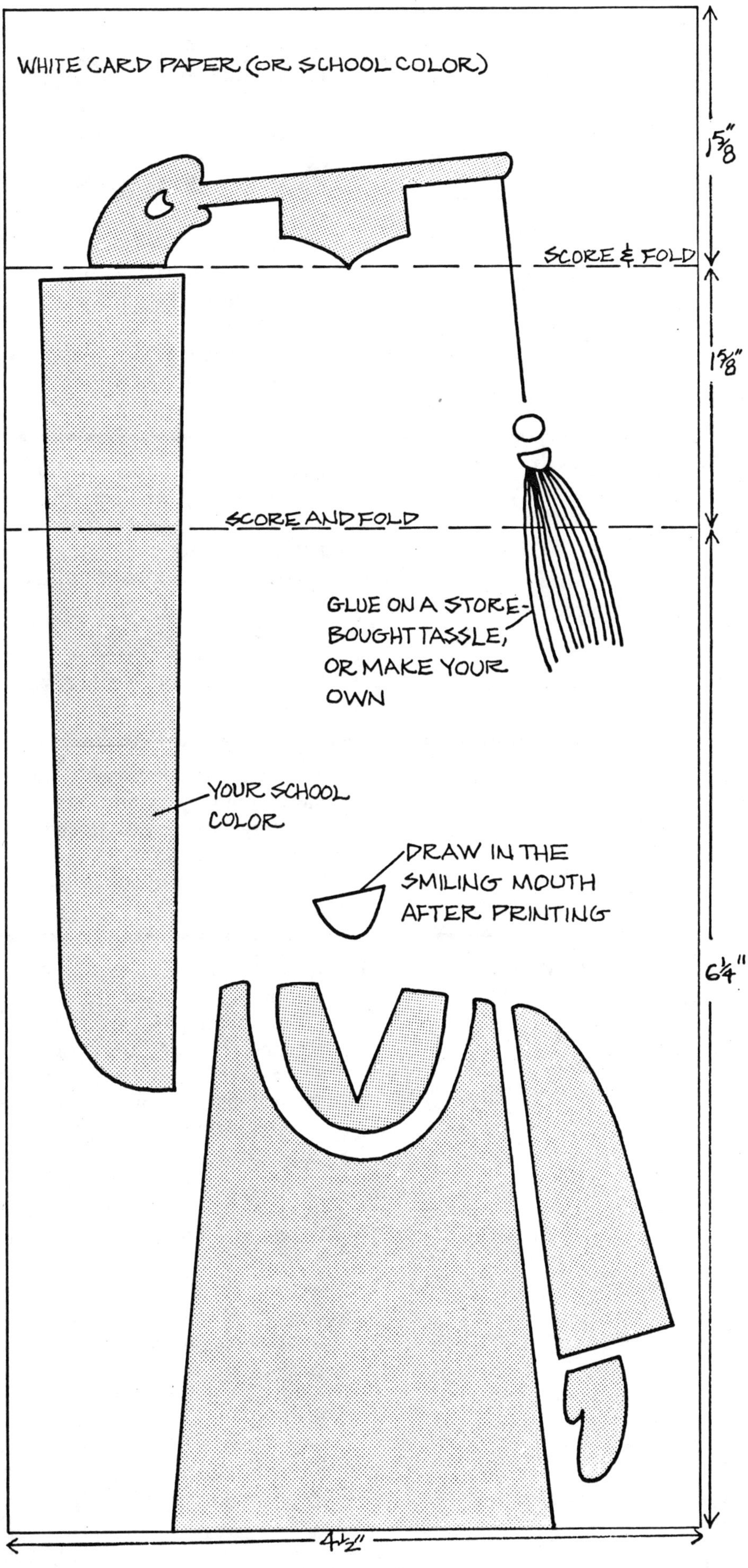

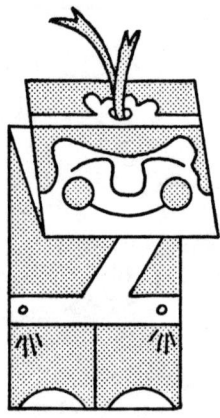

Silk Screen Cards

Appearance: The most professional look, without losing a hand-crafted effect.
Skill required: A steady hand and very careful cutting.
Quantity/Time: After preparation of the screen, up to 200 cards can be made quickly.

MATERIALS

- Recommended paper: medium-weight cover paper (see All About Paper)
- Easy Envelopes
- Plastic-backed, solvent-adhering silk screen film (available in sheets at art supply stores)
- Silk screen film solvent or lacquer thinner (from an art store or hardware store)
- Water-soluble silk screen ink
- Tracing paper
- Cardboard
- Masking tape (1" wide)
- Household cleanser (like Ajax or Comet)
- Cotton balls
- Newspapers
- Paper towels

TOOLS

- Silk screen frame kit with hinged baseboard (from an art store)
- Silk screen squeegee (from an art store)
- X-acto knife (with extra blades)
- Sharp pencil
- Small scrub brush
- Spoon
- Screwdriver
- See individual cards for additonal materials and tools

HOW TO MAKE THE CARD

1-4. Read the general instructions of the Simple Silk Screen section. Then follow steps 1 through 4.

5. Place tracing paper over the card design and trace carefully with a pencil along the edges of the toned areas and thick lines (*both* edges of the lines, see illustration). Also be sure to trace around the rectangular border of the card. The accuracy of your tracing is very important in this process, especially in two-color cards.

6. Tape the traced design onto a smooth piece of cardboard and then tape a sheet of silk screen film over the tracing. The film should be emulsion-side up (dull side) and cut to the size of the silk screen frame, or a bit larger.

7. Now cut out the design with an X-acto knife that has a new blade (replace them often for best cutting), carefully following the design lines you see through the film. Press lightly, since you only want to cut through the thin emulsion layer, not the clear plastic below.
Hint: Cut slowly and patiently with the X-acto knife. Don't drag the blade sideways to get around curves; instead change the angle of your hand or body or silk screen film so that you always cut in the direction of the blade. With practice your cuts will be smooth and show a good printing edge—and your cards will look sensational.

Not enough pressure or a dull blade when cutting will make it difficult to peel off the cutouts; too much pressure and you will cut through the plastic. A few test cuts on the corner of your film will help you find the right balance. If you happen to pierce the plastic where a window will be, no harm is done.

8. After cutting, peel away the thin emulsion layer in the areas to be printed (all shaded areas, or solid black areas, or thick black lines indicated on your card diagram). This leaves clear plastic windows in those areas, creating your stencil.

   Hint: Peeling away the cutouts should be done carefully. Lift a corner of the emulsion with the knife blade and catch the film between your finger and the blade—then lift. A large area can be peeled off with your fingers once you have started a corner. Small pieces (like a nose or teeth) that must remain on the stencil may try to come up with the part you peel away. First make sure you have cut completely around them, then hold them down with the side of the knife blade while you peel all around.

9. To center the stencil underneath the screen, lay a piece of cardboard on the baseboard, the cardboard cut slightly smaller than the screen. On top of the cardboard place the stencil, emulsion-side up, and lower the screen down onto it. The film stencil should fit tightly against the screen. If it doesn't, use additional cardboard below it or hold the screen down until the stencil transfer process is complete.

10. To transfer the stencil to the screen fabric, soak a cotton ball in the silk screen solvent (or lacquer thinner) and take a dry cotton ball in the other hand. Start in one corner of the screen and rub a small area with the solvent; immediately follow this by rubbing briskly in small circles with the dry cotton ball. Continue dissolving and drying small areas until the entire screen has been covered. *The room must be very well ventilated while you are working with the solvent.*

    Hint: Adhering the film stencil to the screen is easy once you get the hang of it. The cotton holds a lot of solvent, which will dissolve your stencil, but if you work fast with the dry cotton ball this will be no problem. Put enough solvent on to wet the area thoroughly, but don't leave it on so long that the stencil dissolves away. If you haven't used enough solvent, when you peel the plastic backing away (step #12) some of the emulsion will not stay on the screen. Try replacing the plastic and putting more solvent on this area. Let it dry and peel again.

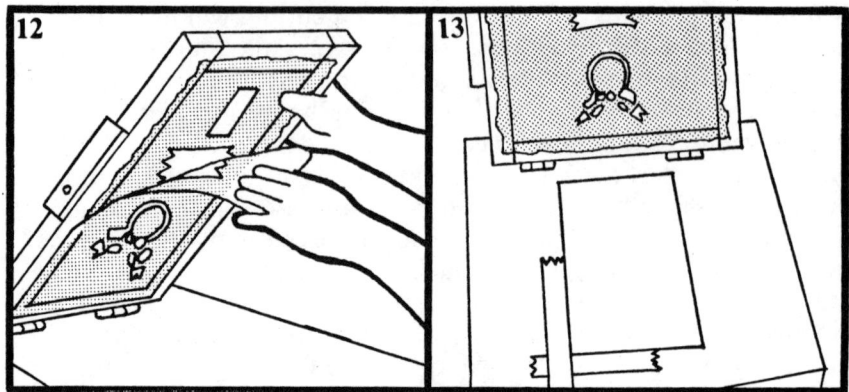

11. Let the screen dry for about ten minutes, keeping it in contact with the film (hold it down or weight down frame with some books).

12. Now raise the screen and peel off the plastic backing on the underside of the film. Peel carefully and you will find the film and your design remaining on the screen. If there are any loose flaps of film at the edges of the screen, tape them to the frame: they will help keep ink from leaking through.

13. Remove the cardboard backing and place a piece of card paper on the baseboard. Lower the screen and adjust the position of the card so that the design is aligned properly over it according to the card design. Put masking tape on the baseboard along two sides of the lower left-hand corner of the card as a guide for later cards to follow. This guide is especially important in two-color prints and should insure that all cards are positioned in the same place and at the same angle. Extra thicknesses of tape will help, but not so many layers as to interfere with printing.

14. Leave the piece of card paper in registration and lower the screen. Spoon out a strip of ink along the hinge edge of the screen and then proceed to print as described in steps 9 through 14 of the Simple Silk Screen section. The process is exactly the same, but the film stencil is already adhered to the screen and will print many more cards than the wax paper stencil (200 or more).

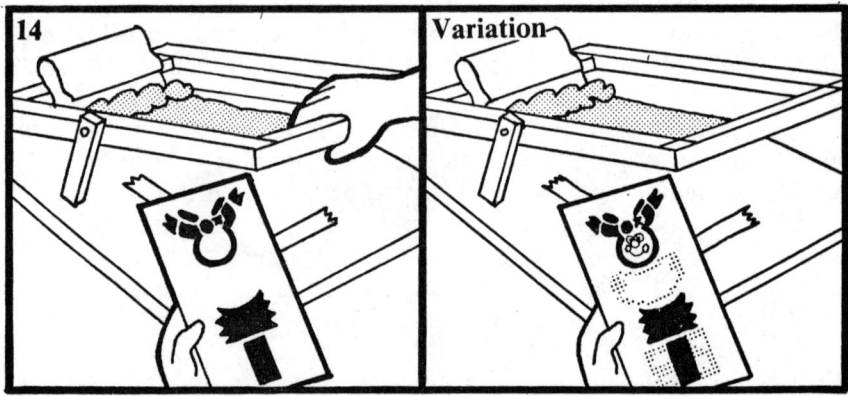

VARIATION TO TRY AFTER MAKING YOUR FIRST CARD

For a two-color card, two stencils are made (one for each color) and the entire printing process is repeated twice (see the Simple Silk Screen section Variation). Cut each film stencil very carefully to make registration of the colors easier. When you finish printing one color—use the lightest color first—dissolve the stencil from the screen. To dissolve the stencil, put some newspapers on the baseboard and lower the screen. Pour the solvent over the screen and rub the stencil with paper towels until it has transferred to the newspaper. Now discard the newspaper and continue rubbing the screen with solvent until clean. Wash with brush and cleanser, and then set aside to dry. When the screen is thoroughly dry, adhere the stencil for the second color to the screen as you did for the first color. To align for printing, lay one of the printed cards on the baseboard and lower the screen. Adjust the position of the card until the design is in register and then make a tape guide for the card paper as in step 13. Now print as before. See the two-color cards in this section.

FINISHED CARDS

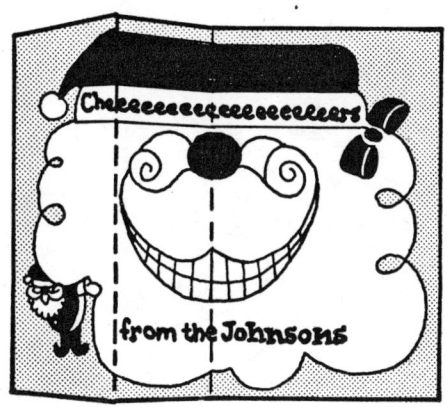

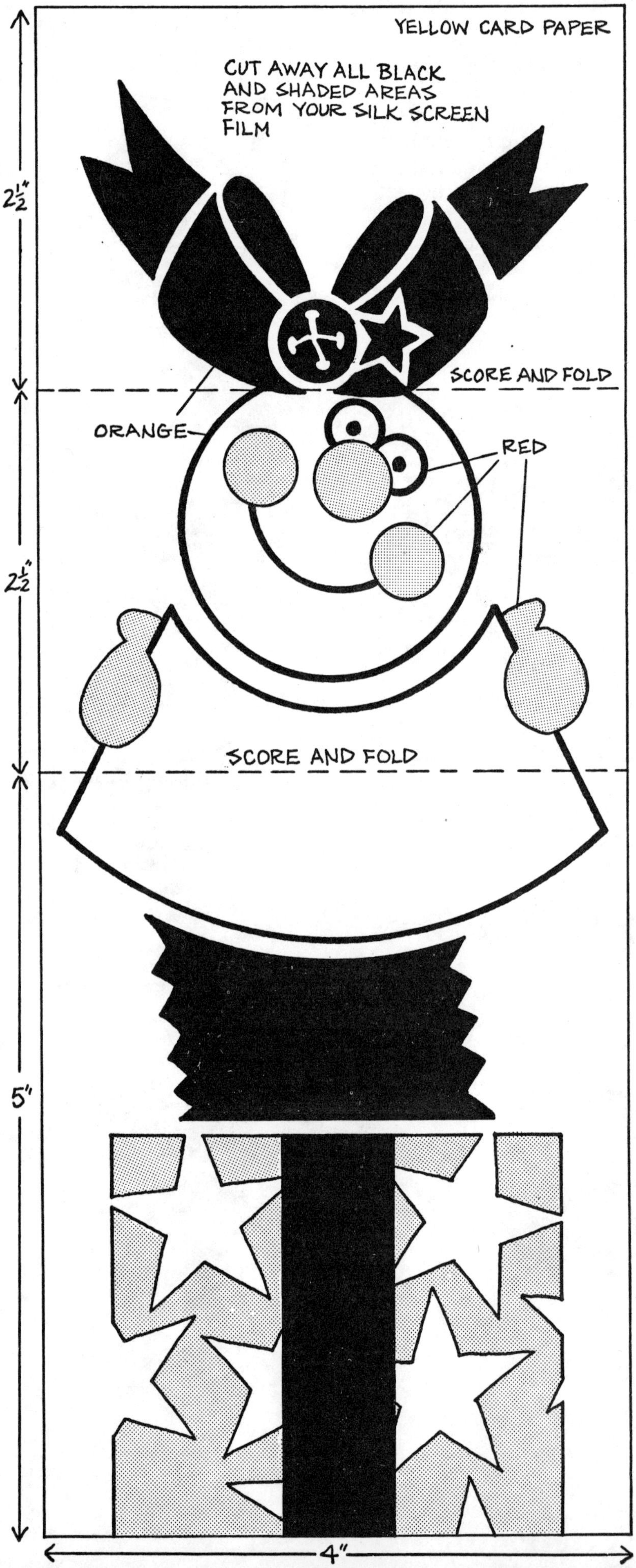

YELLOW CARD PAPER

CUT AWAY ALL BLACK
AND SHADED AREAS
FROM YOUR SILK SCREEN
FILM

$2\frac{1}{2}$"

SCORE AND FOLD

ORANGE

RED

$2\frac{1}{2}$"

SCORE AND FOLD

5"

4"

Surprise! Party Invitation or Birthday Card

- This is a two-color card. See the general instructions Variation for the procedure.
- Cut your card paper to 4½" x 11".
- Make two stencils: refer to the small illustrations of design elements (figs. A and B) and transfer the appropriate elements by tracing the card design. Make your first stencil (fig. A) the lighter color, since it prints first.
- When the ink is dry, trim your card to its final unfolded size (4" x 10"), score, and fold. Your folded card fits into an A2 envelope.

Variation: Use the same stencil to print a unique combination place mat and place card (see illustration). Cut your paper to 11" x 17" before printing. Register the lower left-hand corner of the place mat paper in the card registration marks. Print the first color. Repeat for the second color.

FINISHED CARD

125

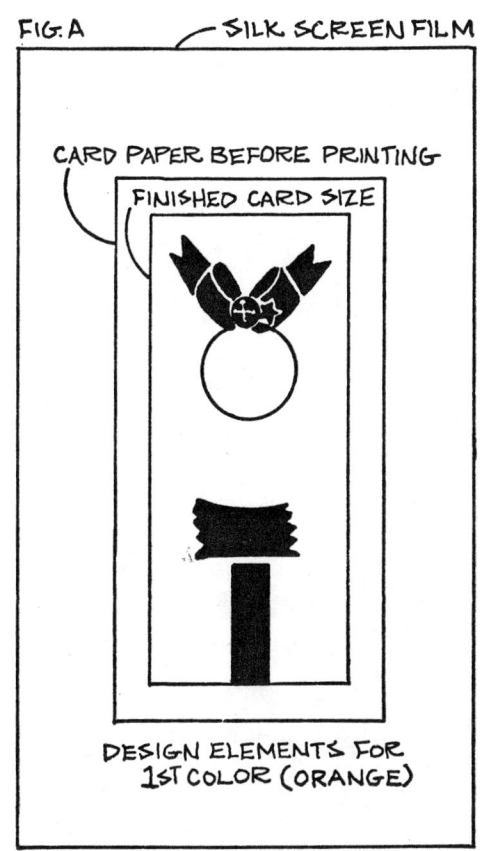

FIG. A — SILK SCREEN FILM

CARD PAPER BEFORE PRINTING

FINISHED CARD SIZE

DESIGN ELEMENTS FOR
1ST COLOR (ORANGE)

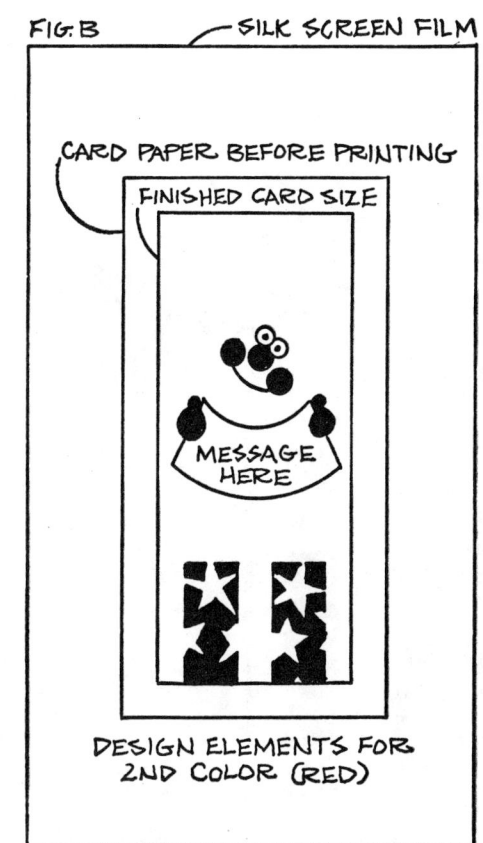

FIG. B — SILK SCREEN FILM

CARD PAPER BEFORE PRINTING

FINISHED CARD SIZE

MESSAGE HERE

DESIGN ELEMENTS FOR
2ND COLOR (RED)

PLACE MAT

DANNY — NAME HERE

11"

17"

ALL BLACK AREAS AND THICK LINES PRINT RED

ALL SHADED AREAS PRINT WHITE

LIGHT OLIVE GREEN CARD PAPER

Cheeeeeeeeeeers

SCORE AND FOLD

SCORE AND FOLD

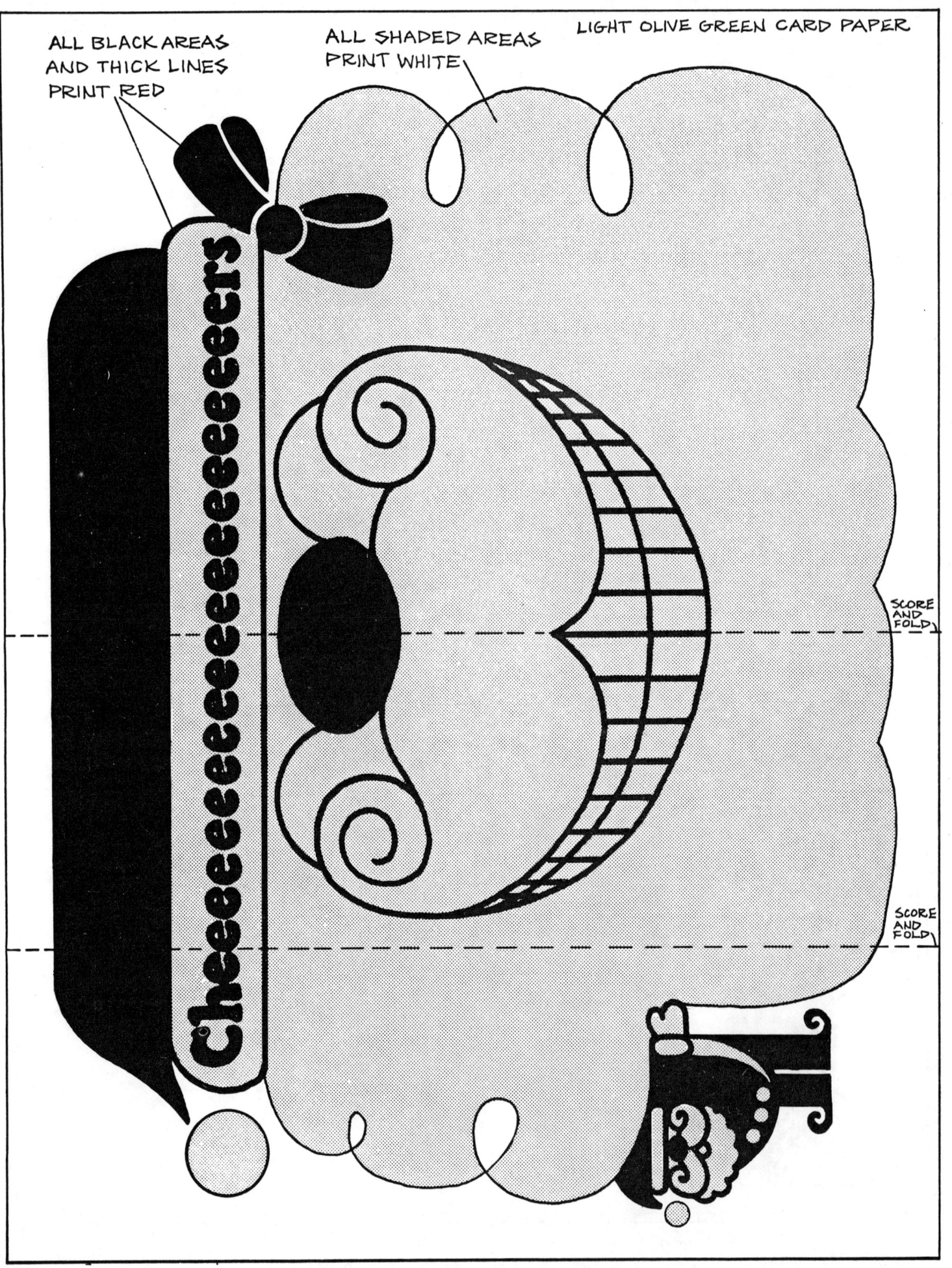

Grinning Santa Card

- This is a two-color card. See the general instructions Variation for the procedure. If you keep a steady hand, and take your time tracing and cutting, Santa will really look like himself.
- Cut your card paper to 7¾"x 10" – this is the final unfolded size, no further trimming.
- Make two stencils: refer to the small illustrations of design elements (figs. A and B) and transfer the appropriate elements by tracing the card design.
- The lettering on the cap is optional—if you take the time to cut it, do it last. You will have gained more control of the X-acto knife. The signature lettering is also optional— take the letters from the Lettering and Typefaces section.
- Allow your card to dry thoroughly, then score and fold as shown.

Your folded card fits into an A8 envelope.

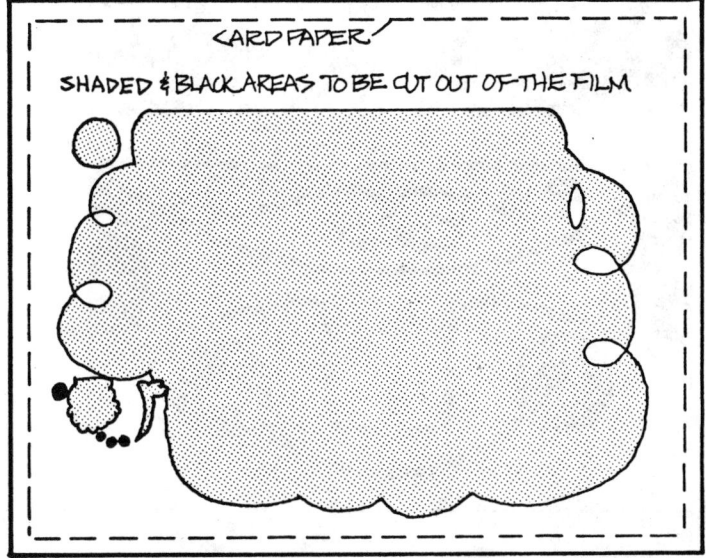

FIG. A DESIGN ELEMENTS FOR 1ST COLOR (WHITE)

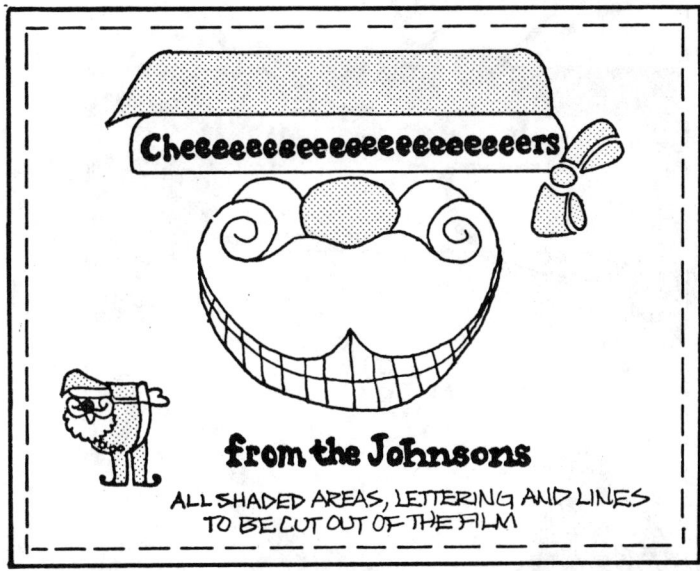

FIG. B DESIGN ELEMENTS FOR 2ND COLOR (RED). MOST OF THIS SCREEN IS MADE UP OF LINES. CUT CAREFULLY.

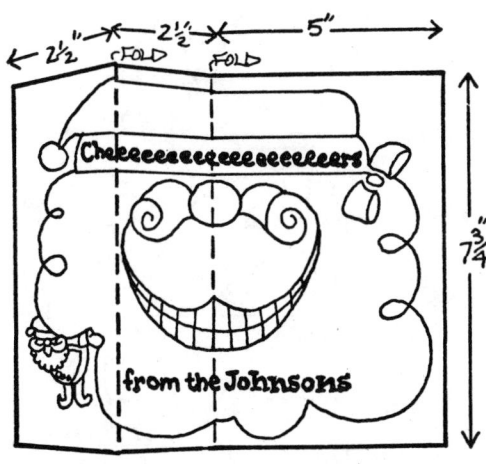

FINISHED CARD OPEN

FINISHED CARD CLOSED

HOLE PUNCH OUT
AFTER PRINTING

RED

$2\frac{7}{8}''$

SCORE AND FOLD

$2''$

CUT ALL
BLACK AREAS
AND THICK
LINES OUT OF
THE SILK
SCREEN FILM

SCORE AND FOLD

MESSAGE
HERE

$5\frac{1}{8}''$

$3\frac{1}{4}''$

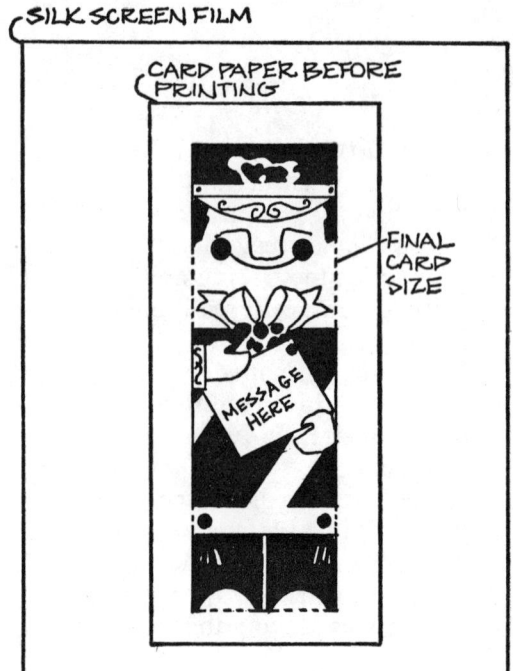

SILK SCREEN FILM

CARD PAPER BEFORE
PRINTING

FINAL
CARD
SIZE

MESSAGE
HERE

Birthday or Father's Day Card

- **Additional material:** ribbon or yarn, hole punch.
- Cut your card paper to 4"x 11".
- Take your time cutting around the eyes, nose, and mouth.
- For an extra touch, punch a hole in the hat and tie some ribbon or yarn through it. This becomes both decoration and handle.
- When the ink is dry, trim your card paper along the printed edges of the design to its final unfolded size, 3¼" x 10". Then score and fold. Your folded card fits into a #6¾ envelope.

THREAD A REAL
RIBBON THROUGH
THE HAT

FINISHED CARD

SILK SCREEN FILM

CARD PAPER

BBQ TIME

CREAM CARD PAPER

USE A JAR LID TO CUT ALONG THIS LINE AFTER PRINTING

THIS LINE DOES NOT PRINT

4"

BBQ TIME

BROWN

CUT ALL BLACK AREAS AND THICK LINES OUT OF THE SILK SCREEN FILM

SCORE AND FOLD

FIG. A

FIG. B

BBQ TIME

BBQ TIME

FIG. C

4"

BBQ TIME

FINISHED CARD

SCORE AND FOLD

4"

1¾"

A Barbeque Invitation

- Cut your card paper to 4" x 9¾"— this is the final unfolded size, no further trimming.
- Note that the design has small details, so cut carefully along your pencil lines.
- Your design will print on the front panel of your card. When the ink is dry, cut around the semicircle as indicated. You can use a drinking glass as a cutting guide (with an X-acto knife) or a drawing guide (pencil the semicircle and cut with scissors).
- Score and fold your card as shown in figures A to C. Write your message on the inside of the card.

Your card is a self-sealer. Just tuck the top panel underneath the semicircle to lock it closed. The address and stamp go on the back.

Variation: Color in the vegetables with felt-tip markers.

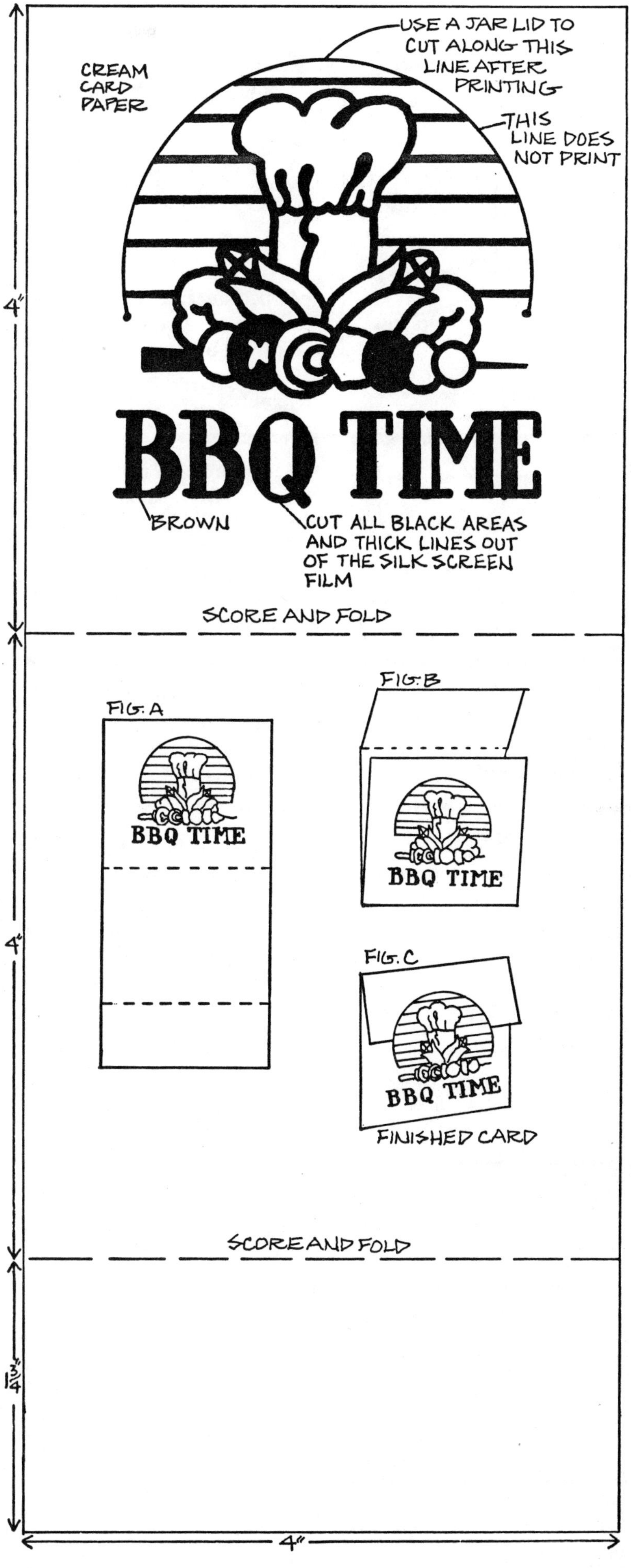

Machine-Printed Cards

Appearance: The design looks handmade. The overall appearance, however, has the uniformity of machine printing.
Skill required: Careful tracing only.
Quantity/Time: An unlimited number of cards can be made very quickly.

MATERIALS

- Recommended paper: medium-weight cover paper—not bond paper (see All About Paper)
- Easy Envelopes (or check with your printer if you want matching envelopes)
- Rubber cement with brush
- White-out ink used to correct typing errors
- White light cardboard
- Tracing paper
- Carbon paper
- Masking tape

TOOLS

- Scissors or X-acto knife
- Ruler
- Black ball-point pen
- Sharp pencil
- Water-soluble, black or red felt-tip marker
- See individual cards for additional materials and tools

MISCELLANEOUS

- "Instant" printer (such as Postal Instant Press)

HOW TO MAKE THE CARD

1. Trace your design onto tracing paper with a black or red felt-tip marker. Trace carefully—what you see is what you get. Hold down the edges of the tracing paper with small pieces of tape so it won't shift position on the design. Be sure you also trace the "crop marks" that are shown on each corner of the design. These aid the printer in centering your design and will not reproduce on your card.
2. Tape your finished tracing onto the white side of a piece of light cardboard which is slightly larger than your tracing paper. To

be sure the paper is absolutely flat, pull each corner down tight before taping.

3. Put any other designs onto your tracing, as required, using rubber cement to hold them down (see How to Glue in Techniques section). Then add your name or message. This can be done in several ways. Handwrite or typewrite your name on a piece of paper and fix in position using rubber cement. Or xerox a clear and sharp copy of the letters from the Lettering and Typefaces section, arrange them to spell your name, and adhere the letters in place on the design. Or use any other "copy" you like from old greeting cards or magazines. The basic requirement for good reproduction is that the letters be dark in color, preferably black or red. They will print in the same color as the rest of your design.
   Caution: Do not use any words or art using blue ink; they will not print. The camera that the printer uses to make your plate does not "see" blue. Blue should only be used for something you don't want to print, such as guidelines. If marked in light blue pencil, guidelines need not be erased before printing since they will not reproduce.

4. Keep your "pasteup" clean. Erase or brush over with white-out ink any smudges, dirt, pencil marks, or pen marks before you have your card printed; otherwise these marks will appear on your card. Remove any rubber cement that shows by rubbing on it lightly with a clean finger or cloth.

5. Choose a printer. The major factor in cost is how many cards you will be printing, but other factors such as paper, ink, and the use of photographs will also be considered in the price. Don't hesitate to ask your printer for advice. Ask to see samples of other work he has done.

6. If you choose the design that uses a photograph, the printer will need to "screen" the snapshot to make a halftone. The cost for this ranges from $7 to $25, depending on the size required.
   Hint: If you show the printer what you have in mind, he can enlarge or reduce the photo as necessary at the same time he screens it—at no additional charge.

7. Choose your paper and ink. Most instant printers have a stock of various colors and weights of paper on hand. They also have paper catalogs from which you may order at a slight additional cost. Choose a paper that will look well with the color of ink you are considering. Don't forget your envelopes!

8. Most instant printers already have black ink on their presses because the majority of their printing is done in black. If you want another color, ask to see an ink-color sample book to find out what your ink will look like on white paper. There is usually an additional "wash up" charge (about $10) when you ask the printer to use any color other than black. This charge covers his time in cleaning the black ink off his press, re-inking it in your chosen color, then cleaning your color off and re-inking with black ink again.

9. When you have finished your pasteup and consulted with your printer about paper and ink, give your "mechanical" (tracing taped to cardboard) to the printer. He will center the design on an 8½" x 11" or 8½" x 14" paper, according to the guidelines (crop marks) indicated on the design.

10. Tell him your choices of paper (color and size), envelopes (if you are ordering from him), and ink (color). Also tell him how many cards he should print and ask to have them trimmed to the required size when the printing is done.
11. When the cards are finished, color them with felt-tip markers or pencils.
12. Then score, fold, and cut your card according to the instructions for each specific card.

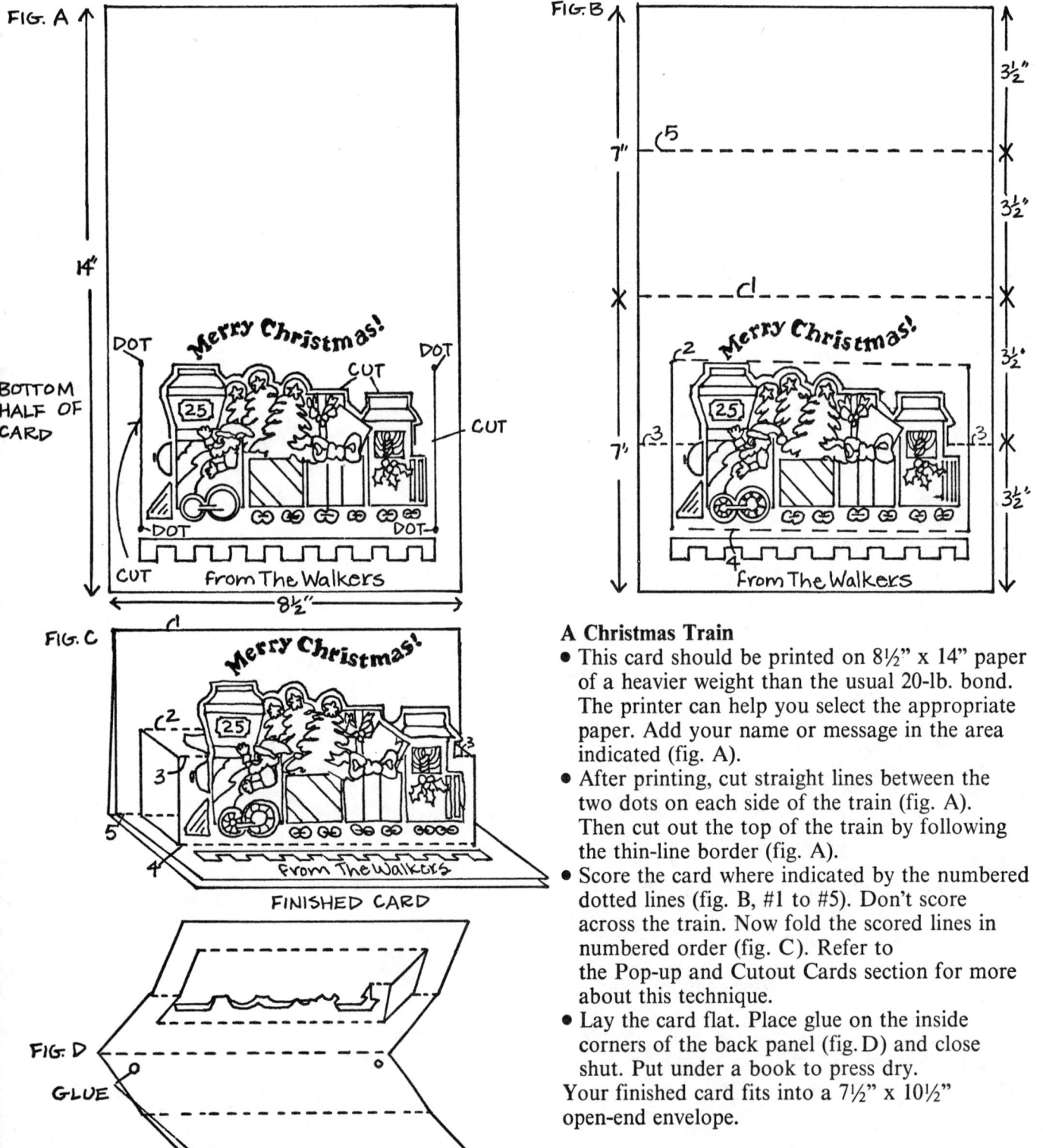

FIG. A

14"

BOTTOM HALF OF CARD

DOT   DOT   CUT
Merry Christmas!
CUT
CUT
25
DOT   DOT
CUT   from The Walkers
8½"

FIG. B

3½"
7"   5
3½"

1
3½"
2   Merry Christmas!
7'   3   25   3
3½"
4   from The Walkers

FIG. C

1
Merry Christmas!
2
25
3   3
5
4   from The Walkers
FINISHED CARD

FIG. D
GLUE

A Christmas Train

● This card should be printed on 8½" x 14" paper of a heavier weight than the usual 20-lb. bond. The printer can help you select the appropriate paper. Add your name or message in the area indicated (fig. A).

● After printing, cut straight lines between the two dots on each side of the train (fig. A). Then cut out the top of the train by following the thin-line border (fig. A).

● Score the card where indicated by the numbered dotted lines (fig. B, #1 to #5). Don't score across the train. Now fold the scored lines in numbered order (fig. C). Refer to the Pop-up and Cutout Cards section for more about this technique.

● Lay the card flat. Place glue on the inside corners of the back panel (fig. D) and close shut. Put under a book to press dry.

Your finished card fits into a 7½" x 10½" open-end envelope.

TRACE THESE CROP MARKS FOR THE PRINTER

WHITE CARD PAPER

DON'T TRACE THESE DOTTED LINES

SCORE AND FOLD

SCORE AND FOLD

RED INK

SCORE AND FOLD

Merry Christmas!

TRACE THE BIG DOTS

CUT ALONG THIS LINE

SCORE AND FOLD

BOTTOM HALF OF CARD

DON'T TRACE THESE DOTTED FOLD LINES

TRACE THESE CROP MARKS FOR THE PRINTER

25

DESIGN B
PRINTS GREEN
GLOSSY WHITE CARD PAPER

A Christmas Stocking
- This card can be printed in one or two colors.
- One color: Trace design A, add your message, and take to printer.
- Two colors: Trace design A and B on different pieces of paper. Add your message to the design that will print the color you want for it. Take both mechanicals to printer.
- Print on 8½" x 11" paper. The card does not fold.

Your printed card fits into an 8¾" x 11½" catalog envelope.

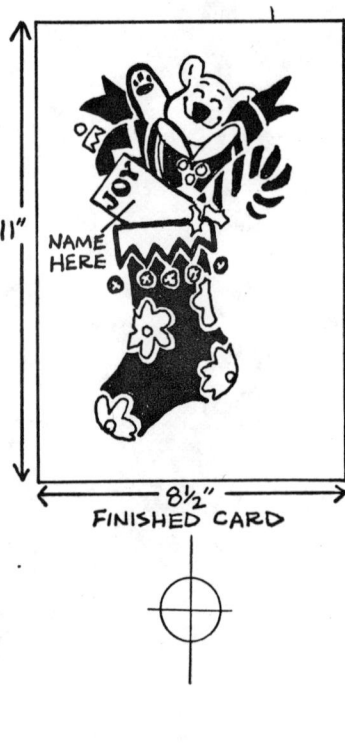

11"

NAME HERE

8½"
FINISHED CARD

BE SURE TO TRACE <u>ALL</u> REGISTRATION MARKS. THEY ARE FOR THE PRINTER TO REGISTER THE TWO COLORS. ASK THE PRINTER TO REMOVE THEM AND THIS COPY BEFORE PRINTING.

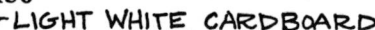
LIGHT WHITE CARDBOARD

TRACING PAPER

Have a
Merry Olde
Christmas

YOUR NAME HERE

YOUR MECHANICAL

OVAL CUTTING GUIDE

PHOTO

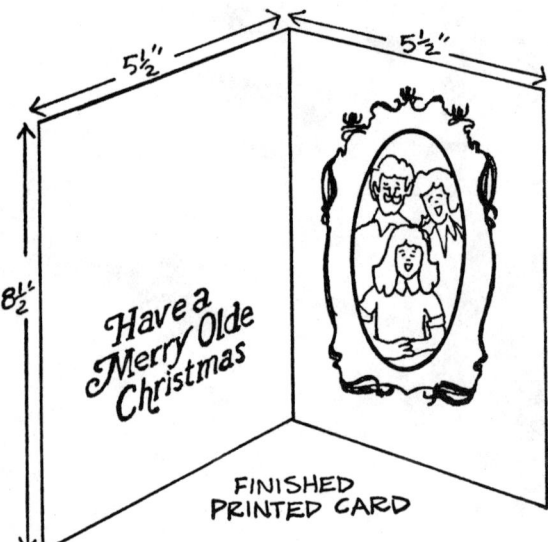
5½"   5½"

8½"

Have a
Merry Olde
Christmas

FINISHED
PRINTED CARD

FIG. A

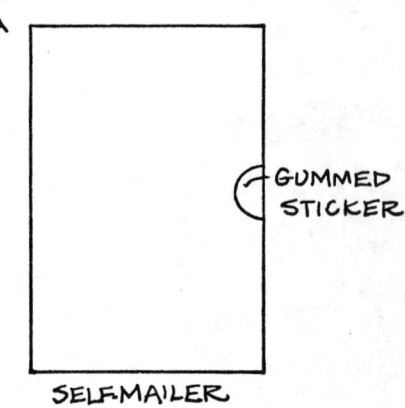
GUMMED
STICKER

SELF-MAILER

Old-Fashioned Christmas Card

- **Additional material:** gummed stickers
- Take your own black-and-white photo. Look at some old family photos to see how to imitate an old-fashioned pose and see the Photo Cards section for professional shooting tips.
- Trace the decorative border design and oval onto tracing paper, giving special attention to the oval that will frame the photo.
- Make a cardboard cutting guide (see Techniques section) in the shape of the thin inside oval. Draw and cut carefully—this will be used to cut your photo.
- Mount the tracing onto white light cardboard, add your message, and take your mechanical and cutting guide to the printer, along with your photo. At the same time the printer screens the photo for printing, he can enlarge or reduce it to fill the frame. Ask him to cut the screened photo to the shape of the cutting guide, center the oval photo in your frame, and paste it down for you.
- An 8½" x 11" light brown or beige card paper with black or dark brown ink will give you the appropriate antique look.

Your folded card is a self-mailer, which you can seal with a gummed sticker (Fig. A), or it fits a 6" x 9" open-end envelope.

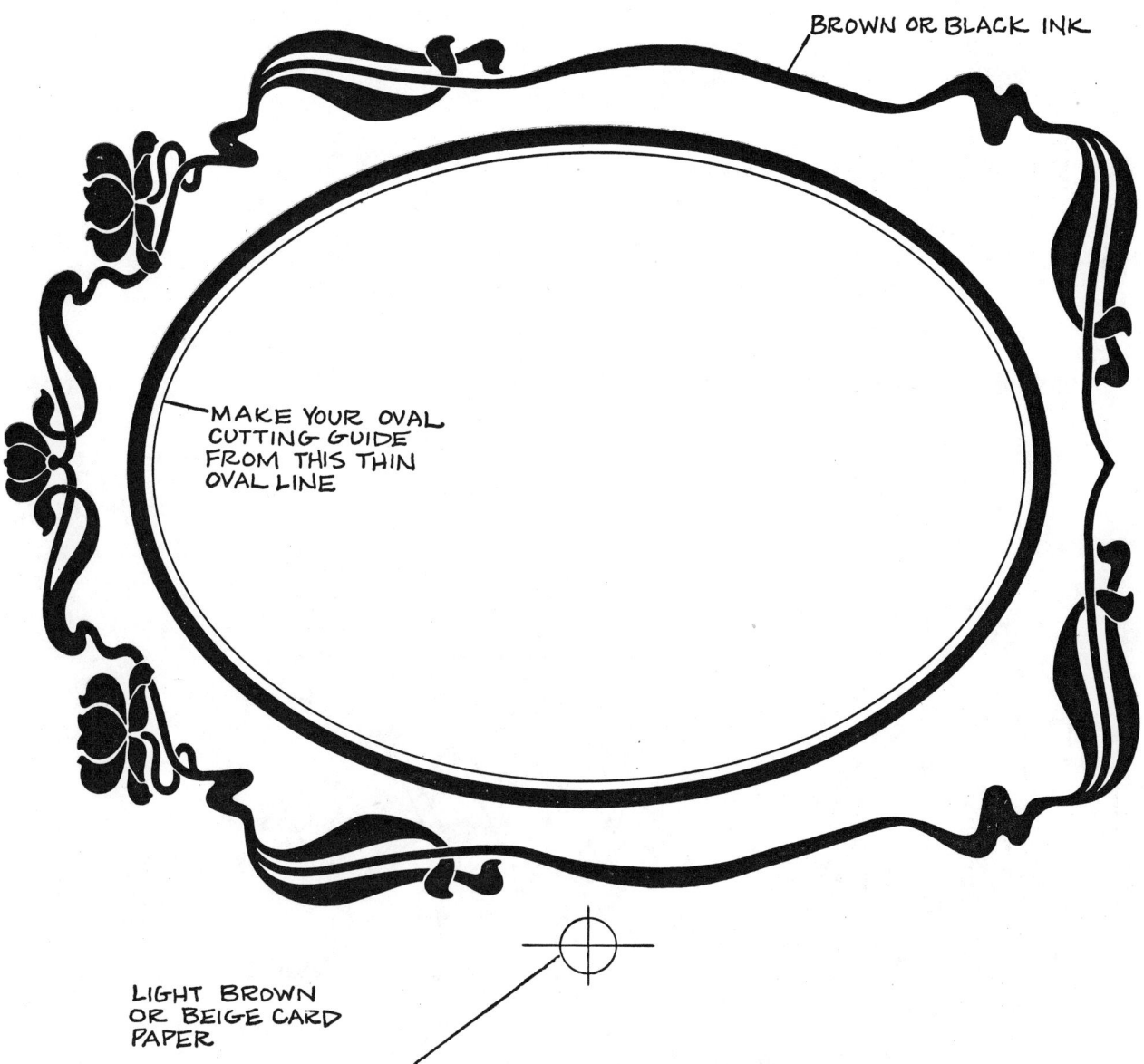

BROWN OR BLACK INK

MAKE YOUR OVAL
CUTTING GUIDE
FROM THIS THIN
OVAL LINE

LIGHT BROWN
OR BEIGE CARD
PAPER

CAREFULLY TRACE THIS CENTER
MARK ONTO YOUR TRACING PAPER.
IT INDICATES THE EXACT CENTER
OF YOUR CARD. TELL THE PRINTER
NOT TO PRINT THIS MARK, BUT TO
USE IT TO CENTER THE DESIGN
ON AN 8½" X 11" CARD PAPER.

TRACE
LETTERING
CAREFULLY

Have a
Merry Olde
Christmas

YOUR NAME

Christmas House-to-House

- Trace the two design pages carefully so that that they will line up correctly when they are taped to the light cardboard. Then add your message.
- Print your card on 8½" x 14" paper.
- After printing, your card can be colored in with felt-tip markers very effectively.
- Make the gatefold by lightly penciling in the fold marks indicated in figure A (erase these marks later). Then score and fold your card as illustrated in figures B to D.

Your folded card measures 6" x 8½" and fits into an open-end 6½" x 9½" envelope.

TRACE ALL CROP MARKS FOR THE PRINTER

DON'T TRACE THESE DOTTED SCORE AND FOLD LINES

CENTER MARK

WHITE CARD PAPER

From Our House A Very Merry Christmas

PRINT IN GREEN INK

IF YOU DRAW IN YOUR FAMILY (SEE MOVING CARD IN THIS SECTION) USE THIS GUIDELINE. DO NOT TRACE FOR PRINTING.

CROP MARKS

CENTER MARK

FIG. A

←3"→ ←2"→ ←— 4" —→ ←2"→ ←3"→

FOLD MARKS

8½"

FIG. B

FIG. C

FIG. D

FINISHED CARD

WHEN TRACING THE DESIGN
MATCH UP THIS CENTER MARK
WITH THE CENTER MARK ON
THE OPPOSITE PAGE

DON'T TRACE
THESE DOTTED
SCORE AND FOLD
LINES

CROP MARKS

And A Happy New Year To Your House

WHEN TRACING THE DESIGN
MATCH UP THIS CENTER MARK
WITH THE CENTER MARK ON
THE OPPOSITE PAGE

CROP MARKS

140

YELLOW CARD PAPER

BLACK OR RED INK

YOUR STREET HERE

USE AS GUIDELINE FOR FAMILY

Christmas Card or Moving Announcement

- First trace your family: Draw a light blue pencil guideline at the bottom of your tracing paper and then align it with the guideline on this page. Trace a figure for each member of your family onto the bike, using the holiday figures for a Christmas card. The figures are interchangeable, so you can put them on the bike to correspond to your own family.
- Then trace your house: Place your traced family figures over the house design (on the opposite page) or the Christmas House-to-House card in this section. Align the guidelines and trace the design. Be sure not to draw through your family.
- Now tape your tracing to the cardboard.
- Take your finished mechanical to the printer and ask him to center the design on 8½" x 11" paper (house design, fig. A) or on 8½" x 14" paper (Christmas House-to-House, fig. B).
- After printing, your cards can be colored in with felt-tip markers very effectively.

Mail your card unfolded if you use the house design on the opposite page. It fits into an 8¾" x 11½" catalog envelope. If you use the Christmas House-to-House card, fold the gatefold as shown in the card instructions there. Your card then fits an open-end 6½" x 9½" envelope.

141

FIG. A

11"

MESSAGE

8½"

FINISHED CARD

FINISHED CHRISTMAS HOUSE-TO-HOUSE CARD

FIG. B

11"

14"

GUIDELINE

GUIDELINE FOR FAMILY

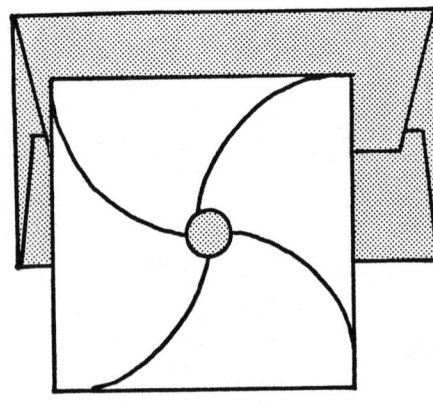

Easy Envelopes

The envelope is part of your message. It should build excitement and anticipation—it should whet the receiver's appetite. Of course you can buy ready-made envelopes in all colors, sizes, and shapes (the accompanying charts will help you select what you need).

But handmade envelopes are more intriguing, more personal and they get opened first.

The instructions in this section will show you how to make envelopes for any size of card.

POST OFFICE RULES

Post office regulations are subject to change, but in general these following rule-of-thumb guidelines give you ample room to make your envelope as creative as your card, and still get friendly service from your post office person.

SIZE

You can't mail envelopes smaller than 3½″ x 5″. Envelopes larger than 6⅛″ x 11½″ carry a postal surcharge; call your local post office for information.

COLOR

Any light color that doesn't make it hard to read the address and postmark is acceptable. The post office frowns on brilliant-colored envelopes or hard-to-read color combinations.

ADDRESS LOCATION

The address should be located in the lower portion of the address side parallel to the length of the envelope. The return address should appear in the upper left corner. In many cases slight variations are allowable, but always check with your local post office before mailing.

CHOOSE YOUR ENVELOPE

These actual-size charts give you standard envelope sizes and shapes along with their correct names. Just match the length and width of your card to those of the envelope and head for a stationery store. If none of these envelopes will do, or your card won't fit, then make your own.

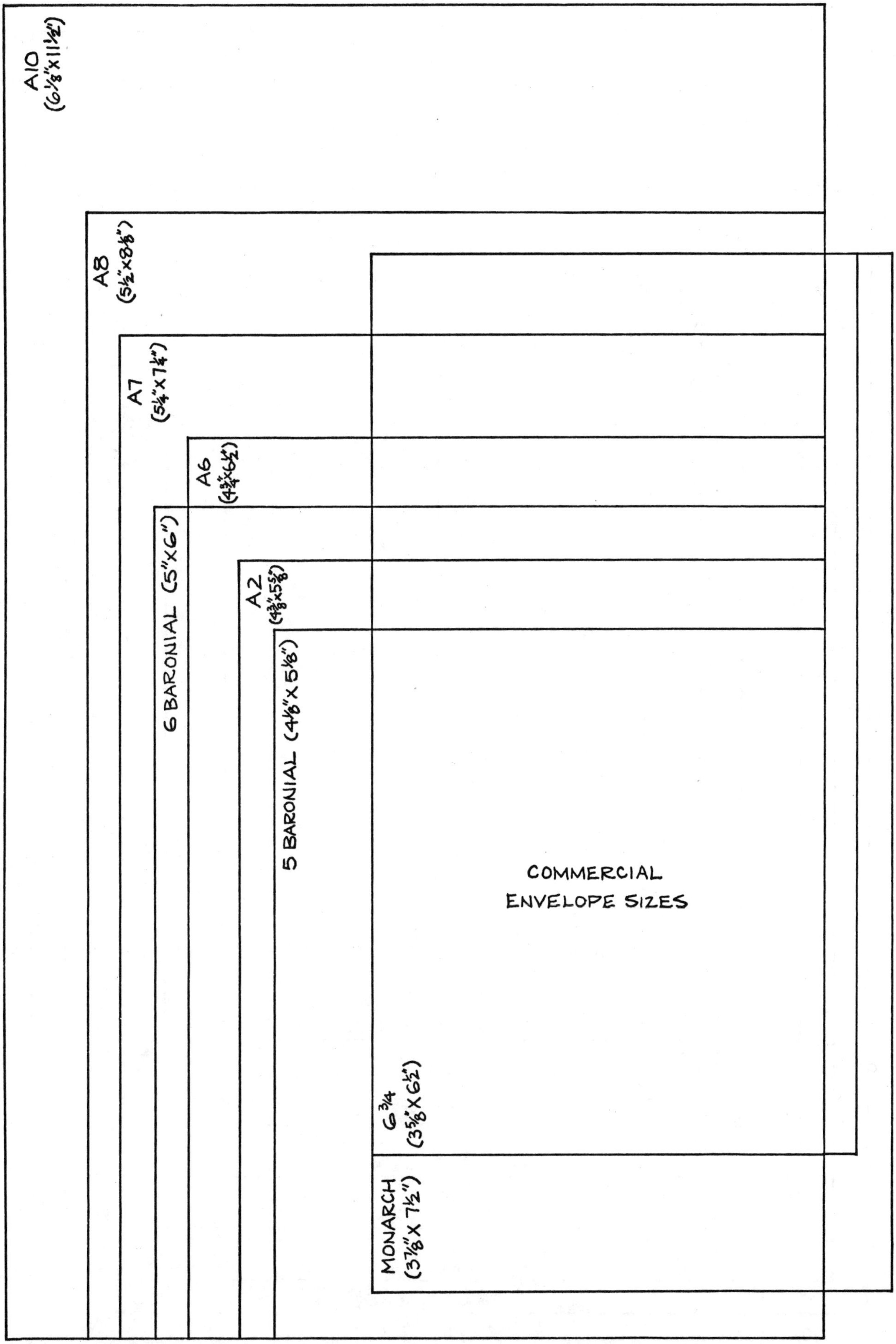
A10 (6⅛"x11½")
A8 (5½"x8⅞")
A7 (5¼"x7¼")
A6 (4¾"x6½")
6 BARONIAL (5"x6")
A2 (4⅜"x5⅝")
5 BARONIAL (4⅛"x5⅛")
6 ¾ (3⅝"x6½")
MONARCH (3⅞"x7½")
COMMERCIAL
ENVELOPE SIZES

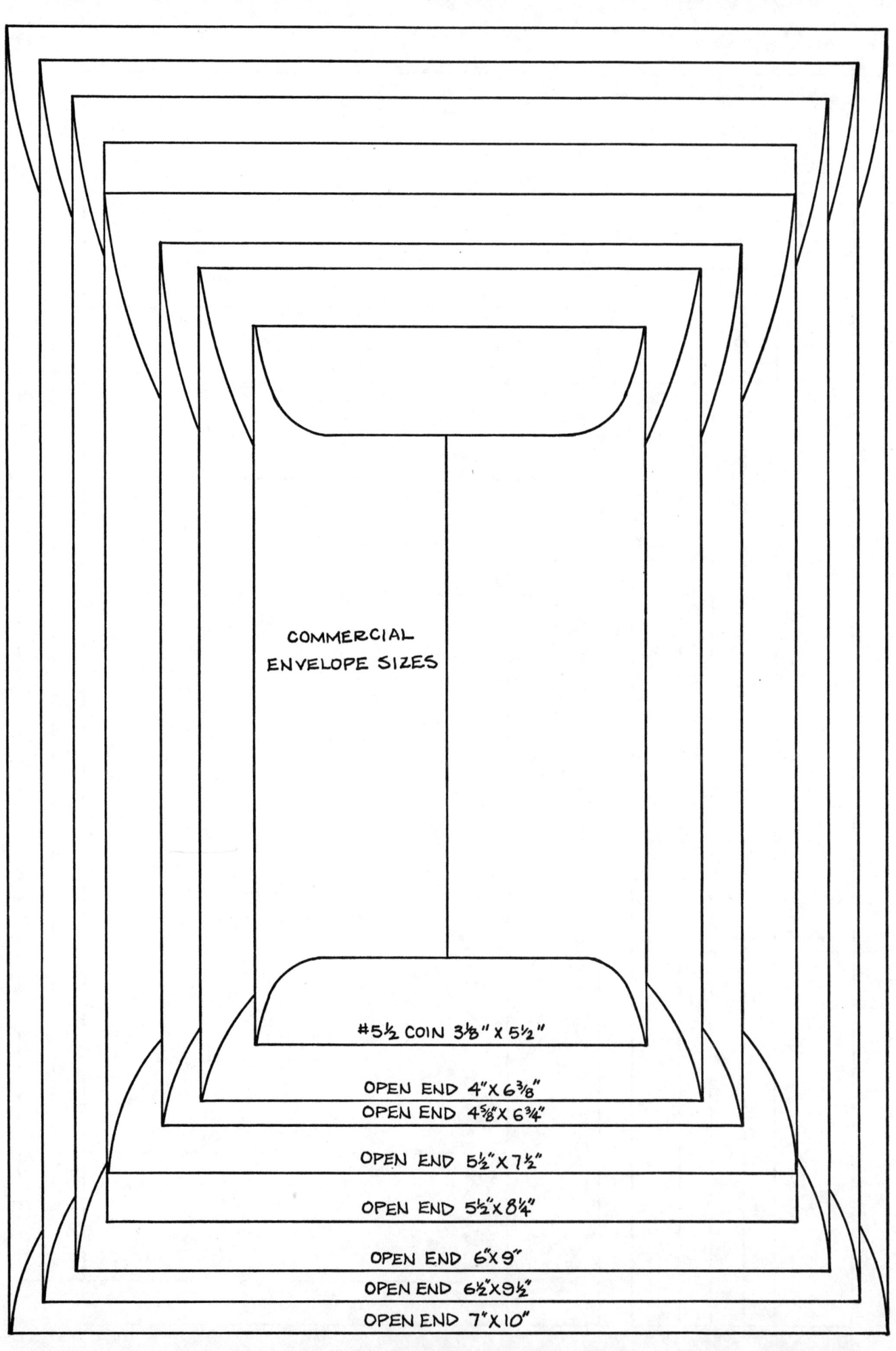

COMMERCIAL
ENVELOPE SIZES

#5½ COIN 3⅛" X 5½"

OPEN END 4" X 6⅜"
OPEN END 4⅝" X 6¾"

OPEN END 5½" X 7½"

OPEN END 5½" X 8¼"

OPEN END 6" X 9"

OPEN END 6½" X 9½"

OPEN END 7" X 10"

This elegant envelope is easy to make and unusual. It will fit and compliment any square card in this book.

MATERIALS

- Recommended paper: medium-weight, white or colored cover paper; or coated paper
- Heavy card paper or light cardboard
- Gummed stickers

TOOLS

- X-acto knife
- Scissors
- Sharp pencil
- Ruler (or straightedge)
- Saucer, dinner plate, or other circular object (for a cutting guide)

HOW TO MAKE THE ENVELOPE

1. Find a saucer, dinner plate, or other circular object whose diameter is the same size or larger than the longest side of your folded card.
2. Place the saucer upside down in the center of a commercially cut (all corners must be right angles) sheet of heavy paper or light cardboard that is at least *twice* as long and wide as the saucer diameter.
3. Pencil a circle around the saucer and remove the saucer.
4. Now fold one edge of the paper back onto itself, keeping the edges of the part being folded square with the edges of the remaining part, until the fold reaches the edge of the pencil circle. Crease the fold flat.
5. Unfold and repeat on the three remaining sides. The circle is now surrounded by a square.
6. With the paper unfolded flat, use a ruler (or straightedge) and a pencil to draw a line from one corner of the square diagonally across the square to the other corner. Repeat from the remaining corner diagonally to the other remaining corner. Where the two pencil lines intersect is the middle of the square.
7. Place the upside-down saucer on the paper so the edge touches the center point of the square and each of two adjacent corners (see illustration).
8. Use an X-acto knife to cut a semicircle around the saucer from one corner of the square to the other corner, but don't cut through the circle. Repeat for the other three sides of the square. You now have your envelope cutting guide.
9. Check the guide by folding one flap over the next inward in a clockwise direction and tucking the flap underneath the first flap

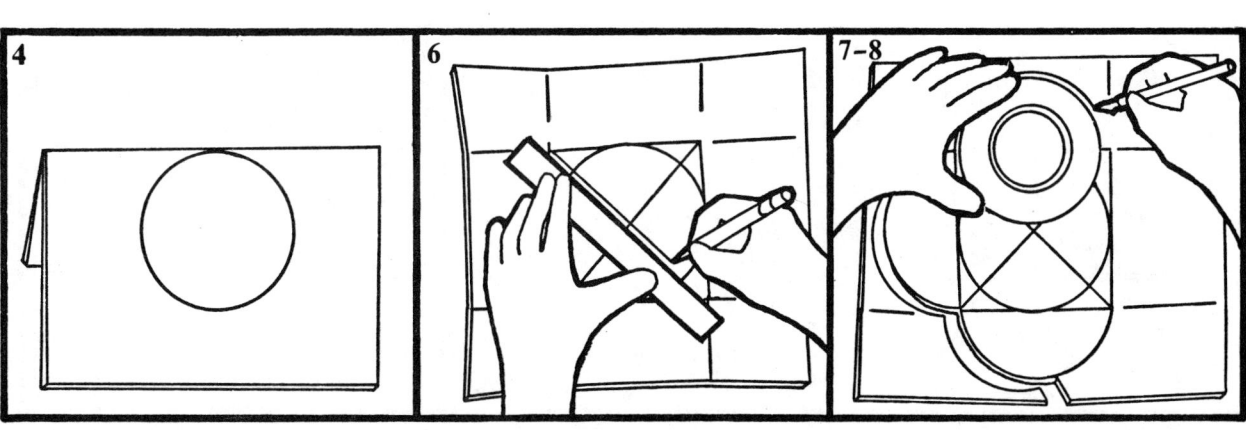

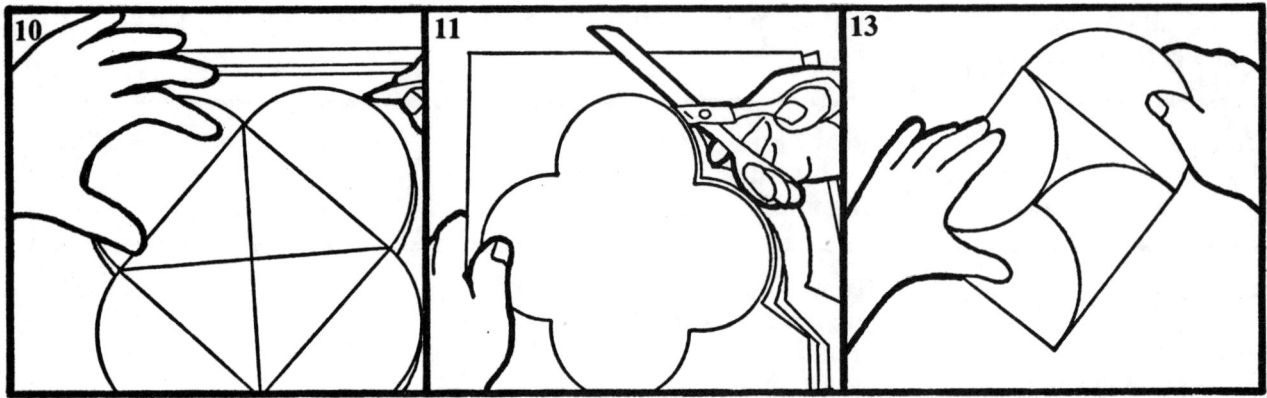

to close the envelope. Now unfold and use as a cutting guide for your envelopes.

10. Place the unfolded guide on your envelope paper and trace around it with a pencil.
11. Cut out the envelope with scissors.
12. Score your paper and fold the flaps inward as in step 9.
13. Seal the center of the pinwheel with a gummed sticker (after you put your card in!).

A SIMPLE ENVELOPE	This simple envelope is attractive and has a traditional design. It will fit any rectangular card in this book.

MATERIALS	• **Recommended paper: medium-weight, white or colored cover paper; or coated paper**	• **Heavy card paper or light cardboard** • **Gummed stickers**

TOOLS	• **Ruler** • **X-acto knife**	• **Scissors** • **Sharp pencil**

HOW TO MAKE THE ENVELOPE

1. Place your finished folded card in the center of the heavy paper or cardboard.
2. Use a pencil and ruler to draw lines parallel to the four card edges ¼" away from each edge. Extend these lines well beyond the ends of the card.
3. On each short side of the card, draw a line parallel to your first line and 1" outside of it. Make this outside line only as long as the width of your card.

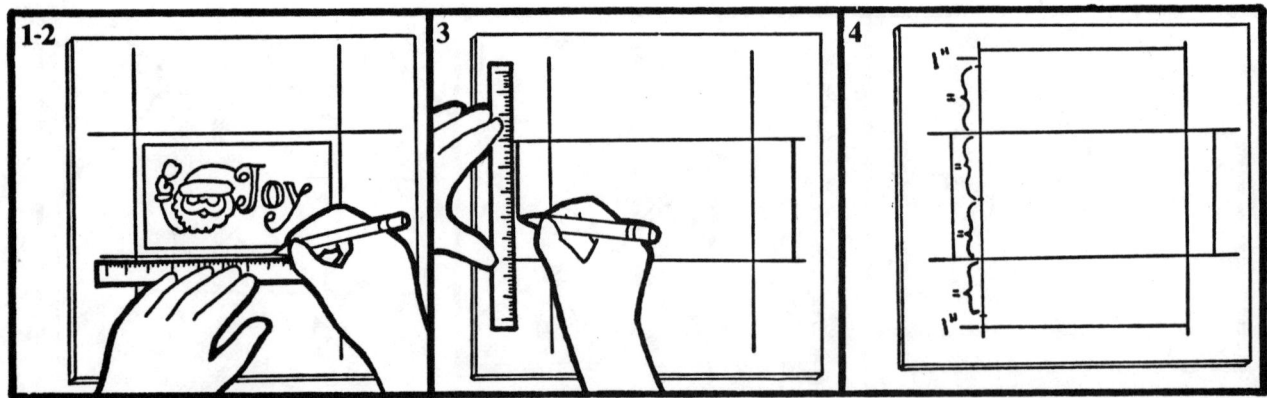

4. On each long side of the card, draw a line parallel to your first line and one-half the width of the card plus 1" outside of it. Make this outside line only as long as the length of your card.

5. Measure on the outside line of your card length ½" inward from each end, and mark the points (four marks), as shown. Then draw a line from each of these marks toward the card to the corners. These lines complete the outline of your envelope cutting guide.

6. Cut out the cardboard cutting guide using a ruler and an X-acto knife, or scissors.

7. Place your guide on the envelope paper, hold the layers firmly together, and cut around the guide to cut out your envelope.

8. Score the envelope as shown, fold, insert your card, and seal with a gummed sticker.

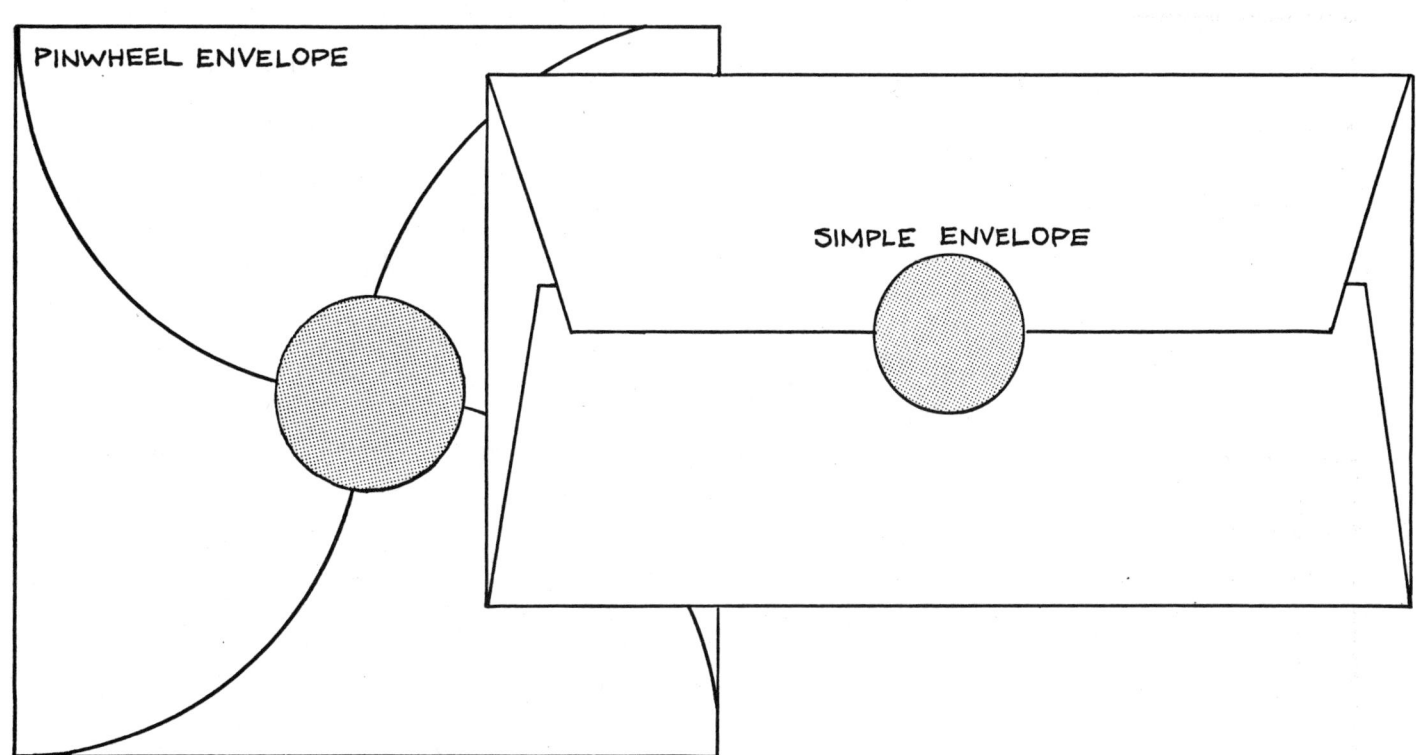

PINWHEEL ENVELOPE

SIMPLE ENVELOPE

All About Paper

Paper is the basic material of any card. Make your card in the same way but change your paper, and you have a different card. The right paper can also make the job easier and faster, and the finished card more beautiful. By referring to the general paper categories and information presented in this section, you can find just the right paper for your design and card-making technique.

PAPER WEIGHT

Recommended papers in this book are designated as *heavy, medium,* or *lightweight.* These weights denote the thickness of the paper and are specifically labeled in pounds—the higher the pound designation, the thicker the paper. Some examples of paper weights:

> Lightweight paper: 12 lb. parchment tracing paper,
>   20 lb. bond typing paper
> Medium-weight paper: 50 lb. to 80 lb. text paper
> Heavy-weight paper: 80 lb. to 120 lb. cover paper

Paper is also referred to in two major weight groups—text and cover (terms taken from the book industry). Text papers are usually lighter in weight (thinner) than cover papers.

PAPER SURFACE

In addition to its weight, the surface of the paper is an important factor in the effect you can get when you use it. The following general categories summarize the qualities of the most common types of paper.

COATED AND HARD-SURFACED COVER AND TEXT PAPERS

These papers are recommended for all card making techniques. Whether glazed, shiny, or dull, these papers have a coated or polished surface. They have the highest quality when used with printer's inks, silk screen inks, India ink, and thick paints, where the ink or paint sits on top of the paper and looks very crisp and sharp. They are especially good for machine-printed cards. They do not, however, readily absorb water-based inks or colors. Thin waterpaints will puddle up and must be carefully blotted to leave color on the paper. These papers should always be scored before being folded to prevent cracking along the fold.

UNCOATED AND FELT-FINISH COVER AND TEXT PAPERS

These papers are recommended for all card-making techniques. Most papers fall into this category, including lightweight cardboard, construction paper, bond paper, charcoal paper, mat board, and most types of drawing paper. Paints and inks will be absorbed by this paper and the image will have a slightly fuzzy edge. This edge is perfectly acceptable. Experiment before making your cards. A small dab of water or ink on the paper will show you its absorptive characteristics.

These papers are recommended for Collage, Pop-up and Cutout, Paper Doily, and Stained-Glass-Look Cards. They are usually hard-surfaced, very thin, and will pucker and warp if too wet. Tracing paper, origami paper, colored tissue paper, and onion skin paper fall into this category. These papers can be used very effectively for Collage Cards because of the bright colors available and the "bonus" colors that result when two colors overlap. Use a glue stick or spray adhesive for best results.

THIN PAPERS

These papers are recommended for Collage, Embossed, Pop-up and Cutout, and Paper Doily Cards. They have a very loose weave which allows them to absorb paint and ink very readily. Rice paper, watercolor paper, and blotter paper are good examples.

HIGHLY ABSORPTIVE PAPERS

These papers are recommended for Collage, Pop-up and Cutout, Paper Doily, Letter Cutout, and Photo Cards. They have a thin metallic layer which is usually smooth and reflective, or slightly textured. Because of an extremely hard surface, many paints and inks will "crawl" or puddle up and not adhere to the surface. For instance, silk screening can be accomplished only if the paint is screened on very thickly. If you want to Machine-Print foils, take them only to an experienced printer who will use special inks. The effect is attractive and unusual, but the process can be very costly. The most effective use of foil in this book is in Collage or as the basic card paper in Pop-outs and Cutouts. Foils should always be scored before folding to prevent the thin foil layers from breaking.

FOIL PAPERS

These papers are recommended for Collage, Pop-up and Cutout, Paper Doily, Letter Cutout, Stained-Glass-Look, Photo, Simple Silk Screen, and Silk Screen Cards. They have a velvety surface on one side. You can print on flock by Silk Screening with good results, but most other reproduction methods must be applied to the opposite side of the paper. Flocked papers work very well as card paper for Collage and Cutouts, or as a paper to mount Linoleum and other prints on.

FLOCKED PAPERS

These papers are recommended for all card-making techniques. They are medium absorptive and usually come in medium and heavy weights, ideal for card paper. Each side of a duplex paper is a different color. Usual color combinations are brown and ivory, green and gold, gray and dark gray, gray and green, blue and green, gold and orange, orange and red, brown and dark brown, and most of these colors and white.

DUPLEX PAPERS

These papers are recommended for Collage, Pop-up and Cutout, Letter Cutout, and Paper Doily Cards. Acetate is a clear or frosted plastic sheet that is available in several weights. Mylar is like acetate, but it has a highly reflective mirrorlike surface. Most paints and inks will not adhere to acetate or mylar, so if you want to use them, ask your art supply dealer for the appropriate paints and inks. Cloth gloves should be worn when working with these papers to prevent leaving fingermarks.

ACETATE AND MYLAR

Lettering & Typefaces

CALLIGRAPHY

1. There are several ways to add your name or greeting to your card. The easiest is to handwrite your message, using a ball-point pen, felt-tip marker, or Speedball or Osmoroid lettering pen set (see Glossary). These sets come with an assortment of interchangeable pen points which can give your handwriting a calligrapher's flair. And they allow you to use colored inks.

TRANSFER TYPE

2. If you are making one or a few cards or are doing Machine-Printed cards, you might want to use "instant lettering" or transfer type. These are sheets of letters that can be purchased from an art supply store and come in a wide variety of type styles and sizes. To transfer the letters to your card paper, first draw a light pencil line on your paper where you want your name or greeting to appear. Remove the protective paper backing from the sheet of transfer type. Line up the bottom of each letter with the pencil line and press it down with your finger.

3. Using a dry ball point pen or other thin burnisher, shade back and forth across the entire letter using light pressure. Peel the sheet back smoothly and the letter is transferred onto your card. Repeat with each letter. Mistakes can be removed with adhesive tape or a pencil eraser.

4. When the entire word is down, fix it firmly to your paper by placing the backing paper on top of the word and rubbing with the side of your thumbnail.

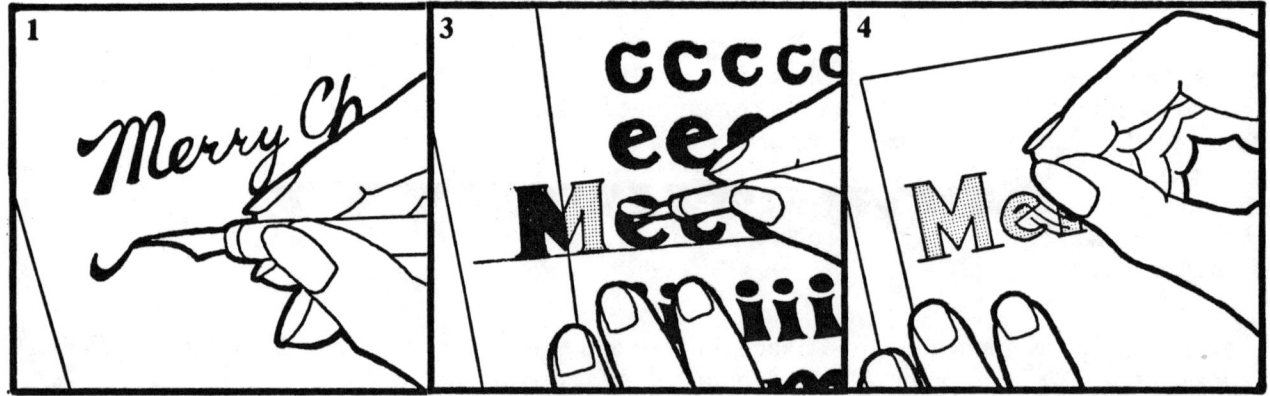

HOW TO TRACE A MESSAGE

The letters in the accompanying alphabets are the same size and style as shown on designs throughout the book. Here's how to transfer them.

Materials depending on tracing technique: sharp pencil, tracing paper, ruler, felt-tip markers, nonreproducible blue pencil, rubber cement

For Individual Cards Use the tracing paper transfer technique in How to Transfer in the Techniques section. Draw a straight line across your tracing paper and align it with the bottoms of the letters of the alphabet you have chosen. Trace around the first letter of your message with a sharp pencil. Then move the tracing paper until the next letter in your message lines up with the previously traced letter. Be sure the pencil line is still aligned. Trace that letter and continue, keeping the space between letters constant, until your message is complete. Now fill in the letters with black or colored felt-tip markers.

One tissue will make several message transfers before you need to reshade the back of the letter tracings.

For Machine-Printed Cards Draw a straight line with a light blue, nonreproducible pencil onto tracing paper. Lay the tracing paper on top of the alphabet and align the pencil line with the bottoms of the letters. Use a black or red felt-tip marker to trace and fill in the first letter of your message. Then move the tracing paper until the next letter in your message lines up with the previously traced letter. Be sure the pencil line is still aligned. Then trace the second letter and continue, keeping the space between your letters constant, until the message is complete. Now cut out the message and rubber-cement it onto your pasteup.

You need not erase the pencil line because blue will not show up when the card is printed.

SELECTED TYPEFACES

ABCDEFGHIJKLMN
OPQRSTUVWXYZ
abcdefghijklmn
opqrstuvwxyz
1234567890 &.,:;''?!-—*.$$¢¢

To Mom Love To Dad
Congratulations!
It's a Girl Boy
Best Wishes from the
Happy Birthday
Join Us for the Fun of It!

ABCDEFGHIJKLMN
OPQRSTUVWXYZ
abcdefghijklmn
opqrstuvwxyz
1234567890 &.,:;'"?!-—*

Best Wishes
To Mom To Dad

◆▶ABCDEEFFGHIJKLM

NOPQRSTUVWXYZ◀◆▶

1223344556677889900

&&..,:""""?!_*$$¢ ◆❈❈◆ ❦❙❙❦

GREETINGS SURPRISE!

AA AABBCCGD DEEFFGGHH

IIJJKKKLLMMMM MNNN N

OPPQRRRR RSSST TGUU

VVWWXXYYYZ

abcdeffi f fighhijkklmnnopqrrnr

sstuvwwwfxyy z

&&..,:;""""?!--*$$¢¢   1234567890

Happy Holidays From the

Making Cards in Quantities

EVERYONE CAN HELP

Your organization can make and sell greeting cards for fun and profit. The more people working, the faster the card-production process.

Group activities allow specialization. Form a card-production line. The more artistically inclined people can work on the card designs and artwork. The mechanically inclined can handle the actual printing and production of cards. Others can round up materials and do the selling. There's plenty of work for everyone—cutting, folding, packaging, mailing, handling finances—and the work goes quickly.

GETTING YOUR MATERIALS

Each person can be responsible for getting a specific material, but if you are turning your profits over to a charity, try to get your card materials donated to you. Contact art supply stores, ink companies, paper companies, or distributors for whatever you need. It might be possible to get materials donated from several sources. Use the donors' names and companies in advertising and publicity releases. Remember to send your donors a thank-you note on one of the cards you have made.

BEST TECHNIQUES

Certain processes lend themselves to large-quantity card production. Probably the best method, because of its production ease, quality, and salability, is silk screening (see Simple Silk Screen and Silk Screen sections). Another good method is the linoleum block print (see Linoleum Print section), using an inexpensive block printing press available at an art supply store. For very large quantities or a different effect, you can have your design printed in one color by a professional printer (see Machine-Printed Cards section). Then your cards can be dressed up by hand by making a collage of bits of colored papers, fabric, and foil, or by coloring with markers or pencils. This printing method is relatively simple, but you will have the added expense of the printing unless you can get this service donated.

PERSONALIZED CARDS

Personalized greeting cards are an attractive service you can offer your card buyers. To print their name or message in gold or silver, use a hot-foil stamping machine, which is what many gift or department stores use to personalize wedding napkins and matchbooks. You can rent a machine or borrow one from the store that sells you the foil.

You can also personalize cards by using an inexpensive rubber stamp kit with interchangeable letters. Or perhaps a talented member of your group can do hand lettering (use an antique style) or has a very elegant handwriting. Writing should be done with an Osmoroid or Speedball pen set (available at art and stationery supply stores). With either of these sets you can get a variety of styles and line thickness.

When you are personalizing cards, be extremely careful—it is easy to make mistakes. Be sure everything is spelled correctly and all words and letters are lined up properly on the card. If you are hand lettering, use a light pencil guideline that can be easily erased. If you are using a rubber stamp, use a cardboard guide to make sure all of your impressions are straight and in the same position on each card. *Always let someone else review your work for errors before you begin printing.*

Once your cards are made, you are ready to package them. Matching handmade envelopes (except for self-mailers) will enhance your cards and can be less expensive than buying envelopes (see Easy Envelopes). You can sell your cards individually or in packages of five to twenty-five. Group your cards by occasion or mix them— for example, notecards, Christmas cards, and party invitations. Then simply tie a pretty ribbon around the cards and include a small notecard with your name, address, and phone number for reorders.

PACKAGING

Try selling cards at community or social gatherings—Christmas bazaars, PTA meetings, church club parties—but don't neglect your relatives, friends, and acquaintances.
Hint: Publicity is invaluable. Merchants might let you put up posters or displays of the cards inside their stores—after all, you already have the know-how to produce professional-looking posters and flyers from your card-making experience. (Be sure to give participating merchants a free box of cards.)

You can also try to get free publicity for your project by sending a press release and sample card to local newspapers and TV and radio stations. The press release should state who you are, what you are selling, and what the money will be used for (a specific project or charity makes the release more newsworthy). Mention where the cards can be purchased or ordered. Add that they are handmade, what kind of assortments you offer, and how much they cost. Be sure that the top of the release states the date on which you would like the news to be released.

SELLING

The best way to figure out how much to charge for your cards is to add up all of your expenses, including materials for the cards and promotion, and divide the total by the number of cards you plan to

PRICING

156

make or have already made. This will give the cost per card.

Now do a little market research. Go to a stationery or card shop and look at their cards. Notice the quality and price range. Assume that your cards are equivalent to the higher-quality commercial cards, since yours are handmade and you are a charitable or nonprofit organization. Your price per card should be close to the price of the higher-quality card—or perhaps a little higher, depending on your cost. But try to keep your prices reasonable. It is easier to sell reasonably priced cards in quantity.

The profit your group has made is the difference between your selling price and your cost per card. The time given by your group members is not calculated, of course, but it is time well spent.

Please Note: All of the designs in this book are copyrighted. If you are making cards for your personal use or for a nonprofit organization to use or sell, you need not get permission for their use. If you wish to use the designs to make cards to sell commercially, you must obtain written permission from the publisher and the authors. Any other use of the designs is strictly prohibited.

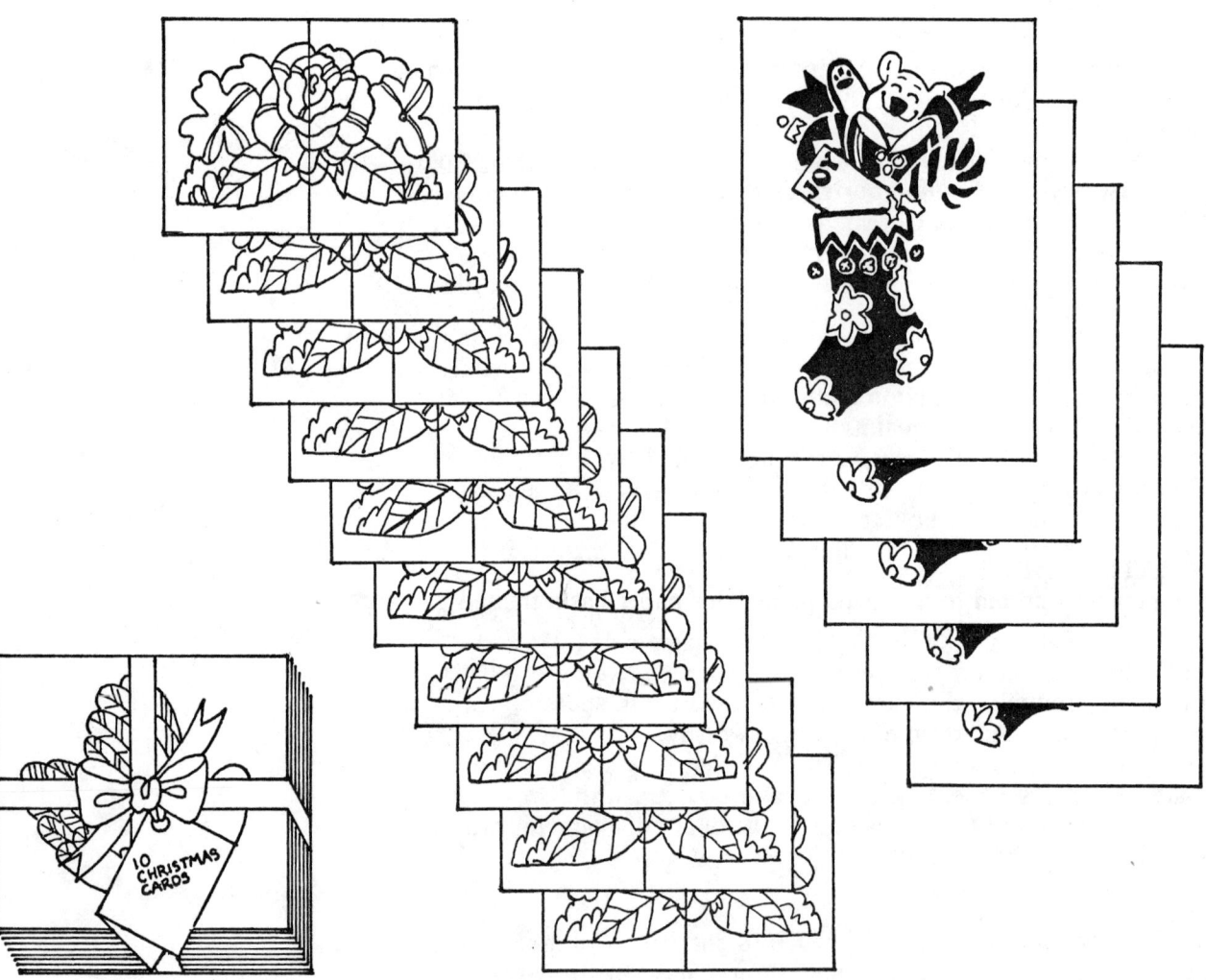

Glossary of Terms & Tools

ACCORDION FOLD
A paper fold that is pleated in a back and forth manner so that it resembles the folds of an accordion.

BASEBOARD
A bottom piece of cardboard, plywood, or masonite. In silk screening it is the smooth surface to which the screen frame is hinged and on which the card paper rests. In embossing it is the bottom piece of cardboard on which the embossing guide cutouts are glued.

BENCH HOOK
A metal tool that hooks onto the edge of a table to hold a linoleum block in place while it is being cut. Can also be used as an inking plate.

BOX BOARD
A lightweight cardboard that has a smooth white surface on each side.

BRAYER
A rubber roller connected to a handle, used to apply printing ink to the linoleum block printing surface.

BURNISHER
Any tool with a smooth surface used to apply pressure to transfer letters or numbers from a transfer-type sheet.

CAMERA READY
A printer's term indicating that preparation of the pasteup is complete and ready to be photographed for printing. See Mechanical.

CHARCOAL PAPER
A soft, textured paper available in muted pastel colors. Sold in sheets and pads.

COATED PAPER
Sometimes referred to as glazed paper, this paper has a treated surface, usually of clay, and comes in a wide range of colors.

COLLAGE
An artistic arrangement of bits and pieces of paper, fabric, or foil glued onto a surface.

CONSTRUCTION PAPER
The familiar, rough-textured paper that is available in many colors.

COPY
A generic term for any words—typewritten, typset, or handwritten—pasted on the artwork for machine-printing.

CROP MARKS
Pencil or ink lines drawn on the outside of the printing area to guide the printer in centering, printing, and cutting.

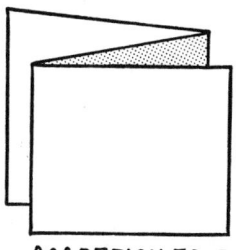

ACCORDION FOLD

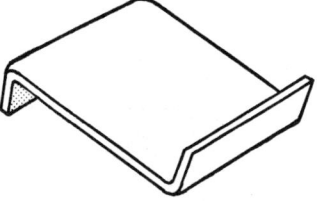

BENCH HOOK

BRAYER

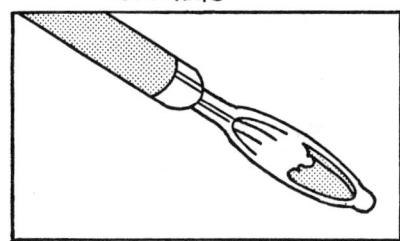

BURNISHER

158

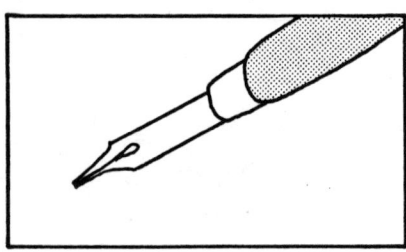

CROW QUILL PEN

DOCTOR PH. MARTIN
WATERCOLORS

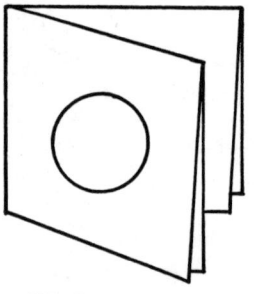

FRENCH FOLD

CROPPING
A photographic term. Parts of a photo are masked so that what remains appears to the best advantage.

CROW QUILL PEN
Brand name of an inexpensive pen that must be dipped in ink to use.

CUTTING GUIDE
Any object used as a guide for cutting a specific shape. The cutting tool is run around the contour of the guide after it has been placed on the material to be cut.

DAY-GLO
A brand name for coated papers and fluorescent paints which can be brushed on or used for silk screening. The colors are intensively bright and most effective when used sparingly.

DESIGN ELEMENT
Any portion or piece of a total design.

DOCTOR PH. MARTIN WATERCOLORS
A brand name of high intensity liquid watercolors and dyes that can be purchased in small bottles.

DOILIES
Commercially produced, lacelike paper, sold in packets in party or stationery stores. Available in several colors.

DRAWING GUIDE
Any object that is used to guide a pencil while drawing a design: a ruler, a jar lid, a dime, a plate.

EMBOSS
Raising a design above the paper surface (without the use of ink or paint) by bending and stretching the paper between two design shapes.

ERASABLE BOND PAPER
Bond paper from which ink and pencil marks may be easily erased. It is recommended for Crayon Melt Cards because it gives the melt a glossy look.

FLOCKED PAPER
Paper that has a fine velvety surface. Very effective in making Collage Cards.

FLUORESCENT PAINT
See Day-Glo.

FOILS
Papers with a thin metallic layer.

FRENCH FOLD
A paper fold that enables a design that is printed on only one side of the paper to show (after folding) on both the outside and inside of a card.

GATEFOLD
A paper fold that enables a card to open from the center.

GLUE STICK
An adhesive made in solid stick form that does not curl very lightweight paper because it is not wet when applied.

GUIDELINES
Lines that determine a shape or explain the function of a design part. Such lines also may indicate areas to be cut, colored, or folded.

GUMMED STICKERS OR TABS
These stickers are produced in a variety of colors and shapes and can be used to seal envelopes or selfmailers. Notarial seals, available at stationery stores, are especially decorative.

HALFTONE
A photograph that has been screened for printing. Screening means that any photograph to be machine printed must first be broken up into small, solid black dots. This is done by photographing it again through a glass screen made up of finely etched lines.

ILLUSTRATION BOARD
A heavy-weight cardboard with good quality paper laminated on one side. It is available in two forms: hot press, which is extremely slick and smooth, and cold press, which has a very fine irregular surface. Both take paint and ink very well.

INDIA INK
An opaque, black, waterproof ink used for line drawings. Especially good for machine printing.

INKS (PRINTING)
There are two main types. Commercial inks, used in machine printing, come in a multitude of manufactured or blended colors. Most printers have a book of ink-color samples you may examine. The other inks fall into the arts and crafts category and are used for handmade printing plates, such as linoleum and paraffin blocks. They are available in art supply stores in several colors and can be mixed to make up almost any color you choose.

LACQUER THINNER
A group of solvents to dilute or dissolve lacquers, varnishes, and shellacs. Used as a solvent in silk screening.

LINOLEUM BLOCK
Carved linoleum mounted on wood or particle board. Available in several sizes at art supply stores.

LIQUID WATERCOLORS
Premixed bottled version of conventional watercolors. Usually concentrated. They can be diluted or, for more intensity, used from the bottles. Dr. Martin's Watercolors is a well-known brand.

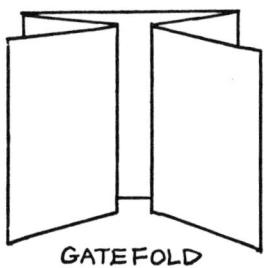

GATEFOLD

HALFTONE

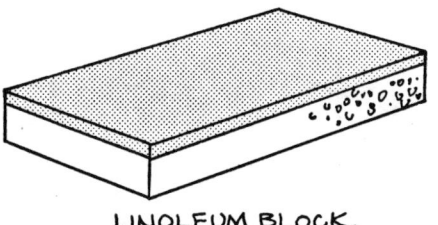

LINOLEUM BLOCK

SPEEDBALL OSMOROID
PENS PEN

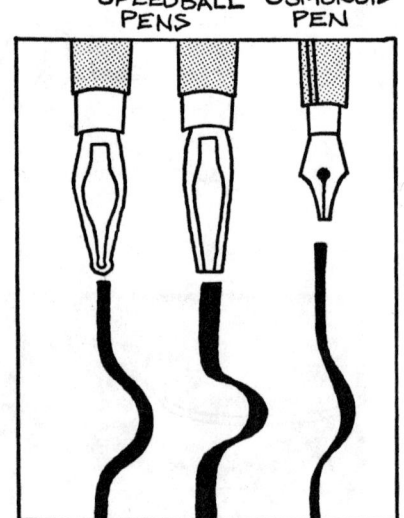

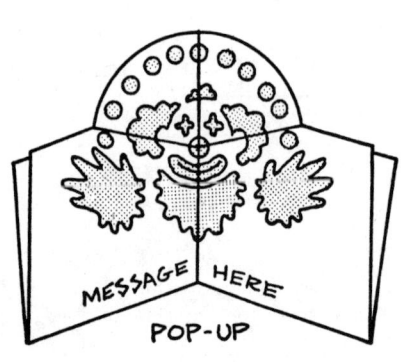

MESSAGE HERE
POP-UP

MAGIC MARKER
A brand name of non-water-soluble dye marker that comes in many assorted colors.

MARKERS (WATER SOLUBLE)
Water-soluble markers are more pencil-like than non-water-soluble markers and are usually sold in sets of assorted colors.

MASKING TAPE
An adhesive tape that is easily removed from hard surfaces. Because of its oiliness, it does not absorb paint and can be used for masking areas where you do not wish paint to appear.

MAT BOARD
A heavy-weight cardboard that has a colored paper laminated on one side.

MECHANICAL
The final artwork and copy for any card that is to be reproduced by machine printing, usually rubber-cemented to cardboard. Also known as a pasteup, though rubber cement is used, not paste.

OSMOROID LETTERING PEN
Brand name of a fountain pen that has an ink reservoir and interchangeable pen points.

PASTEUP
See Mechanical.

PENCIL (LEAD)
Available in varying degrees of hardness. The usual writing pencil is either a 2B if soft or a 2H if hard.

PENCIL (NONREPRODUCIBLE BLUE)
Used on pasteups. Light blue will not photograph; therefore, it can be used for drawing guidelines that need not be erased.

PEN POINTS (SPEEDBALL)
These points are interchangeable and are used with a pen holder. The pen is dipped into the ink, then drawn across a waste piece of paper to remove any excess. Carried by most art supply stores, they are used for calligraphy and can add an interesting look to plain handwriting.

POP-UP
A paper technique that takes advantage of a particular fold or cut to add a third dimension or movement to the card.

POSTER BOARD
Lightweight cardboard with a smooth white or colored paper laminated on one side.

POSTER PAINT
An inexpensive water-based paint that washes off easily.

REGISTRATION
A term referring to the correct positioning of one element in relation to another, either next to or on top of another. It is particularly important when printing two or more colors using any of the printing techniques.

REGISTRATION MARK

RICE PAPER
Fine handmade papers from the Orient that come in many distinctive patterns, textures, and weights. Excellent for card making if mounted on heavier card paper.

ROLLER
See Brayer.

RUBBER CEMENT
A liquid rubber adhesive. Rubber cement should always be used when preparing a pasteup for machine printing; it does not stain and excess cement can be removed easily by rubbing lightly with a clean cloth or finger. If it thickens, add rubber-cement thinner.

SCORE
An indentation made in the surface of paper with a scoring tool to break the fibers. Scoring makes it easier to fold heavy- and medium-weight paper straight, without tearing.

SCORE

SCORING TOOL
Any object used to score paper or cardboard; a used-up (dry) ball-point pen, a dull nail, a screwdriver, a letter opener, a butter knife.

SCREENED PHOTOGRAPH
See Halftone.

SELF-MAILER
A greeting card that is folded and sealed in such a way that no envelope is required for mailing.

SELF-MAILER

SILK SCREENING
Silk screening is a printing process whereby a stencil is placed on fabric or silk stretch tightly over a frame. A thick silk screen ink or paint is then forced through the fabric onto the surface to be painted by a squeegee drawn across the screen.

SQUEEGEE
A piece of rectangular rubber that is set into a wooden handle. Used in silk screening to force the paint through the fabric. Available in many sizes, it should be slightly shorter than the narrowest width of the silk screen frame.

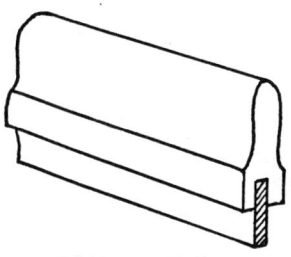

SQUEEGEE

STENCIL
A cutout that masks areas not to be painted, allowing paint to be applied only through the cutout holes. Can be used in making greeting cards in a number of ways. Stenciling and spattering are the two most common.

STENCIL BRUSH

WATERCOLORS

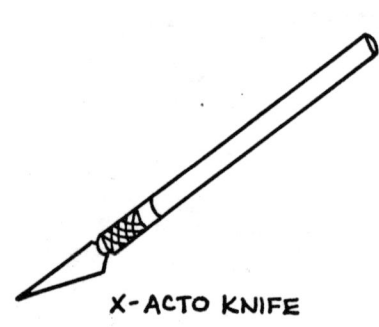

X-ACTO KNIFE

STENCIL BRUSH
A stiff-bristled brush, which holds a minimum of paint, made especially for use with stencils.

STENCIL PAPER
A stiff paper, yet easy to cut, that resists moisture. Commonly called "Oak Tag."

STRAIGHTEDGE
Any guide that helps you cut or draw a straight line. A metal edge is preferable for cutting, a clear plastic edge for drawing.

TEMPERA
Opaque water-based paints. Also known as *gouache*.

TRACING PAPER
A thin, highly transparent paper used for copying designs. Sold in pads of different sizes.

TRANSFER TYPE
Complete alphabet and numbers are available on plastic carrying sheets in many type styles and sizes. They are individually transferred to your card by rubbing with a burnisher. See Lettering and Typefaces section.

WATERCOLORS
Transparent water-based paint sold in tubes or open trays. They are mixed with water and applied on absorbent paper. Hard-surface paper will cause the paint to bead up.

WEIGHT (PAPER)
A designation given to paper to indicate its thickness, usually given in pounds (e.g., 20-lb. bond). The heavier the weight, the thicker the paper.

X-ACTO KNIFE
A brand name for a razor knife. The best type for card making is the slim-handled X-acto with a #11 blade. For best cutting results, change blades often.

Index of Cards by Occasion

Good Luck! from the O'Brian's

OCCASION	CARDS PER TECHNIQUE
Anniversary	
• Collage	1
• Paper Doily	2
• Letter Cutout	1
• Embossed	1
Baby	
• Paper Doily	1
• Pop-up And Cutout	1
• Hand Stamp	1
Barbecue	
• Silk Screen	1
Birthday	
• Collage	5
• Paper Doily	1
• Letter Cutout	2
• Pop-up And Cutout	4
• Photo	1
• Stained Glass	1
• Crayon Melt	1
• Linoleum Print	1
• Simple Silk Screen	1
• Silk Screen	1
Christmas	
• Collage	2
• Letter Cutout	1
• Embossed	2
• Pop-up and Cutout	2
• Photo	1
• Stencil	4

OCCASION	CARDS PER TECHNIQUE
• Spatter	1
• Hand Stamp	3
• Stamp-Out	2
• Stained Glass	2
• Crayon Melt	1
• Paraffin Print	3
• Linoleum Print	3
• Simple Silk Screen	3
• Silk Screen	1
• Machine-Printed	5
Easter	
• Stamp-Out	1
• Stained Glass	1
• Paraffin Print	1
Father's Day	
• Collage	1
• Paper Doily	1
• Letter Cutout	1
• Embossed	1
• Pop-up and Cutout	2
• Photo	1
• Silk Screen	1
Fourth of July	
• Collage	1
• Stencil	1
General	
• Collage	1
• Photo	1
• Crayon Melt	1
• Paraffin Print	1

OCCASION	CARDS PER TECHNIQUE
Get Well	
• Collage	2
• Paper Doily	1
• Crayon Melt	1
• Paraffin Print	1
Graduation	
• Collage	1
• Simple Silk Screen	1
Halloween	
• Spatter	2
Hanukkah	
• Pop-up and Cutout	1
• Stained Glass	1
Mother's Day	
• Collage	1
• Paper Doily	2
• Letter Cutout	1
• Embossed	1
• Pop-up and Cutout	1
• Photo	1
• Stained Glass	1
• Crayon Melt	1
• Linoleum Print	1
We've Moved	
• Pop-up and Cutout	1
• Machine-Printed	1
New Year	
• Stamp-Out	1

OCCASION	CARDS PER TECHNIQUE
Open House	
• Pop-up and Cutout	1
• Linoleum Print	1
Party	
• Collage	3
• Pop-up and Cutout	4
• Stencil	1
• Stained Glass	1
• Crayon Melt	1
• Paraffin Print	1
• Linoleum Print	2
Saint Patrick's Day	
• Pop-up and Cutout	1
Thanksgiving	
• Spatter	1
• Stamp-Out	1
Thank You	
• Collage	1
• Letter Cutout	1
• Pop-Up and Cutout	1
• Stamp-Out	1
• Paraffin Print	1
Valentine's Day	
• Paper Doily	2
• Embossed	2
• Pop-up and Cutout	2
• Linoleum Print	1
Wedding	
• Paper Doily	3
• Embossed	1
• Pop-up and Cutout	2
• Linoleum Print	1